The Dragon
in World Mythology
and Culture

The Dragon
in World Mythology
and Culture

ROBERT M. SARWARK

McFarland & Company, Inc., Publishers

Jefferson, North Carolina

This book has undergone peer review.

LIBRARY OF CONGRESS CATALOGING-IN-PUBLICATION DATA

Names: Sarwark, Robert M., 1983– author.
Title: The dragon in world mythology and culture / Robert M. Sarwark.
Description: Jefferson, North Carolina : McFarland & Company, Inc., Publishers, 2024 |
Includes bibliographical references and index.
Identifiers: LCCN 2024012911 | ISBN 9781476685298 (paperback : acid free paper) ∞
ISBN 9781476652573 (ebook)
Subjects: LCSH: Dragons. | Dragons—Folklore. | Mythology. | Ethnology.
Classification: LCC GR830.D7 S265 2024 | DDC 398.24/54—dc23/eng/20240507
LC record available at https://lccn.loc.gov/2024012911

BRITISH LIBRARY CATALOGUING DATA ARE AVAILABLE

ISBN (print) 978-1-4766-8529-8
ISBN (ebook) 978-1-4766-5257-3

Front cover images: *top* © Landscape Hero/Shutterstock;
clockwise from left © robuart/Elena Zakhariya/kao/Charisia//ESousaOnline/Shutterstock

Printed in the United States of America

*McFarland & Company, Inc., Publishers
Box 611, Jefferson, North Carolina 28640
www.mcfarlandpub.com*

To my nephews,
Maxwell, Henry, and Owen:
May you never stop loving dragons

Table of Contents

Acknowledgments

I would be remiss if I neglected to acknowledge the very extenuating circumstances under which this book was written, along with my thanks to those who assisted me in bringing it to fruition.

By the time the contract for *The Dragon in World Mythology and Culture* was signed, in late June of 2020, Covid-19 had been raging throughout the world, and especially in the United States, for over three months. At the time of this writing (late 2021), over 800,000 people have died from the virus in the United States alone, the highest national subset of more than 5 million victims worldwide. Though vaccines have already provided a great deal of relief and hope, I sincerely hope that, by the time you read these words, this plague has been brought even further under rein.

As for my personal experiences with this disaster, besides the disruptions to my normal routine, and a certain unmistakably ambient sense of anxiety, I have been spared from any substantial hardship. I consider myself extremely fortunate and privileged not only to have been able to keep my principal source of income without interruption during these trying times, but also to have the good fortune to work exclusively from home. This was, in a manner of speaking, also a blessing as regards the writing of a book: I always had something to keep me occupied while virtually all other non-professional activities ground to a halt. And though access to the physical collections of academic libraries was greatly curtailed due to social distancing policies, many thanks are due to the Fulton County Public Library, and especially the Metropolitan Branch in southwest Atlanta, its librarians, and other library workers for providing reliable service on a curbside-pickup basis during that time.

I am also extremely grateful to my two graduate-level almae matres, Brown University and the University of Illinois Urbana-Champaign, for providing digital access to the high-quality academic databases without which this book simply wouldn't have been possible.

For their insights into this book's subject and other research help, I owe the following individuals a significant debt of gratitude:

For their guidance, teaching, discussions, advice, and citations in the field of area-studies bibliography relating to this book's subject, I thank Joe Lenkart, Steve Witt, and Kit Condill of the International and Area Studies Library of the University of Illinois Urbana-Champaign; and Mr. Tesfaye Wolde-Mehdin of the University

Library at large. And to Paula Carns, of the same institution, I thank you for being the first to encourage me to explore the dragon motif and its many permutations more deeply. Many thanks are also due to Dr. Mark Purcell and Will Hale of Cambridge University Library's Rare Books and Early Manuscripts Department. They took time out of their busy schedules to not only welcome my group and me, but also to thoughtfully introduce us to a selection of literary treasures from the inner sanctum which is their charge.

I thank my old college-radio friend and long-time Japan scholar Errol Packard for his invaluable insights into the Japanese language, Japan's treatment of the dragon, and that country's (pop) culture in general. For his equally rich insights into the Greek language and culture (both ancient and modern), I am very grateful to my friend and high-school classmate Dr. Peter Giannopoulos for several enlightening exchanges by phone and text. And to my great friend of many years, Matt Lunkes: I always appreciate your thoughts and feedback regarding the science fiction and fantasy genres, among the many other topics of our conversations over the last twenty-plus years. You always challenge me to go further and deeper, both personally and professionally, and for this I consider myself lucky to count you as a friend. Many thanks are also due to my other interview subjects for their insights and perspectives.

For offering up their kitchen table and quiet home in which to work while they were away, in addition to looking after my own home during my recent absences, I thank my dear neighbors, Lina and Herman.

For thoughtful feedback on the manuscript, and for generally being such an affirming, kindred-spirit presence in my life, I thank my friend and fellow Grant Parker (Atlanta), Dr. Joan Carson, professor emerita of linguistics and former associate provost of Georgia State University.

For their patience and professionalism in guiding this project from a vague idea to a viable proposal and beyond, many thanks are due to Natalie Foreman, Layla Milholen, and the entire editorial team at McFarland.

And to my spouse and partner, Catherine Winner Manci, with whom it has been a pleasure to spend endless days, whether in or out of quarantine: I love you. I am forever thankful for your support, patience, and wisdom as I navigated this process for the first time. Thank you for letting me take over the dining-room table for a while.

Preface

In 2016, when I was a student in the Graduate School of Library and Information Science (now the School of Information Sciences, or iSchool) at the University of Illinois, I took a course on the general topic of rare books and manuscripts. One day, in the reading room of the university's Rare Book and Manuscript Library, as a class we viewed several illuminated manuscripts from the medieval period, along with other holdings of interest. At some point, I came across hand-painted illustrations in one of the manuscripts. The images were remarkable: I found myself almost incredulous at these approximately six-hundred-year-old pages' still-brilliant bursts of color, including rich hues that nowadays would be classified in terms such as cadmium blue, ox-blood red, and Kelly green. One of these illustrations featured the image of a certain Christian saint being devoured by—and simultaneously bursting out of the stomach of—a dragon.

I had a thought, so I asked, of no one in particular, "Did medieval Europeans believe that dragons were actually … real?"

Our professor, Paula Carns, after a moment of contemplation, responded, "That's a good question. That would make for an excellent topic for a research paper."

So began, quite unexpectedly, my first dive into the eons-long anthropological journey of the dragon. The result, at that point, was indeed a short paper, mostly focusing on the creatures' use in medieval iconography, per the course's focus. I came up with a few satisfying answers to my original question—specifically, that yes, medieval Europeans truly believed dragons were real—but I also knew that I had only scratched the surface. The larger topic of humans' relationships with the archetypal monster loomed.

About a year and a half later, in March of 2018, I was slated to give a fifteen-minute talk on dragon lore and its relation to modern popular culture. My presentation was primarily based on my previous graduate-level research and was to be given at the Popular Culture Association/American Culture Association (PCA/ACA) annual conference in Indianapolis.

At the start of my trip from Atlanta to Indianapolis, I had first stayed for a few days at my brother's home in the suburbs of Chicago before leaving by bus for the conference. While finishing up the slides for my talk, I took a desultory look away from my computer screen and towards both my brother's and sister-in-law's (and their children's) bookshelves. What I found was both astounding and, simultaneously, perfectly prosaic: Dragons. Everywhere. On the books' covers. In their titles. Dragons were scattered throughout multiple works of fiction for both children and adults. There was even a dragon-shaped bookend. And that's not even to mention their sons'—my three nephews'—many other dragon-themed toys, books, and video games in their bedrooms upstairs, as well as downstairs, in the basement rec room.

While on the bus to Indianapolis for the conference, I texted my brother and asked him to ask two of my two older nephews, Henry and Owen, three and a half and six years old at the time, respectively, why they liked dragons so much.

The responses came quickly.

> OWEN: "Because they look like dinosaurs with wings." (Besides its face value, this statement is notable in that it establishes that he understood that dinosaurs and dragons are *not* one and the same.)
> HENRY: "Because they fly and I like them."

Sometimes, though not often, the appeal of a cultural phenomenon is as straightforward as this: We like cool things because they are cool. And cool things are cool because they are, in some way or another, awesome—rather, possessing elements of awe. But within this ostensible simplicity, I've found, lie the massively varied cultural accretions of many thousands, if not millions, of years of human history and prehistory, likely stretching back to an age before humans could be accurately called *Homo sapiens*. From deep within this mountain of collective humanity emerges the answer to the riddle of why dragons continue, up to this day, as a recurring figure which variously elicits awe, terror, good fortune, frivolity (more recently, at least), or, quite often, some dynamic combination thereof.

As such, this book's objectives are threefold: (1) To track the evolution of dragon motifs and legends in human cultures throughout their recorded histories; (2) To present a comparative analysis of the distinction between the major Eastern and Western dragon mythologies (and where/how they may overlap historically and/or geographically); and (3) To document and interpret the ways in which these motifs and legends have emerged, fused, diverged, disintegrated, mutated, or exploded into the twenty-first century as it nears the end of its first quarter.

At this early point it would be prudent to clarify that not *all* human cultures contain a mythological beast that may be easily categorized as "dragon" (or even generally dragon-like). However, virtually all cultural traditions do include stories of monsters of some kind, most of which bear at least a striking resemblance to some present or at least evolutionarily relevant threat or other source of awe, animal or otherwise. This is why I am confident in taking on such a wide swath of inquiry, which includes elements of anthropology, folklore, "classical" literature, linguistics, pop culture/media studies, the internet at large, and other fields: wherever there are stories about (or representing) human affairs, there are gods, heroes, and villains. And then there are monsters. Due to their wide cultural and geographical diffusion (not to mention their longevity), dragons happen to be the monster par excellence of humankind. And depending on the culture and/or story, dragons may be gods, heroes, or villains, too. Even before the advent of globalization, as we will see, the diversity of their manifestations was vast.

In more recent decades, and particularly in the industrialized West, much of dragon lore—some of which had either been forgotten or was otherwise primarily relegated to children's books and other juvenilia starting in the end of the nineteenth century (see Chapter 9)—has come roaring back, a reversal made more acute with the steady improvement of audio-visual technologies. Particularly as regards visual media, cutting-edge computer-generated imagery (CGI) has resulted in a much higher potential for the suspension of our disbelief and thus has signaled an equally heightened enthusiasm for terrifying or otherwise awesome dragons. And with my apologies to the original and, admittedly, impressive-for-his-time Godzilla (originally named *Gojira*; see Chapters 3 and 8), no longer must we giggle and squirm through excruciating scenes of awkwardly suited actors or stop-motion clay figurines. With movies and television series leading the fore of this renewed interest—it bears noting that we are currently living in what many critics consider the Golden Age of Television—other media have followed with warp-speed enhancements to both quantity and quality. Many of these phenomena are considered in Chapters 9, 10, and 12.

But the organic human imagination is the engine that will propel the dragon into the future, regardless of the software or hardware used to produce it. And this is where my deeper interest in the topic lies: Where might we take the dragon that we haven't before? And where has it already gone that we may not be as familiar with, relative to our respective sets of cultural knowledge and experiences, on both the individual and collective levels?

Furthermore, I attempt to assess the myriad manifestations of the dragon through not only geography but also language. To that end, I employ a genetic or evolutionary, diachronic socio-linguistic model predicated upon the well-attested theory that the species *Homo sapiens* originated in eastern Africa, where our collective forebears also first attained language and other important biological and behavioral traits. Our species then migrated to other areas both outside and within Africa in multiple waves over many millennia, before eventually inhabiting all the major landmasses of the planet, save Antarctica. But for my purposes, the intrigue lies in the details of how we, modern humans, as members of ethno-linguistic groups (some closely and some only very distantly related to others) have influenced each other, whether genetically, culturally, linguistically, or through all of these and even more vectors. This intersectional framework allows for a clearer interpretation of not only the traits that emerge among populations in relatively homogenous isolation, but also that of the hybridization so prevalent among groups impacted by colonization, creolization, assimilation, pop-cultural or other media influence, and other anthropological and social phenomena resulting from modern globalization. In Chapters 2 through 4 this approach is manifested in the various sets of distinct languages analyzed, several representing each of the major geographic regions of the world.

Finally, a few notes on the word "dragon" itself. It was introduced into English via French (*dragon*) and Latin (*draco*), but it is ultimately of Ancient Greek origin. Through English, unequivocally the current global lingua franca, "dragon" has also infiltrated many—but by no means all—of the various dragon myths around the world, even to the point that *dragon* has either replaced or now complements an indigenous term. The ultimate source of that Greek noun, *drakōn* (δράκων), is grammatically derived from ἔδρἄκον (*edrakon*), a stem of the verb δέρκομαι (*derkomai*), "to see clearly."[1] (An alternate though perhaps overly poetic rendering of this verb into English has been cited by one scholar as "to glance dartingly."[2]) Considering the almost exclusively serpentine associations (to snakes and not legged lizards) of the Greeks' dragon myths (Chapter 6), themselves based on both common perceptions and mythological re-imaginings of snakes, the senses of "gazer" or "sharp-sighted one," or perhaps even "onlooker," "watcher" would be apposite.

Dragons as we commonly know them now are more than unblinking snakes that stare down their prey and other foes—they are, at least nowadays and in the West, much more often gargantuan and mystical quadrupedal monsters. But they are nevertheless still linked to the more mundane snakes observed by the ancients. And this distinction reveals much about how very heterogeneous are the components of the Western dragon, whether reptilian, mammalian, avian, or other. In the Germanic tradition, for example, even invertebrates such as worms may be added to the milieu; one placed on a hoard of gold, a common leitmotif holds, may likely grow into an enormous and avaricious dragon. The unifying concept is that common animals can become both grand and magical if given the right circumstances. Since gold was so rare and thus highly sought-after (not to mention aesthetically pleasing as jewelry and other accouterments), it stands to reason that it could not only change men's fortunes, but also transform beasts.

Introduction

During a recent trip to England, I couldn't stop running into dragons.

In London, the coat of arms of that great political and commercial capital loomed large with its two silvery draconic specimens. Their wings were veined with the red cross of St. George, bane of dragons and patron saint of England. In addition to their wings, the two heraldic monsters also proudly bore a shield bearing yet another St. George's Cross, seemingly in thrall to their kind's famous Christian adversary.

Later, at Leadenhall Market, similarly silvery dragons appeared to be on the loose in three-dimensional form atop the gilded columns found throughout that ancient (but fully modernized) bazaar. The statues peered down at us menacingly from over thirty feet above.

In a great hall of the Victoria and Albert Museum, a massive pine altarpiece, created in Valencia, Spain between 1420 and 1425, depicted the exploits of that same legendary, dragon-slaying saint, George. This time his reptilian foes were portrayed through a medieval and militantly Christian lens—Spain's Muslim inhabitants, soon to be fully evicted from the Iberian Peninsula, were framed quite clearly as the dragon.

An hour-long train ride away from London, at the University of Cambridge, thanks to a pair of its very generous librarians my friends and I had the good fortune to view yet another English dragon. In the University Library's rare-book and manuscript reading room, I gingerly turned to the entry for St. George within a perfect copy of an extremely rare incunable, one of the highly valuable printed books published within the first fifty years of the print medium (1450–1500). Specifically, this was a perfect copy of the very first printed English translation (by William Caxton, England's first printer), from around 1483, of the thirteenth-century hagiographer Jacobus de Voragine's *The Golden Legend* (*Legenda aurea*). The accompanying illustration, a woodcut print, depicts George as he stomps an armored foot onto the two-legged dragon's neck, his lance thrust valiantly into its gaping maw.

Even the national flag of the United Kingdom, the world-famous Union Jack, that ubiquitous and layered symbol of Britishness—especially leading up to the coronation of a new monarch (Charles III, on May 6, 2023)—was a constant reminder of England's patron saint and the dragon of which he was such a bane (quite often, in the neck). St. George's red saltire cross is also found on England's national flag, itself a component of the Union Jack. Banners and bunting of the latter were to be found seemingly everywhere we went. More of this connection between English national identity and the legend of St. George the Dragonslayer is explored in Chapters 5 and 12.

When I returned home to Atlanta, I recalled the mascot of a nearby neighborhood to my own: East Atlanta, with its Eastern-style dragon, adorns lawns, porches, and doorways. The dragon even has a name: Sang Bu.

***

Each time that I returned to this project during its development over the last few years, I found that it had something new to teach me about mythological monsters,' and especially dragons,' ability to reflect some of our deepest-seated human instincts. Sometimes, what I encountered was trivial yet fun, as in the cases of the many dragons created for the entertainment of children over the years, and their various escapades (Chapter 9). This set of attributes may speak to a universal attraction to wonder, especially during our childhood years. Other cases were more poetic and epic, as in the many dragons or dragonesque monsters of ancient folktales from around the world (Parts I and II). These speak to ambitions towards the heroic and the profound—the human impulse to make a positive impact on those we care about. And others still were somewhere in between the latter two groups, yet not at all— strange and revealing examples interwoven in the popular culture of one place or many, among a human species now more connected through technology and culture than ever before in its history (Part III). And, in other cases, a dragon was somehow just cool, weird, or funny. It served a narrative purpose as a totem both familiar and malleable. I have endeavored to include many of these "miscellaneous" dragons as well, especially in Part III.

Regardless, each example opened fresh insights into our collective imaginations, fears, and motivations, especially as they pertain to our capacity for that most ineffable of human sentiments: awe.

The awe of creatures both fantastical and actual begins early in our species' evolutionary journey. For example, many ancient humans once believed serpents to be immortal, a trait both impressive and uncanny as contrasted with the precarious and relatively brief lives of humans.[1] Or, as the Austrian-born art historian Edith Porada put it, "Serpents ... appear in a double role symbolizing both death and life."[2] What's more, and though not likely to hunt one for prey, many venomous snakes could and still can kill a biologically modern human in an act of self-defense. This sense of awed wariness of serpentine creatures—or hybrids thereof—has accompanied the human species throughout its natural and cultural history. But the aspect of death, or rather the serpent's perceived dominion thereof to the point of immortality or even undeath, though of course scientifically inaccurate, is of essence in many mythological manifestations of the dragon creature, whether beneficent, malevolent, or something more nuanced. It speaks to a very specific type of awe particular to a class of creature that is both special and mighty, a band apart from other life-forms.

As a primary component of the dragon, the serpent inhabits many of our oldest extant stories about ourselves. Across all three of the sacred scriptures of the major Abrahamic traditions—Judaism, Christianity, and Islam—is enshrined a common creation myth that follows a similar pattern, all with a serpent at its core. Thanks to these religions' widespread cultural diffusions, a large proportion of the global population is at least marginally aware of this near-ubiquitous story: it includes a talking serpent, a fruit tree, and a pair of naked humans named (in English, at least) Adam and Eve. Despite its ubiquity, this story nevertheless bears repeating here.

The narrative typically goes something like this: After creating the entire universe, and then Earth, the all-powerful God (otherwise known as *Yahweh* [often transcribed YHWH] or *Allah* in Hebrew and Arabic, respectively) creates Adam, the first human being, out of the soil itself.[3] For his homestead, Adam is provided with the Garden of Eden, a sumptuous tropical paradise. In this utopia the first (hu)man wants for nothing and lives in perfect harmony with the flora and fauna around him. He is so perfectly adapted to this environment, in fact, that he requires neither shelter nor clothing—he goes around Eden completely and contentedly naked, just like all his fellow creatures.

After a time, both Adam and God realize that Adam should have a human companion, and specifically a mate and wife. Cue Eve, whom God creates from one of Adam's ribs. Adam and Eve fall immediately in love. All is extremely tranquil and sublime in such a state of harmony between humans and nature.

This peace is not meant to last. The Devil, incarnated in the form of a serpent, lures Eve to Eden's mysterious Tree of Knowledge of Good and Evil. God had already explicitly yet cryptically forbidden the two humans from eating the fruit growing upon the tree's branches. "Ye shall not eat of it," God had commanded them, "neither shall ye touch it, lest ye die."[4] It was His only rule. But with cunning and lies, the devil-serpent talks Eve into tasting the forbidden fruit. "Ye shall not surely die," it now assures her, "for God doth know that in the day ye eat thereof, then your eyes shall be opened, and ye shall be as God, knowing good and evil."[5] But besides its supposed powers of apotheosis, Eve discovers as she takes a bite, the fruit is also exceptionally delicious. Thrilled by its delectability, as well as by the lack of any apparent consequences for breaking Eden's only law, Eve convinces her husband Adam to taste the fruit too.

Fast-forward to several generations later. The now clothed and miserable progeny of Adam and Eve have still not lived down their ancestors' fateful mistake. Banished from Eden for breaking God's law, all humans now live in a world of shame, violence, greed, deception, and myriad other vices. They have fallen from God's grace. Adam and Eve's son Cain has even slain his own brother, Abel, in cold blood. Dystopia reigns. As later detailed starting in Genesis Chapter 6 with the story of Noah and his ark, it would take a worldwide flood, many generations later, to cleanse

Depiction (in statuary and mural) of Adam, Eve and the Serpent of Genesis 3, Sacro Monte di Varallo, Piedmont, Italy (jack1986/Shutterstock.com).

the Earth of such sinfulness and restore it to even a modicum of the godly state of man before the Fall.

All because of that one piece of fruit. And the snake that "sold" it.

But let's return for a moment to that snake, the Serpent of Eden. For it is through this form that Satan, the antithesis of God and godliness, subverts the otherwise perfectly calibrated order of things.

What do we know about this creature? The type of serpent in question, as common interpretation has it, is a large, tree-climbing snake. This could perhaps indicate something along the lines of the green tree python of New Guinea and Indonesia (*Morelia viridis*), but any large arboreal snake will suffice as a model. It dwells in the Tree of Knowledge of Good and Evil, or at least encamps there temporarily to ensnare unsuspecting proto-humans. Such general representation is all well-established through centuries of textual and artistic interpretation, as well as common folklore. But, according to the Old Testament scholar Robert D. Miller II, there is something more at play. "[T]he serpent of Gen[esis Chapter] 3 is not a snake at all," Miller writes. For it is not until the end of the chapter that the creature begins to crawl along on its belly.[6] Satan's earthly form is no more immune to God's eternal punishment than are humans and, accordingly, is stricken of its limbs only after its transgression against Him and his special creation, humanity: "And the LORD God said unto the serpent: 'Because thou hast done this, cursed art thou from among all cattle, and from among all beasts of the field; upon thy belly shalt thou go, and dust shalt thou eat all the days of thy life.'" The implication is clear that the serpent had, before this alteration, propelled itself in some other way than slithering.

It nevertheless remains ambiguous whether the intention was for the "serpent" (Hebrew: *nachash*, נָחָשׁ) to be a quadrupedal rather than a limbless creature. Of course, a magical, allegorical beast may violate any number of physical and evolutionary precepts depending on the teller and, often enough, the beholder, who may likely later become a teller themself. But the prospect is intriguing: What is a large (possibly), legged reptile with malignant intentions if not, at the very least, a danger to an unsuspecting individual human? And what is a dragon if not the mythological archetype of such an entity?

According to biblical tradition, the dragon was, at least for a short while at the dawn of life on Earth, a wily beast who first tempted fate by trespassing into Eden and then rising from the ground to climb Eden's Tree of Knowledge. After its crime of deceit against the innocent humans, it was then cursed by God back to the ground to forever crawl upon it, now even lowlier than it had begun: prostrate, limbless, and wretched. Like the "earthling(s)" (*Adam/adamah*) who ostensibly joined it in the world of sinfulness beyond the protected realm of Eden, the dragon-serpent is as accursed as the humans are, but in a uniquely demeaning fashion: it eats the dust and filth left behind by all other creatures. In such a state of ignominy, one senses that the creature's resentment and revenge should only continue to smolder and intensify.

As we will see, the serpent is the primary, though not the only, aspect of the dragon. As a chimera, it is essentially hybrid in nature, and not only of animal substance—it may be elemental as well, especially extending to aqueous phenomena such as rain and rainbows. But whether a dragon is slithering, crawling, walking, or flying, its purpose is awe. The principal objective of this book is to measure and scrutinize how much psychic and cultural bandwidth that awe may contain.

PART I

Birth of the Dragon

1

The Dragon Complex

"I made myself," says the dragon. "A long time ago. By deciding to exist, and take up space in the world."
"Is that all it takes for you to be real?" [says the knight-errant.]
"Are you the litany of things you have accomplished?"[1]

Everyone knows what dragons are, what they look like. This comes despite the fact, of course, that no one has ever seen one. To a major extent dragons and their ilk are *the* default monsters—the familiar, fantastical foes (and friends, heroes, etc.) which populate the shadowy realms of tall tales told throughout the world. Yet rarely do we think of where they came from. They just seem to … be. Such a tautology as seen in this chapter's epigraph ("I made myself") may reflect the self-evidence of what a dragon represents in a familiarly poetic or symbolic sense, but it also presents a larger quandary: How might we solve a riddle that, though perhaps easily dismissed as little more than child's play on the surface, compels our species with its perennial appearances?

The purpose of this book, as I've stated, is to explore, through the lenses of various media, both modern and ancient, how exactly the dragon's "self-creation" first came about, and then gradually and sometimes drastically morphed over time. As we will see, the dragon's cultural evolution tracks remarkably close alongside our own as a species. This "big dragon energy," then, is part and parcel with the very force by which populations of human beings have spread and overlapped throughout the world, altering landscapes and each other in the process, all the while telling stories about ourselves and our relationship to the awesome.

(Kanye) West Meets East

On April 25, 2018, the rapper, producer, entrepreneur, Christian preacher, and provocateur Kanye Omari "Ye" West sent a tweet.

"You don't have to agree with trump [*sic*]," West wrote, "but the mob can't make me not love him. We are both dragon energy. He is my brother. I love everyone. I don't agree with everything anyone does. That's what makes us individuals. And we have the right to independent thought."[2]

Whenever the paths of West and Donald J. Trump have crossed, even digitally, a maelstrom of media outrage and speculation almost invariably erupted. And this tweet was no exception. With that statement, the phrase "dragon energy" entered the lexicon of global popular culture. (As of the time of writing, the term redirects to the "Politics" section of Kanye West's entry on the online encyclopedia Wikipedia. org, though those two words are nowhere to be found therein.[3])

Only a few hours after West posted this tweet, in which had named but not explicitly "@"-tagged President Trump, the President retweeted West's comment along with a comment of his own: "Thank you Kanye, very cool!" This short, non-committal response, reminiscent of a patronizing but distracted father, has become an internet-meme phenomenon unto itself.

What did Kanye West mean by "dragon energy"? Where did he get this phrase from, if not his own mind? On the crowdsourced site UrbanDictionary.com, the top entry for this phrase, posted about a month after West's now-infamous tweet, states, "You have to have dragon energy to understand what dragon energy is."[4] Considering the deep-seated, ubiquitous nature of the dragon mythos, such a tautology is perhaps permissible. But to reference an eons-old mythological creature in the context of supporting the most controversial American president and former president of the modern era, if not ever, is telling. In the case of Kanye West, dragon energy is *iconoclasm*—perhaps sometimes or even often for its own sake—whether political, artistic, or otherwise. It is a rejection of propriety, of the norms of etiquette, and of the strictures of any and all authority figures, whether real or perceived.

Simultaneously, this same "dragon energy" does have a much older and more established provenance than just Kanye West's Twitter feed, one that he had likely encountered in an early chapter of his own life.

Starting at the age of ten, in 1987, Kanye West spent his fifth-grade year with his mother, Dr. Donda C. West, then a professor at Chicago State University, in Nanjing, Jiangsu Province, China. Dr. West taught English at Nanjing University on an instructor-exchange program while young Kanye attended a local school. As the only foreign student in his class, Kanye was immersed in Chinese culture and language, his mother reported in her memoir. He also reportedly studied tai chi. Though, according to Donda, Kanye would later forget all the Mandarin he had picked up during that year, this immersive cross-cultural experience must have left an indelible mark on him, as it most certainly would on any ten-year-old child.[5]

Though communism and atheism have officially reigned in China since Mao Zedong's takeover of 1949, old traditions die hard. The precepts, philosophies, and aesthetics of Buddhism (introduced to China around 200 BCE) and, more anciently, Taoism and Confucianism, remain inexorable components of the predominant Han (Mandarin) culture of the People's Republic of China. In Taoism in particular, and in Chinese culture broadly, the dragon represents creation and the life-force of nature.[6] Is it possible that, decades after his year in China, West was pondering something related to this Chinese/Taoist theme shortly before tweeting about Trump?

Writing for *Business Insider*, Shana Lebowitz provides further context, particularly by quoting from Tin Yat Dragon, an "online temple" of Taoism.[7] In a December 12, 2017, post, the latter site's authors state, "In Fung Shui, we talk about the dragon energy all the time, Lung Hei 龍氣. This dragon energy is actually the pre-heaven energy that comes from nature, which goes into things in reality and charges up everything." The concept, the post further explains, also figures into the communal movements of organisms (including "the sperm"), inorganic particles, and even, remarkably, "the line of people who are lined up for black Friday sales outside of Best Buy." The dragon—and its energy—is a metaphor for them all, as well as for the Chinese people and "the thing [*sic*] they emphasize on—togetherness and united minds."[8] It is possible that Kanye West was aware of such concepts, even if dimly remembered, due to his early exposure to Chinese thought.[9]

The day before he posted his now-infamous "dragon energy" tweet, on the morning of April 24, 2018, West had written the following verse, a standard haiku if not for its extra fourth line:

> dragon [dragon emoji] energy
> Natural born leaders
> Very instinctive
> Great foresight[10]

Less than twenty-six hours later, Kanye tweeted about sharing this special kind of energy with the American president. The reaction of social-media users and mass-media pundits alike was swift and, not surprisingly, highly divided along political lines. Whatever his original inspiration, the power of dragons was on his mind. And after these two dragon tweets, that power was on the minds of millions more.

Perhaps this is one of the truest and most durable powers of dragons (and their energy): self-evidence. West did not need to explain what he meant in belabored, academic terms. He assumed, mostly correctly, that his audience would just get it. The target of his iconoclasm, the sacred totem to be smote, was the public's false assumption that he, as an African American man, could only feel an automatic disdain towards the white, aged, Republican Donald Trump. Any preconceived notion or expectation on behalf of the general public, based on West's pattern of known behavior, has posed a constant source of frustration to him and, therefore, also a source of artistic fodder. He has seemed constantly at the ready to destroy his own image in the process. Before he can destroy, though, he must transform from the body of a mere mortal to that of a rare, ferocious, and—of course—energetic dragon. As he rapped on a 2015 track, "Everybody know I'm a motherfucking monster."[11]

Then again, dragons perhaps aren't as rare as Ye might like to think. In fact, they are everywhere. As team mascots, decorations on clothing, and corporate logos. As fearsome foes and loyal friends in books and songs and shows and films for children and adults alike. As emoji (as in West's own tweet above), tattoos, and on national, regional, municipal, and other flags. And yes, even as aspirational,

Shown here flanked by the press at a meeting in the White House Oval Office, Washington, D.C., on October 11, 2018, Kanye "Ye" West (left) and Donald Trump (right) (as NFL Hall-of-Famer Jim Brown looks on) would both go on to be candidates for president of the United States in 2020. Six months before this meeting, the pair had shared a public Twitter exchange in which West popularized the phrase "dragon energy" (Ron Sachs–CNP/Shutterstock.com).

iconoclastic metaphors. Dragons populate our dreams and haunt our nightmares. Throughout the world, the dragon (or something generally fitting that description) has been a major recurring figure in virtually all human cultures and mythologies. And although this imaginary creature has had many of its traits altered or even, if temporarily, neutered in the West—from evil incarnate, to docile friend or pet, and back again to a more menacing figure—one factor remains: we keep reinventing and reimagining it, seemingly *ad infinitum*. And while the West (the geo-cultural region, not the rapper) has become markedly less superstitious—and, according to recent polling, less religious—over the last century,[12] it appears that the factual, anthropological foundations of dragon myths, and thus why we still enjoy watching or reading or thinking or writing about them, are much, much older than any of the world's organized religions.

During the writing of this book, on July 4, 2020, Kanye West entered the race for president of the United States as an independent. Later that year, both West and his Republican opponent, Donald Trump, lost the election to the Democratic candidate, Joe Biden. West continued to provoke controversy on various issues using Twitter and other social media platforms, but is now banned from most for anti–Semitic content as of late 2022.[13] Trump, however, was "permanently" banned from the platform on January 8, 2021, following his inflammatory statements regarding the insurrection of the U.S. Capitol two days prior … until Twitter's (now X's) new owner Elon Musk reinstated him by fiat on November 19, 2022. Trump has refrained from using the platform, however, in favor of his own TruthSocial.

Both Vile and Puerile

Concurrent to the recent surge in superstitious belief discussed in this book's introduction, mythical beasts—and the mysticism that often surrounds them—and especially dragons, have become wildly popular in the realm of entertainment. This is fueled in large part by the meteoric rise in popularity, starting in 2011, of the dragon-heavy high-fantasy television series *Game of Thrones* (HBO), based on the *A Song of Ice and Fire* (*ASOIAF*) novels by George R.R. Martin (first published in 1996). Six decades prior, in the works of J.R.R. Tolkien (1892–1973), an indispensable influence on Martin and countless other creators, the dragon Smaug in *The Hobbit* (1937) had reinvigorated the motif, priming the fantasy-laden English-language literature of the twentieth century for more new specimens. The presence of mighty, war-ready dragons in the *ASOIAF* franchise and their importance to the overall story arc are of note for their bringing of ages-old mythology to the fore in provocative and dramatic ways for a modern and discerning audience. (As such, this franchise will be discussed at length in Chapter 10.)

But this trend is a sign of a stark departure from the previous trajectory. In contrast to Martin's massive, fire-breathing, bloodthirsty trio of Drogon, Rhaegal, and Viserion—those dragons whom Khaleesi Daenerys Targaryen, their "mother," incites to dragonfire with a shout of "*Dracarys!*"—docile, child-friendly versions of dragons had begun to appear in the late nineteenth and very early twentieth centuries, Hollywood-dominated media landscape. As seen in such works as the folk ballad (1963) and subsequent animated film (1978) of "Puff, the Magic Dragon," a marked trend of declawing and infantilizing the once exclusively fearful, demonic beasts emerged. Disney's ancillary character Figment—a friendly, cat-sized purple dragon that has appeared at Disney World's Epcot Center in Orlando, Florida, since 1983—is adorable enough to be a plush toy. And the 2010 animated children's film *How to Train Your Dragon* (and its sequels in 2014 and 2019), about a beloved domesticated dragon in a storyworld loosely inspired by Norse lore, is at present a favorite of both children and their parents. Even the original Godzilla, a dragon-like monster first introduced in Japan in 1954 as *Gojira*, has a certain cuteness to him, at least to modern eyes. These, along with other such whimsical representations of what otherwise, historically, would be considered Satan or otherwise evil incarnate, represent a general trend in the West that corresponded with producers' capitalizing on the vast market potential of children and thus child-friendly entertainment. Noting this shift, the twentieth-century Argentine writer and librarian Jorge Luis Borges (1899–1986) elaborated on the sullied status of dragons in *The Book of Imaginary Beings*. He concluded that after many millennia of glory dragons had become childish ("puerile"). "Time has considerably tarnished the prestige of Dragons," he wrote. "…[It is] perhaps the best known though also the least fortunate of fantastic animals."[14]

This domesticated manifestation of the dragon, at least as its primary form in popular culture, appears to have been a somewhat short-lived anomaly, however. The psychic presence that dragons have occupied in previous human eras throughout the world, Borges continued, was quite substantial. In addition to their generally fierce, demonic reputation in many locales, many truly believed that they existed. Even natural philosophers referred to them in earnest as late as the mid-sixteenth century, including the Swiss polymath Konrad Gesner in his *Historia Animalium*, a zoological encyclopedia published in five volumes between 1551 and 1587.[15]

Gesner (or Gessner), a physician and professor of Aristotelian philosophy, indeed wrote of the dragon in scientific terms alongside real animals. However, the folklorist Phil Senter tempers Borges' claim and attests that, by Gesner's time and the Renaissance in general, dragons were not fully or truly believed in by the learned, at least not as the ferocious and gargantuan monsters of lore. Rather, Gesner, as a man of science who of course had never *actually* seen a dragon, living or dead, understood and described them as merely a kind of very large snake. Snakes and other reptiles composed an animal class well known and observed by Europeans; it stood to reason that gargantuan and even magical reptilian species probably existed in far-off, lesser-known realms like Sub-Saharan Africa or the Americas. Another phenomenon of the early-modern age was the tendency to acknowledge dragons' existence based on textual precedent. The creatures were earnestly included in many manuscript texts (and their illuminations) held by the elite intelligentsia. These medieval Christian bestiaries and classical Greco-Roman treatises were often complemented by cabinets of curiosities, sometimes populated by elaborate taxidermic hoaxes.[16] At that moment in history,

Conrad Gessner (or Konrad Gesner, 1516–1565), depicted here in the engraving by Tobias Stimmler which is featured on the fifty-franc bill of Switzerland. The Swiss polymath Gessner represented the dragon as a real creature in his five-volume treatise, *Historia Animalium* (Janusz Pienkowski/Shutterstock.com).

Gesner's hedging was a sign of respect for the erstwhile titans of ancient thought—few yet dared to tear down wholesale the claims of vaunted ancients such as Aristotle or Pliny the Elder or Thomas Aquinas. Better to err on the side of monstrous creatures roaming the still-hazy fringes of Europeans' perceptions and knowledge of the wide world. It would require the innovations of the Swedish polymath Carl Linnaeus in the mid-eighteenth century for all serious Western scientists to strictly rely on well-documented, empirical evidence, all but obliterating the possibility of dragons' literal existence.

But despite scientific progress, the dragon remained and remains. Though perceptions may continuously change or branch off into new directions, what persists is this hulking figure's lingering presence in the psyche of the majority of human cultures—whether in its malignant or beneficent manifestation—throughout the world. As the Australian-British anatomist and Egyptologist G. Elliot Smith noted in his treatise on the phenomenon, "An adequate account of the development of the dragon-legend would represent the history of the expression of mankind's aspirations and fears during the past fifty centuries and more. For the dragon was evolved with civilization itself."[17] This sentiment echoes the inspiration—whether fully acknowledged or not—of the many scribes and artists who have utilized the dragon in their works, whether in antiquity, the modern era, or what will be our collective future.

East Meets West

The myriad interpretations of "dragon" lie across a wide spectrum but can be most rudimentarily divided into Eastern and Western types. As G. Elliot Smith explained: "[I]f in the West the dragon is usually a 'power of evil,' in the far East he is equally emphatically a symbol of beneficence. He is identified with emperors and kings; he is the son of heaven, the bestower of all bounties, not merely to mankind directly, but also to the earth as well."[18] This distinction nevertheless leaves us with many questions: Did these respective dragon myths in the East and West (itself an imprecise geographic and cultural dichotomy, to be sure), originate independently? And even if they did not, when did this split occur? And why? If we are to assume that the deepest roots of the dragon are shared among our common human and pre-human ancestors, and are not independent coincidences, these are questions worth answering.

At this point it will suffice to maintain that the Western (malevolent) and Eastern (benevolent) types do serve as important guideposts before delving further into more specific, culture-by-culture analyses. There are many exceptions, and though almost all dragons are "by nature" rather fickle, unpredictable beasts, in the broadest terms this East-West dichotomy holds true.

To wit, consider the modern national flags of Wales and Bhutan, each of which features a dragon as its central device.[19]

Wales' *passant*[20] red dragon, or *Y Ddraig Goch* in Welsh, is of the typical Western variety: four-legged, winged, ferocious, demonic even. Its red color is strongly associated with the Welsh people's Celtic heritage[21] and furthermore their distinction from their Anglo-Saxon neighbors and rivals on the island of Britain (the latter are traditionally associated with the color white). Anatomically, the Welsh red dragon displays a suite of detailed and intentional features—it is a classic chimera. In addition to its four separate legs (and not two, plus wings, like some depictions of dragons[22]), it has pointed, quasi-mammalian ears and a scruffy beard. Its nose, however, is more of a rapine beak than a mammalian snout; and its feet wield sharp, avian talons and wings. Spinal protrusions in the form of spikes resemble certain species of lizard, such as iguanas or bearded dragons (genus *Pogona*). A barbed, reptilian tongue and an equally deadly barbed tail threaten from the beast's respective extremities. Taken as a whole, it is most certainly not a creature to be meddled with lightly.

Bhutan's dragon is nowadays white but in its original conception, between 1949 and 1956, it was green.[23] More significant, however, is the dragon's Eastern morphology: more serpentine than saurian; wingless; even more heavily bearded—or feathered, perhaps—than its Welsh counterpart. It carries a jewel in each of its four sets of claws (which each have three digits instead of the Welsh dragon's four). In general, the Eastern-tradition dragon such as the one represented on Bhutan's flag tends to be taloned and serpentine—an enormous, magical, legged snake, often with a head vaguely reminiscent of a shih tzu—wingless, though, as noted by anthropologist David E. Jones, "flight capable."[24]

Flag of the Principality of Wales, or *Y Ddraig Goch* (The Red Dragon) (archivector/Shutterstock.com).

Flag of the Kingdom of Bhutan, representing the nation's so-called "dragon people" or *Drukpa* **(mapsandphotos/Shutterstock.com).**

These two examples are thus highly emblematic of their respective dragon traditions. As we have seen, in the East the creature is a symbol of good fortune and prosperity; in the West, one of terrible ferocity, though not necessarily always adversarial to the beholder. Wielded as a sigil on flags, heraldry, and other identity-marking materials, *Y Ddraig Goch* defends the Welsh homeland and furthermore its cultural and linguistic autonomy from the Germanic English—i.e., the more recently arrived, non–Celtic "Britons," at least in the ethno-linguistic, if not necessarily genetic, sense—at any rate the cultural descendants of those once-hated and perhaps still begrudged invaders, the Anglo-Saxons. In the form of Bhutan's own daemon the beast also protects, but in line with the Eastern tradition seemingly more so through tidings of beneficence than carnivorous aggression or predation against foes. (Tellingly, the Kingdom of Bhutan's endonym, *Drukyul,* translates to "The Land of the Thunder Dragon" and its people *Drukpa* or "dragon people.") Bhutan's dynastic ruler is *Druk Gyalpo*, "Dragon King." For its part, the Welsh dragon legend, as we will see more in Chapter 6, is similarly deeply linked with its people's sense of distinct ethno-linguistic and national independence.

In addition to the Welsh and the Bhutanese, a handful of other people-groups have also integrated dragons into their flags. China, under the Qing dynasty (1644–1912), for a time had as its flag's central device a left-facing azure or blue-green Eastern dragon, otherwise similar in morphology to that of Bhutan, chasing a red pearl on a field of yellow. (More about various "dragon" flags is found in Chapter 12.) And, rather distinct from the other three mentioned usages of the dragon herein, the emblem on the top left of the flag of the tiny Mediterranean island-nation of Malta features an equally minuscule dragon under the horse and lance of St. George, Malta's patron saint. This hagiographic legend, as well as those relating to several other Christian saints involving dragons, will be detailed in Chapter 5.

For now, it suffices: Two very different peoples, the Welsh and the Bhutanese, separated by almost 5,000 miles (8,000 km), use iterations of the same uncannily similar mythic creature to represent themselves as sovereign nations, not only internally, but on the world stage. And whether perceived as benevolent or malevolent is, at this level of representation, at least, irrelevant; all that matters is that we understand the creature, if harnessed, to be the mighty protector of whatever it is that we wish to project, represent, value. This is the power, or energy, of the dragon that Kanye West cryptically alluded to—humankind's most iconoclastic icon.

The Complex Dragon

In the book *An Instinct for Dragons* (2000), anthropologist David E. Jones muses deeply on questions of the dragon's origins, and especially on why we just "get" what a dragon is without a second thought. "The dragon puzzle persists," he begins. "There seems to be no physically based theory to explain why the dragon populates the imagination of peoples in seemingly all cultures. What, after all, is this beast that all the world knows—this creature that never was?"[25]

Even encyclopedists, the supposed arbiters of ultimate meaning, are inconclusive. In the header to its current online entry on the subject, *Encyclopædia Britannica* states, glibly, that "The origin of the dragon is lost in the mists of time[.]"[26] To a certain extent, this appears on its face to be true: Certainly, no one knows exactly when dragons began to be conceived and then artistically represented by human beings. All we can confirm with any certainty is that the figure of the dragon is very, very ancient, if not primordial. If the purpose of this book is indeed to look further and deeper into the true sources of the *phenomenology* of dragons; an incomplete answer would be more than unsatisfying. But before offering a more thorough demystification, a brief survey of the more common preconceptions or assumptions surrounding the dragon is in order.

To us, as modern observers, the parallels and similarities between mythological dragons and once-existent dinosaurs (or perhaps other clades of large prehistoric reptilians such as ichthyosaurs or pterosaurs), may appear a foregone conclusion. After all, both types are enormous, saurian, and presumably bloodthirsty (if not at least awesome in size and power). Folk wisdom has it, then, that ancient as well as early modern observers must have beheld the fossilized skeletons of these great beasts that, as we now know, indeed walked, swam, and flew throughout the Earth of over 65 million years ago. The logic then follows that our human ancestors, as prehistoric amateur paleontologists, must have imagined the fossils of these dinosaurs, ichthyosaurs, or pterosaurs as living, breathing creatures, rarely seen but likely still extant, whether nearby, in distant realms, or both.

The term *dinosaur* (a novel Greek compound meaning "terrible reptile") did not exist until British anatomist Richard Owen coined it in 1841. Before then, the various (and often isolated) bones of large, extinct beasts were indeed sometimes stumbled upon. But it was more likely that these fossils were attributed to giant humanoids or otherwise mysterious beasts, and not necessarily what we might refer to as "dragons."[27] And, it should be noted, in many parts of the world fossilized remains of large, extinct reptiles, mammals, or other megafauna were simply invisible and unknown, buried deep within layers of soil and stone, if not wholly nonexistent: fossilization is a relatively rare phenomenon that requires many specific biological, chemical, and geological conditions to occur. The consideration of megafauna fossils by ancient humans may be a piece of the puzzle, but it is surely not the only piece.

Another theory is that perhaps we, as the only extant case of what was once several humanoid species, retain on a virtually if not truly genetic level a reminiscence of a long-extinct (but once human-contemporary), dragonesque predator. This gargantuan and marauding beast from our evolutionary and collective past continues to haunt our psyches, according to the still-debated theory of the collective unconscious. Like all other traits extant in the modern human genome, so the theory maintains, our fears are also the result of the processes of evolution. "These ancient images are restored to life by the primitive, analogical mode of thinking peculiar to dreams," wrote the Swiss psychiatrist and philosopher Carl Gustav Jung (1875–1961) in the essay "The Relations Between the Ego and the Unconscious" (1928). "It is not a question of inherited ideas, but of inherited thought patterns."[28] Unless deluded by literal interpretations of mystical or figurative writings, we may readily acknowledge that dinosaurs and humans were never coexistent. Yet other types of large predators may have fit the bill: large birds, saber-tooth cats ... perhaps even giant, post-dinosaurian lizards or snakes were all (and in some cases still are) our evolutionary contemporaries. Dragons are thus, so Jung's theory holds, a manifestation of that evolutionarily and culturally—though, again, not directly—disseminated inheritance of a phobia of our natural predators, even after these have mostly ceased to be existential threats.

Through the lens of both zoology and anthropology, David E. Jones furthers this theory. The anthropologist contends that the fullest explanation indeed lies in our evolutionary past in a way that is deceptively simple, though obscured to the point of outright oblivion. This obfuscation is due to our species' full or at least partial departure from the dynamics that our distant ancestors once maintained with our original African habitat and its common fauna. The mythic dragon's physiognomy, then, is so universal because it is, more than anything else, a composite of the three types of real animal that most threatened our distant, though collective, human (and pre-human) ancestors. Furthermore, the dragon documents a response to an ancestrally shared experience as the common or at least occasional prey of the three predator classes. These three classes are as follows: The eagle (raptor), the leopard (big cat, or, more generally, any large carnivorous mammal, possibly including bears and wolves), and the snake (serpent). All of them were, many millions of years ago, common predators of the distant ancestors of modern humans. And together, the three form what Jones calls the "dragon complex."[29] Though not without its strong detractors, this hypothesis is at the very least worth considering.[30]

Jones' assessment dovetails with the conclusions of classical folklorist Adrienne Mayor, who recommends that a greater respect and mutual understanding exist between academic science and folk knowledge, especially as regards the former towards the latter.[31] The nineteenth-century British biologist T.H. Huxley (also known by his nickname, "Darwin's Bulldog") tended to agree: "Ancient traditions," he wrote in 1863, "when tested by the severe processes of modern investigation, commonly enough fade away into mere dreams: but it is singular how often the dream turns out to have been a half-waking one, presaging a reality."[32] If we are all indeed descended from a vulnerable yet resourceful species (or several species) of primate that originated in or around the Rift Valley of Eastern Africa, all three component animal groups—raptor, big cat/carnivore, serpent—would most certainly have been very real and very constant threats. This was to such a degree, asserts Jones, that this tripartite phobia, passed on by our prehistoric predecessors through the process of natural selection, and though mostly decoupled from its atavistic meaning, is still with us to this day.

To reach us today in the form of the dragon, such an evolutionarily advantageous set of fears would have had to first pass through the lens of storytelling and myth, especially as protohumans, through natural selection, became more and more adept at protecting themselves from physical predation. The residual, ancestral abhorrence towards our erstwhile natural predators, all of which have *almost* (but not entirely) ceased posing existential threats to individuals of our species, was nevertheless preserved across cultures in the visual arts, oral folklore, and then, when and where it existed, the written word. For example, when Christianity and its ministry and scripture spread to the West during the first millennium CE, and its dogma, mythology, and transnational literature accreted, the ancient, familiar dragon was a near-perfect surrogate for Satan/evil, just as Eden's serpent had already established in the Jewish and other Semitic or otherwise Near-Eastern traditions.[33] And today, through much more recent media such as television and cinema, the dragon is again reborn as a mirror of both our values and concerns.

Jones supports his Dragon Complex Theory in several ways. Naturally, an anthropological assessment is the most prevalent throughout his book. But it is also through non-human primatology that his evidence emerges. He focuses on African vervet monkeys (*Chlorocebus pygerythrus*) as research subjects, for they "give distinctive alarm calls at the appearance of three different predators: leopards, martial eagles, and pythons. Further, each of these calls stimulates responses directly related

A leopard hunts a juvenile monkey in the Okavango Delta, Botswana. Such predatory exchanges, according to anthropologist David E. Jones, may hint at the very origins of humans' preoccupations with mythological monsters such as the dragon (Thomas Retterath/Shutterstock.com).

to escaping the predator."[34] Other anthropologists, such as Lynne A. Isbell, have shown that this evolutionary trait, especially in response to snakes, likely extends to before primates even diverged from our other shared mammalian relatives.[35] Most essentially, those individuals, whether proto-simians, true primates, or hominids, who did not respond quickly and appropriately enough to the presence of a snake by fleeing to safety or otherwise fighting back, became prey. And if they had not yet procreated before becoming a meal to such predators, their unique genes would not be passed on. This is Charles Darwin's principle of natural selection at its simplest and most brutally elegant.

But we *Homo sapiens*—and though we are technically apes and share an eons-distant ancestor with all other modern primates, including vervets—are not monkeys. Wouldn't we have forgotten—or, more precisely, *lost* the adaptation for—such obsolete fears long, long ago? Furthermore, vervets are much smaller animals than modern humans, or even protohumans for that matter. This, Jones contends, is a question of relativity: "Dragon combats, or encounters," he writes, "scanned in several pictures and tales reveals that the human is on average about a fifth the size of the dragon. The size of the human relative to that of the dragon compares to that of the ancestral primate and its major predators."[36] Though some descriptions of exceptionally large dragons do exist in traditional folktales, such as those from Japan, China, and Greece, they are indeed the exceptions and not the rule. And it is only in the relatively recent media of live-action and animated motion pictures that dragons have taken on their almost impossibly massive sizes, such as in *Game of Thrones* (the original books as well as the two adapted television series). As harbingers of evil and destruction, at least in the Western tradition, dragons must be plausibly sized, and thus vincible, if a goodly hero such as St. George or Beowulf is to prevail with sword (or lance) and shield.

It is important to note here that, when Jones had first conceived of his theory, he was preparing a lecture on primate behavior, and not on dragons whatsoever. It was only when a page of a book with the images of all these predators happened to fall open that he made his discovery. "Suddenly," he writes,

> in my mind's eye, the three predator images merged. The leopard body took on the outer look of the python, resulting in a large reptilian body with four clawed feet and a mouth full of sharp teeth. When the wings of the martial eagle attached to the shoulders of the blended leopard/python, I saw a dragon![37]

From this eureka moment, Jones followed the dragon thread as it extends further and further away from the prehistoric, protohuman branches of our primate family tree, losing much of its original literal meaning over the thousands of millennia but meanwhile taking on a deeply figurative life of its own. "At a particular point in human evolution, a novel conception," he writes, "'dragon,' enters human consciousness."[38] It is at this point, whenever it may have been in the mists of prehistory, that the dragon, as a simplified stand-in for the three predators, began to shift from the literal to the figurative. By then, the immediate threat was no longer material, for we humans had mostly evolved out of harm's way by virtue of our size as well as the use of primitive weapons and, much later, technologies such as firearms. Though the memory of our three classes of foe was already fading, the solid core of that inherited dread was enough to anchor an entirely new creature in the fireside tales and bedside legends that have continued unabated, as if to remind us to never fully drop our guard against such creatures. They still could, at least in theory, kill and eat us.

Though the various theories of the genesis of the dragon need not be considered mutually exclusive in this book's analysis, classics scholar Daniel Ogden warns of depending too heavily on any easy answers. Of Jones' theory in particular, Ogden is highly skeptical. "His hunt for images that salute this [tripartite] type across a range of historical cultures lacks rigour,"[39] Ogden writes, offering instead the classical (i.e., Greco-Roman) view that the snake or serpent figure is not only vastly predominant, but the ultimate and persistent source of *drakontes*.[40] Indeed, it is necessary to temper Jones' enthusiasm for an almost purely evolutionary model with the more mytho-geological views of Adrienne Mayor, whose study is based on a careful overlay of geography with the records and tales of ancient Greeks, Romans, Scythians, and other people-groups of antiquity. These groups developed at least some of their folklore based on actual encounters with dinosaur fossils, particularly in deserts, that were discernible as the remains of large, ancient animals. The discovery of triceratops fossils in the Gobi Desert, Mayor contends, led to a common visualization of what in English is referred to as a griffin.[41]

A rock python kills a vervet monkey by constriction after concealing itself in leaf litter (Nick Greaves/Shutterstock.com).

Whatever their "true" origin, what is certain is the dragon's lasting resonance as a cultural totem. Whether as a fearful monster; a cuddly friend; a talisman upon a flag, a coat of arms, or a patch of human skin; or furthermore as a resonant metaphor (whether for political or artistic iconoclasm), our primordial, complex relationship with the dragon will only continue to grow more complex and nuanced over time. Regardless of how humans wield technology in increasingly involved, world- and self-altering ways, our shared anthropological, historical, and (pop-)cultural baggage will accompany us. Inside that baggage is a shape-shifting but dependable form that never ceases to find ever more daring and innovative ways to escape.

2

Dragon Myths and Legends
Around the World

Africa, the Middle East/Central Asia, and Europe

With the coming of the light, the good-seekers, the evil-hunters, the kind-hearted, of course they sought me out. The gods who rose up from the depths of that chaos challenged me to battle. But even the gods turned in fear at my might. The humans named me Tiamat, the Serpent, Azhdeha, the Evil One, as if naming things could make them disappear.[1]

We launch our comparative inquiry into the worldwide dragon phenomenon from the premise that *Homo sapiens* first emerged, in the form we recognize ourselves as today, in the Great Rift Valley of eastern Africa (modern-day Ethiopia, Tanzania, and Kenya). It was here in our shared ancestral homeland that the evolutionary changes in physiology and brain size allowed for toolmaking, art, language, and, ultimately, all the elements of humanity that make us evolutionarily modern humans.

From Africa we follow the thread through the deserts and oases of the Middle East and the mountain fastnesses and plains of Central Asia, into the temperate and subarctic forests of Europe. In Chapter 3 we descend into the steamy, tropical Indian subcontinent and to the three major East Asian cultures of China, Japan, and Korea, as well as into Southeast Asia, continuing to hopscotch among the islands, large and small, of Oceania. Crossing the Pacific we make our way, finally, to the Indigenous and Creole cultures of the Americas, once densely wooded and now greatly transformed by European colonization, North, Central and South, before stopping to cover any other ground that we may have missed thus far.

Also important to this analysis are considerations of a philological or etymological nature. As such, I introduce each section in this and the subsequent two chapters with translations of the word "dragon" (or closest equivalent) in several of its region's traditionally or commonly spoken languages. While there is an admitted arbitrariness to where, exactly, ethno-linguistic lines might or should be drawn, the sociolinguistic concept of *Sprachbund* remains germane: any languages in close geographic proximity—and especially in contexts predating modern mass media and telecommunications—tend to converge in objectively measurable ways, regardless of the linguistic affinities of these speaker-groups. (Note that not all languages listed in each section will be investigated in equal detail; rather, I seek to display a cursory sampling in each section's introduction and then present one or more case-studies drawn from that region.)

Africa

Amharic: *zenido* (ዘኒዶ)	Malagasy: *dragona*	Xhosa: *inamba*
Hausa: *dragon*	Swahili: *joka*	Yoruba: *dragoni*
Kinyarwanda: *yoka*	Wolof: *dragon*	

In *The Hero with an African Face*, the African American psychotherapist and Africanist Clyde W. Ford calls attention to one of the most glaring blind spots in mythologist Joseph Campbell's otherwise seminal *Hero with a Thousand Faces* (1949): his bias against Africans. In particular, the source of Ford's consternation and disappointment is Campbell's stated disparagement of African (and more specifically Bantu) folklore and religion, early in his classic text, as "the dreamlike mumbo jumbo of some red-eyed witch doctor of the Congo."[2] Nevertheless, Ford writes, "Campbell's shortsightedness about Africa could not obliterate his immense contributions to mythology, and his omission gave me an opportunity to explore African mythology in a novel and meaningful way."[3] Furthermore, Ford begins his inquiry into African mythology armed with the knowledge, even further reinforced since Campbell's heyday in the mid-twentieth century, of what several branches of science have proven most conclusively: that Africa is the original motherland of all humanity and should be acknowledged and respected as such. "Ultimately," Ford proclaims, "we are all the transformed gold of the prime matter of Africa—all children of some African diaspora—and to these African heroes and heroines we all owe our lives."[4]

Besides its fifty-four independent nations, the geographic continent of Africa contains at least fifteen linguistic supergroups, most of which are consistent with ethnic or tribal identities. All fifteen supergroups fall under one of six major linguistic phyla or "families" (the highest tier of language classification): Afro-Asiatic, Niger-Congo, Nilo-Saharan, Khoisan, Austronesian, and Indo-European. Majority populations of native speakers of these supergroups, under these six great families, in order of their listing above, include the populous Semitic-Hamitic group (including Arabic, Berber, and Amharic) in the continent's north and northwest[5]; Guinean (or Niger-Congo A) in the west (e.g., Ashanti, Yoruba, Igbo) and Bantu (or Niger-Congo B) throughout the equatorial regions and into South Africa (e.g., Kimbundu, Kinyarwanda, Zulu)[6]; several groups of Nilo-Saharan, which, at large, includes the Dinka, Bambara, and Luo[7] languages; Khoisan (e.g., Khoi, Nama, San) in the extreme south; and the unique case of Malagasy, the Malayo-Polynesian language of the island of Madagascar (and its several dialects). In addition, and depending on the area, Indo-European languages such as (the mostly Dutch-derived)

Afrikaans, French, Spanish, Portuguese, English—and, to a lesser degree in Libya, Ethiopia, Eritrea, and Somalia: Italian—are prevalent as *linguae francae* resulting from several centuries of European colonial rule and continued influence.

Africa is a massive and a massively diverse landmass in terms of both its geography and demography. To attempt to describe one "African" culture, even along the continent's six major language phyla, would be an exercise in extreme folly. "Diverse" only begins to scratch the surface, and this equally applies to the continent's mythology and folklore.

As we can see in the cases of the languages Malagasy and Wolof (the latter being one of several spoken in Senegal), the former colonial language of French has provided the source for each of these respective dragons (*dragona/dragon*), just as English has in *dragon/dragoni*, respectively, for Nigeria's Hausa and Yoruba. (The latter two are genetically unrelated). We also see the kinship in the Bantu (otherwise classified as Niger-Congo B) languages of Kinyarwanda (the majority language of Rwanda) in its *yoka* and Swahili's *joka*, despite the centuries of deep Arabic imprinting on Swahili via commerce and colonization, which also correlates to Swahili serving as the lingua franca of much of East Africa.

Ethiopia (historically also known as Abyssinia) was once an empire of multiple ethnolinguistic groups, and to this day its successor state retains a large degree of ethno-linguistic diversity. Ethiopia was also the only significant region of Africa never to be colonized by a western European power during the onslaught of conquest between 1500 and 1900. Though the Kingdom of Italy attempted a colonial takeover in 1895, this quickly failed. In 1935, under fascist dictator Benito Mussolini, however, the Italians were more successful; they launched their campaign from neighboring Eritrea, which they had more successfully colonized since the late nineteenth century. With Ethiopia now under the rule of an occupying foreign power, the Ethiopian emperor, Haile Selassie I (*né* Ras [Prince] Tafari Makonnen, 1892–1975), was forced into exile in England. The imposition would not last for long, as the Italians would practically abandon all their colonial ambitions in East Africa soon after their defeat, along with the other Axis Powers Germany and Japan, in the Second World War. In 1947, Italian colonists and the Italian state finally surrendered all their territorial claims to the region, including Eritrea and parts of Somalia. As a result of this short tenure, Italian language and culture only achieved a modicum of penetration into the region. Amharic is still the reigning lingua franca of the country, as well as that of the ruling elite, which has been the case for almost a millennium.

Amharic and other Ethiopic languages, such as Tigre, Tigrinya, and Harari, hold the distinction of being (Southern) Semitic in origin, meaning that they are more genetically related to Hebrew and Arabic than they are to, say, Swahili or Igbo. Ethiopia has also been predominantly a Christian country since the fourth century CE, with particularly strong influences from the Greek-Byzantine and Egyptian-Coptic Orthodox traditions. All these factors play into the dragon lore and other related mythologies of the region.

Amharic's dragon, *zenido* (pronounced "zendo"), has strong serpentine connotations, semantically consistent with the python or otherwise very large snakes. When it comes to the St. George the Dragonslayer cultus in an Ethiopian and/or Amharic context, we see both parallels to and departures from the Greek and other versions of the legend[8] that warrant further scrutiny. The Amharic-Ethiopian version gained particular prominence between the fourteenth and eighteenth centuries, as documented in contemporary iconography such as manuscript illuminations, mural decorations, and paintings on wood.[9] As attested by Polish scholar and librarian Stanislaw Chojnacki, "There seem to be no icons representing St. George preserved from a time before the fifteenth century and little or no evidence in manuscript illuminations."[10] Regardless, as in the originally Greek version of the tale, and though St. George's grisly martyrdom[11] also has received considerable iconographic attention, the emphasis in Ethiopia traditionally remained on the Christian soldier's seemingly effortless triumph over the noxious and evil dragon who had threatened to devour the unlucky pagan princess of the Kingdom of Silene. Also paralleling the original, the Ethiopian pictorial version of St. George's dragon reflects the shift from a limbless snake to a bipedal and winged dragon (i.e., a wyvern) in the then-increasingly conventional late–Medieval/Renaissance Western style, especially starting around the late fifteenth century. Chojnacki attributes this to the likelihood of foreign and especially Italianate and/or Greek-Byzantine influences on Ethiopian art and artists.[12] By the seventeenth century the transition would be complete in Ethiopia, as elsewhere in Christendom, with the doomed dragon—lance-skewered and trampled under George's mighty horse—regularly exhibiting four legs in addition to a pair of wings.[13]

The once-substantial cultural and iconographic influences on Ethiopia from Europe and the West at large have, latterly, subsided somewhat. With virtually the entire African continent throwing off the shackles of European colonialism as of the end of the twentieth century, along with the erstwhile Abyssinian empire's transition to a federal democratic republic, ties with the old standbys of Orthodox Christianity and Greco-Roman thought and literature have been tempered by a more Pan-African consciousness. The influence of Islamic traditions from Ethiopia's closest neighbors, Somalia, Sudan, and Kenya, has been considerable as well. Fittingly, the specter of dragons, according to my Ethiopian informant, does not pack the same psychic or metaphoric punch that it may have in yesteryear, at least based on the iconographic evidence. Nevertheless, St. George and the dragon still hold significant semiotic power. In 1974, for example, when Haile Selassie I and thus the 2,000-year-old monarchy were deposed, the *Ethiopian Herald* ran an editorial cartoon depicting the famous saint and his foe. As reported by the *Guardian*:

> It showed an Ethiopian Saint George standing at the ocean's edge and throwing spears at a five-headed dragon rearing up from the water. Above the five heads were the words "corruption, bribery, nepotism, inefficiency and embezzlement."
>
> The tail of the monster was shown looping round behind the heroic Saint George with the

Mural of St. George and the Dragon, Ethiopian Orthodox Monastery, Lake Tana, Ethiopia (Glen Berlin/Shutterstock.com).

words "reactionary forces" written on it. And the caption read "The coordinating Committee is facing a Herculean task."[14]

Middle East/Central Asia

Arabic (Standard): *tani(y)n* (تنين)
Berber: *adṛak* (ⵄⴰⵇⵄⴽ)
Farsi (Persian): *ajedha* (اژدها)
Hebrew (Modern): *derakon* (דְרָקוֹן)

Kurdish: *ziha/ejder*
Pashto: *dareegan* (درېگان)
Tajik: *azdaho* (аждахо)
Turkish: *ejderha*

Like Africa, what is commonly referred to as the "Middle East" or "Near East" is anything but monolithic in its culture and language. And where exactly the "Middle East" ends and Central Africa (to its south), Europe (to its north/northwest), and Central Asia (to its east/northeast) begin is, of course, open to considerable semantic, geographic, climactic, and political perspective and debate. Nevertheless, for mere purposes of convenience we may, albeit imperfectly, define this world region as including the lands where both Islam, overall, predominates *and* where the influence of the Arabic language and/or script have penetrated to a significant degree.

Though the far-flung Arab peoples have been uniquely influential throughout the region since their ancestors first migrated out of the Arabian Peninsula in a flurry of both political conquest and religious conversion in the seventh and eighth centuries CE, other major groups include the indigenous (and also Afro-Asiatic, though Hamitic, not Semitic) Berbers of the Sahara; the Indo-European Pashtuns, Kurds, Tajiks, and Persians in and around what is now Iran; and the Turks, Uzbeks, Turkmens, Kazakhs, Kyrgyz, Uyghurs, and other Turkic ethno-linguistic groups throughout Asia Minor and the Eurasian steppes. Add to this milieu another group that, for many centuries, was relatively sparse in number but since the 1940s is again in considerable demographic ascendence: the Jewish people and their reconstructed, revitalized national language, Modern Hebrew, now represented in significant numbers in the State of Israel.

Long before these people-groups would coalesce and evolve into their modern forms, there lived in the fertile, crescent-shaped valley between the rivers Tigris and Euphrates (the "Cradle of Civilization" of Mesopotamia) a people known as the Sumerians. They and their cultural successors, the Akkadians, a demonym which encompasses both the ancient Babylonian and Assyrian peoples and their Semitic languages, would leave an outsized influence. In large part, this was thanks to the biologically abundant riverlands themselves, which allowed these groups to transition from small groups of nomadic hunter-gatherers to complex, agrarian societies capable of "high culture," including the invention of a system of writing.

In the foundational Babylonian cuneiform text, the *Enuma Elish*, the creation of which dates to probably the second millennium BC, we read of the origin of an early Semitic[15] interpretation of how the world was first formed. This genesis was not immediate, but rather progressed through first a mixing (or mating) of elements, such as types of water, and then a war between the old and new gods for supremacy over humankind. At the conclusion of his battle with the elder god Tiamat, the younger or lesser god Marduk splits her inflated carcass with an arrow. (Tiamat is a goddess often portrayed with draconic attributes, hence her inclusion as a female dragon in such modern franchises as *Dungeons and Dragons*.[16]) After Tiamat is slain, "[h]umanity is then put to work for the gods," writes the biblical scholar Robert D. Miller III, "a theme known from earlier Mesopotamian creation myths."[17] But in addition to being her mortal foe, Marduk is also a direct descendant of Tiamat. The genealogy is as follows: Tiamat is the wife of Apsû (the "Begetter" and representative of groundwater); she is also the mother of the Sky and Earth and the grandmother of Anu (the sky-god), Enlil, and Ea. As he is Ea's son, Marduk is thus Tiamat's great-grandson. Tiamat's principal epithet is "Maker," and she also represents saltwater—her name is from the common word for "sea" in Akkadian, also a Semitic language.[18] She is thus a marine creature in her earthly form, both dwelling in and embodying the primordial sea. Marduk's explosion of his great-grandmother's corpse with an arrow after first trapping her with a net and then inflating her with wind symbolizes a rebirth through death—the birth of a new world wherein humans will play an essential part, not in the sea, but on land.

Another creature which fits the description of "dragon" in the *Enuma Elish* is known as the *Mušḫuššu*. This creature, a servant of Marduk, is depicted as a near paragon of David E. Jones' tripartite Dragon Complex described in Chapter 1. It has a scaly, reptilian body and snake-like tongue; leonine forelimbs and paws; and the talons of an eagle as its hindlimbs. The image of this creature, which also serves as the symbol (in a way, the mascot) of Marduk himself, once adorned the Ishtar Gate leading to the inner city of ancient Babylon, in what is now central Iraq. During a German excavation of 1904–14, the remains of that gate were covertly disassembled, transported, and then, in 1918, reassembled at Berlin's Pergamon Museum, where the reconstruction still stands. A smaller replica of the Ishtar Gate was also completed in the 1980s, under then Iraqi president Saddam Hussein, and still stands near the town of Hillah.

There are several parallels between the *Enuma Elish* and Genesis 1 of the Hebrew and Christian Bibles, as well as between the analogous creation story in the Qur'an of Islam. For one, the Middle Eastern/Muslim or otherwise Semitic-dominated

Replica of Ishtar Gate of Babylon featuring images of the dragon-like *Mušḫuššu* of the ancient Babylonian text, the *Enuma Elish*. The recreation, in Hillah, Iraq, south of Baghdad, is smaller than the original and was completed under Iraqi president Saddam Hussein in 1987 (Homo Cosmicos/Shutterstock.com).

cultural areas have been (and still are) inclined towards what we may call the maleficent or Western-type dragon. The Semitic influences on European cultures via their adoption into the corpus of Christian (and, in a few cases such as in the Balkans region, Islamic) literatures and folklores present a major catalyst for virtually all European dragon lore as it has existed since Christianization began in earnest in Europe in the fourth century CE (or, to a much lesser degree, Islamization in later centuries). "Within the Hebrew Bible," explains Robert D. Miller, "snakes more likely stand for sorcery, knowledge, infernal wisdom—the same root [used for 'snake' words] is used for divination...."[19] Along with notions of evil, mayhem, or damnation, the serpent's affiliations with the occult also transmitted practically unabated from the belief systems and mythologies of the city-states of Mesopotamia to, eventually, the farthest outposts of European colonialism. In addition to popular mythology, the contributions of Semitic cultures, and especially the Islamo-Arabic cultural sphere that flourished in the Middle Ages, had far-reaching impacts on the sciences of the Near East and Eurasia as well.

Astronomy, for example, is a discipline which, without the contributions of classical Arab scholars, often working under the direct patronage of powerful regional caliphs, may very well have been lost and forgotten in Europe during the Middle Ages. Though the highly influential Greek-Egyptian astronomer Claudius Ptolemaeus (or Ptolemy; c. 100–c. 170 CE) had documented many of the major constellations of the night sky in his *Almagest* (originally *Mathēmatikē Syntaxis* in Greek), manuscript copies of this text were nearly obliterated in Europe after the fall of the Roman Empire (c. 476 CE) and the ensuing power vacuum of the subsequent centuries. Furthermore, even with access to classical texts, much of the mathematical knowledge necessary to accurately conduct or interpret astronomical studies among Europeans had fallen into decline in the absence of stable centers of higher learning and other factors generally hostile to systematic education during this period, such as political instability.

The transcultural journey of Ptolemy's influential book is imprinted in the name *Almagest* itself: due to Muslim Arab scholars' translation and popularization of the Greek work into Arabic, the text maintains to this day its popular name in a corrupted Arabicization of the Greek word for "greatest"—the Arabic definite article *al* plus *megisti*/μεγίστη. Medieval Arabic preeminence in astronomy, in general, is why the names of a great many stars—approximately ⅔ of those known to humanity since this period[20]—are Arabic in origin. Another impact of the text was Ptolemy's geocentric model of the cosmos, which remained the predominant (and little-disputed) theory of Earth's placement in the heavens for over 1,400 years. It wasn't until Polish astronomer Copernicus (d. 1543) systematically argued for heliocentrism with his monumental tome *On the Revolutions of the Celestial Spheres*, published in 1543, that consensus began to shift, albeit slowly. By the eighteenth century, and not without a great deal of corresponding religious, political, and furthermore demographic upheaval throughout Europe, very few scientists would attempt to argue to the contrary. (Incidentally, a more robust inheritance from Ptolemaic astronomy has been popular astrology, or the Western zodiac. This system is of course still subscribed to by millions, some more earnestly than others, to interpret individual personality traits and romantic compatibilities, among other phenomena.)

The serpent-shaped constellation known as Draco was one of the original forty-eight highlighted by Ptolemy in the *Almagest*, and it is still recognized as such to modern astronomers. Draco is the eighth-largest constellation of all those visible with the naked eye from Earth. Located in the far north of the night sky, the coils of the wingless and limbless dragon—strongly correlated with ancient Greeks' conceptions of the creature, as detailed in the *Greek and Roman* section of Chapter 6—surround Polaris, the Pole Star. Due to natural forces related to the shifting or "wobbling" of the Earth's axis (a process technically known as precession), at one point in the distant past the Pole Star was not Polaris but Alpha Draconis. This star of Draco was also known to the Arabs as *Thu'ban* (الثعبان), their common word for snake or serpent to this day. In Egypt, over 4,000 years ago and thus prior to both the Arab invasion and the shift to Polaris, one of the passageways of the Great Pyramid of Giza was built to line up directly with Thuban/Alpha Draconis because it was then the Pole Star. Alpha Draconis will be the Pole Star once again in about 22,000 years.[21] The star *El-Tanin* (from Arabic التنين, "the dragon"), also known in English as Gamma (γ) Draconis, is positioned in Draco's head, roughly on its "snout." Gamma's neighbor, Beta (β) Draconis or, more traditionally, Rastaban, is so called from the Arabic *ras al-thu'ban* (رأس الثعبان, literally "head [of] the serpent") and could be said to compose the dragon's chin. In chess, the formation known as the Dragon Variation of the Sicilian Defense earned its name due to its similarity to the Draco constellation's general shape.

Another field in which Arabs were preeminent during the medieval era was mechanical engineering. Scholars in this cultural sphere were again prescient in translating and building upon the scientific works of the classical Greco-Roman world, in this case harnessing the discoveries of Hellenic mathematicians such as Euclid and Archimedes. The greatest Arab engineer and inventor of this period was named, in full, Al-Shaykh Rais Al-Amal Badii Al-Zaman Abu Al-Izz Ibn Ismail Ibn Al-Razzaz Al-Jazari (1136–1206 CE). He is better known as simply Ismail al-Jazari. "[Al-Jazari's] innovations," writes one English-language translator and commentator of the inventor's grand opus, "together with the use of components and techniques that were not known in Europe until much later, make al-Jazari's book of the first importance, even though we do not know how much of his work was transmitted to the West."[22] In his famous manuscript, usually translated as *The Book of Ingenious Mechanical Devices*, al-Jazari described and illustrated a particularly notable device: the elephant clock. Intended to stand at over three meters (ten feet) high, the machine is interesting not only for its functional ingenuity but also its array of intentionally symbolic components. The principal "elephant" component, inside of

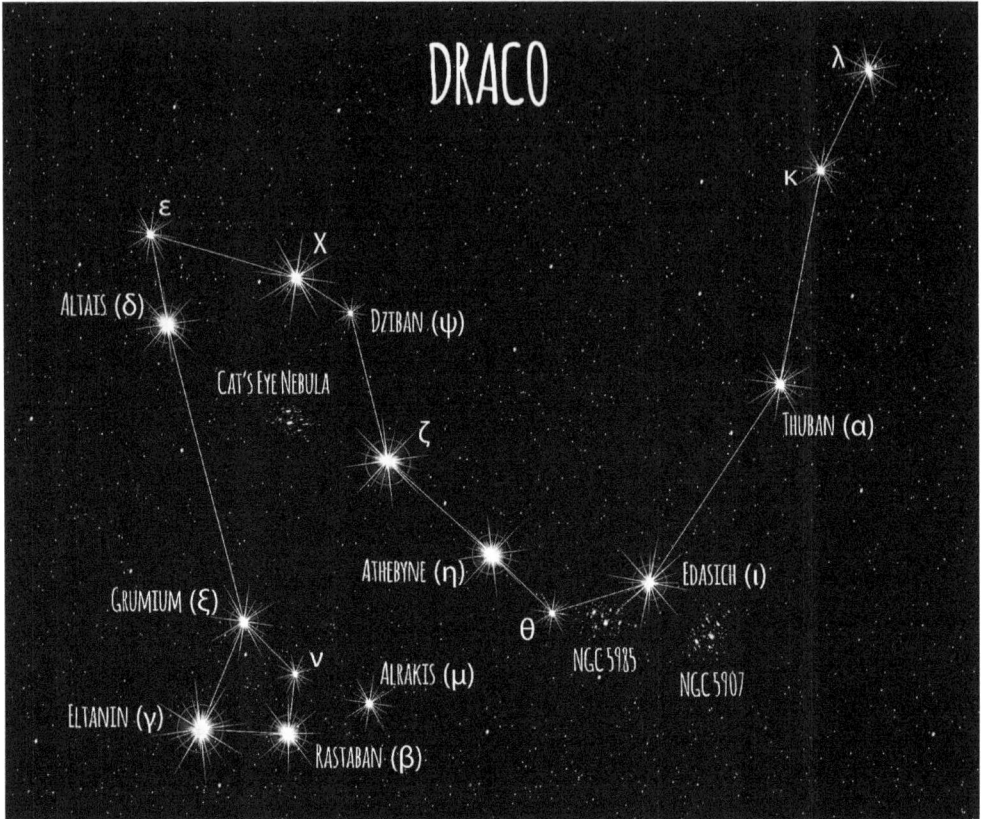

Configuration of the constellation Draco, as seen in the night sky (Jazziel/Shutterstock.com).

which is hidden the water chamber that ultimately powers the clock itself, stood for the Indian and African cultures; its internal water mechanism for the Greeks; the spinning phoenix at the pinnacle for the Egyptians; the intricate rugs and the ball-dropping falcon for the Persians; the turbaned men for the Arabs; and a set of dragons or serpents for the Chinese. Typical of the relatively multicultural spirit of his era, al-Jazari sought to honor the achievements of his many scientific predecessors as well as the specific cultural settings which had nurtured them. Though the word al-Jazari used in his text to describe the Chinese components was indeed *thu'ban* (ثعبان, "serpent" or "snake") and not *tanin* (تنين, "dragon"), according to both al-Jazari's illustrated design and its description the two serpentine mechanisms can clearly be seen as bipedal, mythological dragons and not garden-variety snakes. "Transversely between the centers of the pillars," the scientist wrote, "is an axle on which are two serpents, the claws of each one grasping the axle, its tail around the axle like a ring, its head tilted backwards, the mouth open as if to swallow the head of the falcon."[23] Some versions of the design even show the dragons' limbs as flaring out in the approximate shape of wings, an interesting creative license given traditional Chinese dragons' winglessness.

The Persian dragon, *ajedha* (اژدها), is echoed in Turkish *ejderha,* which was

Medieval Arab scientist Ismail al-Jazari (1136–1206 AD) invented his ingenious elephant clock partially in honor of the scientific achievements of the various civilizations of Asia and Africa. As such, he chose the dragon to represent China. This replica is found at Kasimiye Madrasah, Mardin, Turkey (Tayfun Yaman/Shutterstock.com).

introduced into that language (and practically all other Turkic languages). This is due to the long-standing influence of Persian language and literature on the Near Eastern/Central Asian region in general, especially as Islam became both the predominant religion and cultural conduit among not only the Arabs, but also among the Iranian peoples (almost entirely supplanting the native practice of Zoroastrianism in Persia). Later (between the eighth and ninth centuries CE), as they too converted to Islam, this conduit became the norm among practically all the Turkic peoples of Eurasia as well. For a time, the Persian variety of Arabic script was one and the same as the script of the Ottoman Empire (late thirteenth to early twentieth centuries CE), despite the latter being politically dominated by ethnic Turks from their capital city of Istanbul (formerly Byzantine Constantinople). This usage was also despite the Turkish language being genetically related neither to Persian (an Iranian/Indo-European language) nor Arabic (a Semitic/Afro-Asiatic language) whatsoever; as ever, culture is king and *Sprachbund* may handily overpower genetic affinity given enough exposure and influence. Persian literary and mythological figures, such as the *ajedha,* were thus infused into the lexicons of their genetically unrelated neighbors through cultural diffusion and the general transnational commerce of the Middle Ages in this region.

Though they may have had indigenous terms for the dragon or its ilk, words ultimately derived from the Greek original prevail in Berber (*adṛak,* ⴰⴸⵔⴰⴾ), Modern Hebrew (*d[e]rakon,* דְּרָקוֹן), and Pashto (*dareegan,* دريګن). Modern Arabic maintains its ancient *tani(y)n,* which is also akin to what it was in Ancient Hebrew; the word in Modern Hebrew would have maintained this affinity had external (i.e., Indo-European) influences been less profound (see Chapter 4). Only the stateless Kurds among this group appear to stand out as potentially unique. The three main Kurdish languages, of which the northern variety or Kurmanji is the most widely spoken, have been frequently beset from all sides by the hegemonic forces of the neighboring Arabic, Turkic, and Persian (Iranian) spheres.[24] The Kurds have as their dragon word *zîha,* but even this likely reveals yet another example of *Sprachbund: zîha* is possibly derived from the common Turkic word not for "dragon," but for "snake," *(y)ılan,* where the initial *y* may sound more like a *z* in the mouth of a speaker of an Indo-European language such as Kurdish.[25] What's more, the other common Kurmanji word for dragon is unequivocally Persian, via Turkish, in origin: *ejder.*

Europe

Albanian: *dragoi*	Finnish: *lohikäärme*	Romanian: *balaur*
Basque: *herensuge*	Icelandic: *dreki*	Welsh: *draig*
Bosnian/Croatian/Serbian: *zmaj* (Змај)	Latvian: *pūķis*	

Millennia ago, the continent of Europe was called something else. We don't know what that name was—if there even was a single, definitive name for the whole continent—because virtually all the descendants of those who had already been there for eons were either killed off or assimilated into the societies of the relative newcomers, starting in earnest around 3000 BCE. Those newcomers or invaders are known today as the Indo-Europeans—more commonly still under national or ethno-linguistic categories such as French, English, Italian, Russian, Swedish, Lithuanian, and the others. In the absence of a more accurate nomenclature, the most convenient labels to distinguish these two overlapping, conflicting groups would be, simply, *Old* versus *New* Europeans. However, only one national or people-group of "Old" Europeans remains in any recognizable form, as we will see.

The current scientific hypothesis holds that, at least 5,500 years ago, a group (or related groups) of people originating on the steppes between the Black and Caspian Seas of what today are parts of Ukraine, the Russian Federation, and Kazakhstan,[26] mastered the arts of both domesticating and riding horses. This highly advantageous skillset led to the development of not only the wheel, but furthermore wheeled vehicles like the chariot and cart. Emboldened by such powerful new technologies, these ancestors of the "New" Europeans (also sometimes referred to as the Yamnaya) began to migrate farther and farther west, until, by about 2500 to 200 BCE, they eventually overran the vast majority of what is today known as Europe.[27] As they conquered these new lands on horseback, so too did they vanquish the indigenous peoples there, the Old Europeans, putting most of the males to death while taking the women as wives, concubines, or otherwise rape victims.[28]

After millennia of this near-total dominance, by the start of the Christian Era

The Proto-Indo-Europeans, or Yamnaya, developed technology such as the wheeled, horse-drawn chariot and other vehicles. These innovations gave them a great advantage over other groups when they expanded into various parts of Eurasia, including western Europe, Persia, and northern India. Shown here are the ancient frescoes at Paestum, Magna Grecia (modern Campania, Italy) (BlackMac/Shutterstock.com).

only the Basques (*Euskara*) of northern Spain/southern France had retained their Old European language and ethnic identity, despite the invasions and subsequent linguistic and genetic influx of the New or Indo-Europeans. That the Basques have maintained this distinct language (a true isolate, as far as linguistic research can determine) and national identity to the present day is a remarkable outcome. Their cultural resilience is especially remarkable considering the active repression they experienced under the regime of Spanish dictator Francisco Franco (r. 1939–1975). "Essentially, they should have disappeared as a distinct people," attests the anthropologist and Basque scholar William A. Douglass.[29]

Any other current and long-settled *non*–Indo-European ethno-linguistic populations in today's European continent (i.e., the Finns, Sami, Estonians, and Hungarians—all Finno-Ugric people-groups) would arrive long after the Indo-Europeans in separate waves from the northeast or east by 400 CE, originating in what is today the north of the Russian Federation.

European dragon and other mythological lore, writ large, is consequently hybrid in nature. The underlying Celtic, Germanic, Baltic, Albanian, Slavic, Basque, and other ethno-linguistic cultures of the European continent have virtually all been overlain with literary elements of Roman, Greek (Hellenic), Judaic, or Islamo-Arabic origins, among others. This process was catalyzed after these latter colonial or otherwise hegemonic influences made inroads into traditional homelands, less often through sheer demographic influx than through the forces of commerce, war, empire, language, literature, science, religion, or some combination thereof.

But let us return to the unique Basques. Through their (usually) seven-headed dragon, the *herensuge*, we gain a particularly nuanced insight into the fungible nature of the dragon in the European context.

Firstly, *suge(a)* is the common Basque word for "snake" or "serpent" and thus *herensuge* is a derivation thereof. *Heren-* is a prefix related to *handia*, the common adjective "big." The immediate sense of the word *herensuge* is as simple as "big/great snake," though *heren-* is only used as a prefix in certain rare cases, of which the name of the traditional dragon is one. As Iñaki Arrieta Baro, Librarian of the Jon Bilbao Basque Library at the University of Nevada, Reno, clarifies, "There does not appear to be an agreement about the etymology of the word as a whole," he states, "other than it could maybe refer to the name of a specific creature."[30] A term related to *suge* that is much simpler to parse out, however, is the pre–Christian Basque god known as *Sugaar*, the male counterpart to the goddess Mari. The god's name is a simple combination of the same "serpent" or "snake" as above plus the suffix *-ar*, indicating maleness.

Regardless of etymology, the resonance of the *herensuge* in Basque folklore and mythology is considerable, especially as regards the creature's possible and confirmed links to other dragon legends in the greater Neo-European *Sprachbund*. However, as attested in many traditional works of art, the Basque culture's conception of the *herensuge*, besides its multiple heads, matches more closely the Eastern, wingless form of the *lóng* than that of Western lore. As mentioned, the Basque *herensuge* almost always has seven heads, which generally recalls the Lemean Hydra of Greek mythology, though the latter boasted of nine (of which one was immortal, the hero Heracles would come to learn). More likely an explanation than one of mythological borrowings between Greek and Basque is the existence of a common melting pot of European motifs—whether Old or New or combined—from which many of these tales originally emerged in prehistoric times. "[T]here seems little doubt that for the Occident, at least," the American folklorist Stith Thompson wrote, "the dragon legends are organically related."[31]

One narrative, included in a volume of traditional Basque folk tales collected by nineteenth-century British scholar Wentworth Webster, appears to bear out this affinity. In "The Grateful Tartaro and the Heren-Suge," as related in the late nineteenth century by a Basque woman from Labourd, a suburb of the seaside city of Biarritz in the French Basque Country, the core of the story aligns uncannily well with the common folk-tale motif known as "The Dragon Slayer" (ATU Type 300[32]). The central content of this traditional Basque tale—which Webster warns may have been absorbed from or otherwise highly influenced by a (non–Basque) French version—centers around a dragon-slaying prince in exile and is, in essence, also what composes the entirety of the St. George the Dragonslayer legend of Christian hagiography (described and analyzed in Chapter 5). Besides the detail of St. George being an itinerant prince rather than an itinerant soldier, what distinguishes "The Grateful Tartaro and the Heren-Suge" from the traditional St. George tale is its set of uniquely Basque elements. These include a rather helpful and dignified one-eyed ogre, or the eponymous "grateful Tartaro" (contrast with the invariably doltish, vile, and bloodthirsty Greek Cyclops), as well as a talking, even somewhat reasonable seven-headed dragon of the uniquely (for Europe) Basque variety. Webster speculated that there may have been a direct point of cultural contact between the Greek Cyclops and its approximate Basque counterpart, the Tartaro.[33] The evidence that the folklorist presented in support of this hypothesis, however, is too scanty to be conclusive.

The collected Basque tales in Webster also contain certain interesting rhetorical devices, as seen in the tale's introductory sentence. "Like many of us who are, have been, and shall be in the world," it begins, "there was a king, and his wife, and three sons."[34] Or consider this, the first line from another *herensuge* tale collected by Webster, "The Fisherman and His Sons": "Like many others in the world," it echoes, "there was a fisherman who lived with his wife."[35] Even in translation these small but important flourishes express the unique qualities of a particular narrative tradition. In this case, the sentiment that we are meant to feel is one of an immediate affinity or at least general familiarity with the characters who are about to be introduced. The following passage from "Grateful" yields yet another memorable turn of phrase, one embedded in the following action sequence:

[The hero, Petit Yorge,] leaps on his spirited horse, and they fight more fiercely than ever [with the seven-headed *Heren-Suge*]. The horse leaped as high as a house, and the serpent, in a rage, says to him,

"*If I had a spark of fire between my tail and my head*, I would burn you and your lady, and this horse and this terrible dog."

The young man says,

"I, if I had the good-scented water under my nose, I would cut off one of your heads, and the horse another, and the dog another."[36] [italics added]

"If I had a spark of fire between my tail and my head..." stands out as a monstrous utterance as equally iconic as (if not more so than) "Fee-fi-fo-fum, I smell the blood of an Englishman!" of *Jack and the Beanstalk* fame. (Perhaps only Smaug of Tolkien's *The Hobbit* can best the Heren-Suge in the dramatic eloquence department.)[37] As the Indo-Europeanist Calvert Watkins wrote, "Language is linked to culture in a complex fashion: it is at once the expression of a culture and a part of it."[38] On display is the genius of not only the individual speaker, but the Basque imaginary as expressed through the Basque language.

One additional point on the narrative is worthy of mention here. The extended version of "The Dragon Slayer" motif—also referred to by Stith Thompson as the "Dragon Rescue"—, or rather, the wider narrative in which this simpler motif is often embedded, is known as "The Two Brothers" (ATU Type 303). As will also be elaborated in Chapter 5, this much longer and more nuanced ancient story template contains material that stretches far into the background of the character St. George the Dragonslayer, as well as into his future. In the traditional version, "George" also has a twin brother. And in the Basque version recorded by Webster, "The Fisherman and His Sons," the dragon-slaying figure has not one but *two* brothers.[39]

Specifically, the brothers are identical triplets. Otherwise, the congruence with the template as described by Thompson is unmistakable: A childless fisherman catches a magical, talking fish. The fish is grateful to the fisherman for sparing his life two times, but the fish finally accepts its fate the third time it is caught, though with a caveat. "Well, then, since you will carry me home," the fish says,[40] the fisherman must feed one piece of him to his wife, another to his mare, and another to his bitch. The rest he should bury in his garden under a tree. Not long after, in turn first the fisherman's bitch, then his wife, and then his mare all give birth to identical triplets (again, identical *twins* in most other versions). The significance of the burial of the piece of fish under the tree is that from then on, its leaves will suddenly fade and fall should anything unfortunate happen to any of the fisherman's three boys. (In the Basque version, the alerting device is not a tree, however, but a well on the fisherman's property that will start to boil in case of emergency. We may assume that the fisherman threw a piece of the fish into the well, though this is not explicitly mentioned in the version recorded by Webster.[41]) Each boy (whether there are two or three), then, has his own horse and his own dog.

Once he comes of age, one of the human triplets ventures out into the world to seek his fortune on his own. As Thompson summarizes, "He sets forth with his sword, horse, and dog, and after a while arrives at a royal city. *From this point on the story is identical with The Dragon Slayer tale [...] but after the marriage with the princess the narrative proceeds [...]*"[42] As we will see in Chapter 5, due to his proselytizing agenda the pious and chaste Christian soldier George does not marry the princess he rescues, but otherwise the details are a match. In "The Two [or Three] Brothers," the longer story's progress is contingent on the first son marrying the rescued princess after first proving to her father, the king, that he has indeed slain the marauding dragon. He does so by presenting the dragon's seven (in the Basque case) tongues; he had cut the tongues out of its heads right after cutting them off its necks with the help of his horse and dog. Otherwise, a scheming, by-standing coachman (or, in the Basque case, a charcoal-burner) would have gladly taken the credit (and the princess's hand) by presenting the dragon heads that he had merely scavenged from the scene of the battle.

The narrative continues further as the first son goes missing on his wedding night (or at some point afterwards). He has been trapped in a castle by an old witch and must be rescued by his identical brother(s) and his/their animals, who pose(s) as him in order to solve the case and set things right again.[43] Essentially, the significance of the brothers' identicality is that they must remain true and loyal to their first brother even when everyone else, including the first brother's lusty new wife, is unaware of the mix-up. (The very basic moral here is that one should do the right thing even when it might be easy to get away with doing the wrong thing.) What these many parallels ultimately exemplify is that though the Basque conception of the dragon likely emerged from its own autochthonous, non– and pre–Indo-European tradition, as exhibited in this folklore, at least, it has been thoroughly brought into the milieu of its surrounding Indo-European neighbors, just as Webster had suspected.

Lastly, the conception of the *herensuge* as a wingless, primarily serpentine (and therefore less mammalian or avian) dragon is of interest. This may, at least at first blush, be related to the Basque culture's unique genetic and chronological status as contrasted with all other nations of Europe. Is it possible that such an isolated people-group's more Eastern-style dragon is yet another survival from the pre–Indo-European era and locale from which they originated? Before the arrival of the Yamnaya invaders, it is tempting to envision outside influences upon the Proto-Basques' cultural sphere as having been relatively minor, with mostly localized and homogenous elements predominating. But it is impossible to know with much certainty about the dynamics of an era so shrouded in the mists of time. It is plausible that the evolutionarily acquired aversion to snakes among humans and our primate forebears may be expressed in a fashion that we might consider more elemental or animistic in certain cases, just as it is in the Far East, Australia, and in the Indigenous Americas, for example. In its various oral and literary interpretations, though it is primarily malevolent the Basque *herensuge* does appear to lack many of the trappings of the otherwise standard Christo-European dragon. Even more telling of this potential cross-cultural affinity, the mighty Basque serpent-god Sugaar, much like the many manifestations of *lóng* in China, possesses a highly auspicious aspect: he is the life-giving yet tremendous bringer of storms and thunder.[44] In the recent children's fantasy chapter-book, *The Basque Dragon*, author Adam Gidwitz clearly expresses this auspiciousness. The series' two young heroes are tasked with protecting cryptozoological wonders such as a (in this case, one-headed) *herensuge* against a pair of greedy corporate polluters, the Schmoke Brothers, who are clearly modeled after Charles and David Koch.[45] The moral is that nature is right and good; even monsters deserve to be protected if they are of nature.

Further instances and details of European dragon lore and etymology are included in Chapter 6.

3

South Asia, East/Southeast Asia, and Oceania

South Asia

Bengali: *ḍrāgana* (ড্রাগন)
Gujarati: *ḍrēgana* (ડ્રેગન)
Hindi: *ajagar* (अजगर)
Marathi: *ḍrĕgana* (ड्रॅगन)
Nepalese: *ḍryāgana* (ड्रयागन)

Sinhalese (*Sinhala*): *makarā* (මකරා)
Tamil: *tirākaṉ* (டிராகன்)
Telugu: *ḍrāgan* (డ్రాగన్)
Tibetan: *dru* (འབྲུག)

What is immediately evident from the above list is the influence, via British colonialism and postcolonialism, of English on many of the languages of the Indian subcontinent and its environs. Though clearly adapted to match the phonologies of these languages (excepting the equivalent words in Sinhalese, Hindi,[1] and Tibetan, which do not share this etymology), the Greek-derived *dragon* has replaced what anciently would have been terms derived from more localized lexicons and folklores. Nevertheless, the dragon lore of South Asia is to this day rich and furthermore highly embedded in the cosmologies and mythologies of the region's ancient belief-systems and literatures, and especially those of Hinduism and Buddhism.

Many South Asian or Indic mythological traditions can be traced as far back as the Vedas (written *c.* 1500–900 BCE), the ancient texts which compose the pillars of both Sanskrit literature and the Hindu religion. The Vedic Sanskrit word *Makara* refers to a creature with the more specific connotations of "sea dragon" or "water monster." This is the source of the common "dragon" *makarā* (මකරා) in Sinhalese, one of the two primary languages (along with the Dravidian language Tamil) of Sri Lanka. According to the Vedas, Varuna, the god of the sky in the Hindu pantheon, rides a crocodile named Makara. Like many other dragons, Makara sometimes also displays a certain hybridity, such as possessing a fish's head or an elephant's trunk, along with its more reptilian traits. Besides serving as Varuna's personal mount, Makara may also serve the same function for other Hindu deities. As we saw in Chapter 2 with Tiamat of the Babylonian *Enuma Elish*, Makara was also a primordial creature capable of both creation and destruction. However, as Kenneth Dobson and Arthur Saniotis point out, "Unlike the Greeks and Babylonians, the Hindus did not conceive of the precursors [i.e., titans or primordial gods] as having been conquered or demoted when the next era/generation came along. But the predecessors were more obscure and primordial."[2] This trope appears to be congruent with Hinduism's great tolerance and even celebration of a large and dynamic pantheon, which by most counts comprises thirty-three principal *devas* or gods and many lesser deities and other beings.[3]

Related to Makara are the Nagas. These legendary, snakelike beings were later exported from India, especially via Indo-Buddhist missionaries, to Southeast Asian countries such as Thailand, Cambodia, and Viet Nam (or "Indo-China"), where they proliferated in art and literature along with many other elements of originally Indic lore and culture. As such, these mythological beings will be detailed further in the following section of this chapter. For now, it bears mentioning that the Nagas are more explicitly associated with snakes, and specifically cobras, than with the more crocodilian Makara. "These were demi-gods in various serpentine forms," Ernest Ingersoll wrote of Nagas, "uncertain of temper and fearful in possibilities of harm, whose 'kings' lived in luxury in magnificent palaces in the depths of the sea or at the bottom of inland lakes."[4] Vedic writings also include mentions of marauding strangers, foreigners who were referred to as "Naga men" or simply "Nagas." The likely allusion was that, among the members of the elite Brahmin class who composed the Vedas, these mysterious folk were particularly notorious for being cobra-worshipers, i.e., non–Hindu animists.[5]

East/Southeast Asia

Burmese: *nagarr* (နဂါး)
Cambodian (*Khmer*): *neak* (នាគ)
Chinese (Mandarin): *lóng* (龍 or 龙)
Filipino (*Tagalog*): *dragon*
Hmong: *zaj*
Indonesian/Javanese/Malay/
 Sundanese: *naga*

Japanese: *ryū, tatsu* (竜), *doragon* (ドラ
 ゴン)
Korean: *yong* (용)
Thai: *mạngkr* (มังกร)

As mentioned above, the concept of the Nagas was imported to southeast Asia from India. *Naga* even became the default word for "dragon" in Malayo-Polynesian languages such as Bahasa Indonesia, Javanese, and Sundanese. Burmese, with its *nagarr*, shows this affinity as well. The wandering Buddhist missionaries of the first millennium CE clearly succeeded in spreading not only their spiritual philosophy, but also components of the folklore and mythology of their Indian homeland and forebears. Even as other major religions, such as Islam and Christianity, rose in prominence in many areas of maritime southeast Asia did this Hindu-Buddhist (and Jain) motif remain highly embedded.

Temple Naga Stairway at Doi Suthep Temple, Chiang Mai, Thailand (jaboo2foto/Shutterstock.com).

Such a manifestation was prominently showcased in the recent animated Disney film, *Raya and the Last Dragon* (2021), written by Americans Qui Nguyen, of Vietnamese descent, and Adele Lim, of Chinese-Malaysian descent. The setting, in the fictional land of Kumandra, is a composite of several Southeast Asian countries and their traditional cultures. The eponymous last dragon, named Sisu and voiced by Chinese American comedian Awkwafina, is visually very much from the Naga tradition: she has an almost equine head, two rhinoceros' horns, leonine paws and mane, and a fishlike tail; she is proudly an excellent swimmer. She is the only dragon left unpetrified after evil spirits called the Druun have cast their spells on her brothers and sisters. The stone dragons depicted in the film were inspired by the statuary commonly seen on the grounds of many Buddhist temples in Thailand, Laos, Cambodia, Viet Nam, Myanmar, and other areas of what was once known as "Indo-China"—the area south and southeast of China proper that came under the influence of Buddhist philosophy and other Indic cultural exports.

In the Japanese language, a seahorse is literally a "dragon's spawn" (*tatsunō-toshigo*, written either タツノオトシゴ or 竜の落し子). In her short story "Where Europe Begins," the transnational Japanese novelist Yoko Tawada elaborates on this etymology: she refers to her home country as a "child of Siberia that had turned on its mother and was now swimming alone in the Pacific … a seahorse, which in Japanese is called *Tatsu-no-otoshigo*—the lost child of the dragon."[6] (It should be noted that the Japanese archipelago does also generally resemble a seahorse.) Though of course references to dragons are found in names for animals, plants, minerals, and beyond in many languages throughout the world, this case stands out as displaying a notably poetic potential.

The Eastern, beneficent dragon maintains an integral presence in Japanese folklore. And though many of its attributes were introduced into Japan long ago, like so many other cultural phenomena either from or via China, the various manifestations of the dragon in Japan are distinctive. These distinctions become particularly acute as Japan has emerged in the last century as a cultural and technological powerhouse on the world stage, one that has managed to both preserve many of its ancient traditions while also welcoming and assimilating many disparate elements from the West.

What instantly stands out in the list of terms above is that Japanese has three common terms for the dragon. The first two, *ryū* and *tatsu*, are indigenous, but the third, *doragon* (ドラゴン, written in the *katakana* script used for words of foreign origin) is borrowed directly from English. Furthermore, *doragon* is used specifically to indicate the Western, malevolent dragon, the image of which has been subsumed into the Japanese imaginary and exists in tandem with the indigenous, beneficent variety. The high frequency of such borrowings evinces the strong influence that the languages and technologies of the West, and especially of the United States, have had on modern Japanese. This influence is also seen in the island nation's popular culture in general, a trend that began during the second half of the twentieth century and continues in earnest into the present day.

"The Japanese use English words to express concepts for which they have no equivalents" writes Japanese language expert Namiko Abe. "However, some people simply prefer to use English expressions for practically [*sic*] or because it is fashionable."[7] All of this more recent cultural hybridity traces back to the United States' nuclear-bombing and subsequent defeat of the Empire of Japan in 1945 at the culmination of the Second World War. The devastation of the cities of Hiroshima and Nagasaki would cast a deadly, radioactive pall, as well as a deeply psychological one, over the Japanese people. Meanwhile, the pseudo-colonial military rule of the victorious Americans engendered an uneasy peace.

In his book *How to Hide an Empire: A History of the Greater United States*, historian Daniel Immerwahr details how, after the Second World War, the United States shifted its burgeoning imperial aspirations from the acquisition and direct governance over colonized lands to a more indirect policy. It achieved this through its worldwide network of military bases, international commerce, and furthermore through an array of world-beating technology on which cultural and ideological content could be transmitted. Japan, which was occupied by the United States military under General Douglas A. MacArthur from 1945 until 1952—the nation's very constitution was rewritten by American civil officials—was uniquely placed to witness this dramatic transition. In the literal ruins of their own empire, writes Immerwahr, Japanese start-up corporations began to adapt the innovations wielded by the American occupiers to their own local needs and aspirations, essentially reverse-engineering American ingenuity. These enterprising individuals filtered what they had ascertained through the lens of a post-war, "nothing-to-lose" mentality, and, in many cases, improved upon the very American devices and methods that they were emulating. As seen in the origin stories of Japanese companies such as Sony (not to mention Toyota, Yamaha, Mitsubishi, etc.), this proved to be a model that has not only succeeded locally, but thrived internationally.[8]

The Japanese people's prolonged suffering from the detonation and radioactive fallout of atomic bombs, which killed hundreds of thousands of its civilians, inspired a massive artistic reckoning. Through the cinematic genre known as *kaiju* ("strange beast"), of which it is considered one of the first examples, the 1954 film *Gojira* earnestly expresses this national trauma. Though now sometimes considered to be in the realm of camp, *Gojira*'s producers attempted to present an unequivocal and urgent warning to the rest of the world on the dangers of nuclear weapons as the Americans blithely, it seemed, continued their test-bombing in the South Pacific. In English we know the franchise spawned by *Gojira*, now in its seventh decade, as *Godzilla*.

Is the monster known as Godzilla a dinosaur, a dragon, or something else? Practically speaking, Godzilla's original physical appearance was dictated by the constraints of the miniature-model-based special effects of the period: an actor in a rubber suit was much more manageable than engineering a prehensile, Eastern-style dragon that was also awe-inducing on the big screen. Godzilla's barrel-chested and thick-armed physiognomy—almost as if it were the offspring of a crocodile and a gorilla—was thus the franchise's standard until computer-generated imagery could produce more realistic saurian features. But in the Japanese original, it is implied that the 165-foot-tall reptilian represents some kind of transitional species between ichthyosaurs and dinosaurs: "It's believed that during [...] the Cretaceous period," reports one of the film's heroes, paleontologist Professor Kyôhei Yamane, "a rare intermediate organism was evolving ... from a marine reptile into a terrestrial animal."[9] We also learn that the creature was already known to the natives of the film's fictional Odo Island, off the coast of Japan. In ancient times, so it is revealed, Gojira would occasionally emerge from its aquatic lair to feast on the large schools of fish just offshore. The islanders explain to the team of investigating scientists that in such cases their ancestors would then be forced to appease the monster by sacrificing a young girl set adrift in a boat. What has changed of late is the underwater detonation of hydrogen bombs (the Americans are not specifically named), an act which has not only disturbed and infuriated the otherwise dormant creature, but furthermore made it radioactive. After Odo, the megalopolis of Tokyo is the seemingly unstoppable leviathan's next target.

Along with much creative license, of course, what directly inspired such dramatic plot points was the series of actual detonation of H-bombs in the Pacific by the U.S. Atomic Energy Commission after the Second World War; nearly seventy such tests were conducted between 1946 and 1958. Odo Island is thus a very thinly veiled reference to Bikini Atoll (among other atolls), in the then American-controlled Marshall Islands of the greater Pacific archipelago of Micronesia. Starting in the mid–1940s, the tiny island was made uninhabitable by several detonations leading up to that of a fifteen-megaton hydrogen bomb called the "Bravo shot" (or Castle Bravo thermonuclear weapon test) in 1954.[10] The fallout of the latter was so widespread that the crew (and catch) of a Japanese fishing boat, *F/V Lucky Dragon 5* (*Daigo Fukuryū Maru*/第五福龍丸), or simply *The Lucky Dragon*, fell victim to its radiation while out plying their trade. All aboard suffered from acute radiation syndrome (ARS) and one crewman died. After the news broke, the Japanese population at large was duly incensed about the American tests, acutely compounded by the horrors of Hiroshima and Nagasaki of less than a decade before. All these events inspired Japanese producer Tomoyuki Tanaka and director Ishiro Honda to focus their now-iconic *kaiju* film on the nuclear menace and furthermore on the dangers of humans' meddling with the laws of nature. It can be reasonably argued that such science-fiction-fueled monster franchises as *Jurassic Park* would not have been conceived without Tanaka's and Honda's groundbreaking achievement.

Its urgent topicality aside, certain elements of *Gojira* are firmly rooted in the ancient folklore of Japan. Namely, *Gojira* was likely inspired by *Ryūjin* (龍神, loosely "dragon being" or "dragon person"), the tutelary deity or *kami* (神) of the sea who is, as his name clearly implies, also a dragon (*ryū*). Like *Gojira*, *Ryūjin* dwells deep below the surface of the ocean in a space virtually inaccessible to humans; *Gojira* is described as dwelling in a geologically ancient strata of the ocean floor. *Ryūjin* possesses not only great magical and physical powers but also dominion over the tides; like the mighty *Gojira* he should never be disturbed or disrespected, lest his wrath be unleashed. This mythological link also helps to explain why *Gojira* is seemingly able to breathe underwater.

In *Godzilla, King of the Monsters!*, the 1956 American localization of *Gojira*—actually, more of a heavily revised splice-job with a superimposed American protagonist named Steve Martin, played by Raymond Burr—none of the original's anti-nuclear messaging remains. "The Japanese *Gojira* was a protest film," writes Immerwahr, "hammering away at the dangers of the U.S. testing in the Pacific. The English-language *Godzilla*, by contrast, was just another monster flick."[11] The vast majority of Americans, especially during those hopeful and prosperous years of white Middle America immediately following the war, were mostly ambivalent, if not oblivious, to the environmental and societal havoc being wrought by their government many thousands of miles away. Since 1954, Godzilla has gone through dozens of Japanese-produced sequels (with their American localizations) and, since 1998, a handful of reimaginings exclusively produced by Hollywood studios. Bringing together two of cinematic history's most reliably popular gargantuan monsters, the most recent of the latter was 2021's *Godzilla vs. Kong* (Warner Bros.). In a return to the Godzilla franchise's original anti-nuclear message, in 2016 the original Japanese studio Toho Co., Ltd. released *Shin Gojira* (*Godzilla Resurgence*). The plot of this

Godzilla, or *Gojira* in the original Japanese, it may be argued, represents a fusion of both Western and Easter dragon types. But the monster's film debut clearly transmitted a political and environmental message from the Japanese perspective concerning the horrific consequences of detonating radioactive weapons. This statue in Osaka, Japan depicts Godzilla in his original manifestation of 1954 (UsaPyon/Shutterstock.com).

recent installment was directly inspired by the disastrous March 2011 meltdown at the Fukushima Daiichi Nuclear Power Plant, triggered by a massive offshore earthquake and its subsequent tsunami.[12]

In recent years, consumers and hobbyists in the West have taken more of an active interest in Japan and Japanese culture than ever before—a marked reciprocation in what was previously a mostly asymmetrical exchange. Such "Nipponophilia" has been particularly fueled among young people by the global rise in popularity of manga and anime, or Japanese comics and cartoons, respectively. As reported by *The Wall Street Journal*, among users of the Duolingo language-learning app in the United States and United Kingdom in 2021, Japanese was the fastest-growing language. Most of these learners are between the ages of thirteen and seventeen and their most common reason of interest, according to the company, is to better understand the various Japanese pop-culture media that they consume.[13] Yet comics and cartoons may and often do easily lead to further investigations into all things *Nihon*, including the unique island nation's history, folklore, mythology, and religious beliefs. For example, a curious learner might wonder why the mystical "dragon balls" of the popular cartoon franchise *Dragon Ball Z* are wish-granting—in a word, beneficent—as opposed to something more sinister and occult, as such objects would likelier be in a Western fantasy.

Oceania

Fijian: *gata*	Samoan: *tarako*	Warlpiri: *warna*
Hawaiian: *mo'o*	Tahitian: *'ōfī*	Wikmunkan: *Taipan*
Maori: *tarākona/ taniwha*	Tongan: *moko*	

According to the linguist and ethnologist Robert Blust, the ultimate anthropological origin of the dragon may lie less in our evolutionary forebears' fraught relations with predatory beasts than it does in a particular meteorological phenomenon. "[A]lthough the dragon exists in a more or less independent idea in Europe, the Near East, India, the Far East, North America, and Mesoamerica," Blust writes, "in Africa, Southeast Asia, and Australia it almost invariably appears as an alter-ego of the rainbow."[14] Particularly in the case of the Aboriginal peoples of Australia is this construct prevalent, as first reported by A.E. Radcliffe-Browne in a pair of articles published in 1926 and 1930, respectively. This "rainbow serpent" of Australia is variously named *Taipan*, *Julunggul*, *Kunmanggur*, and others, depending on the ethno-linguistic group. The manifestation displays an equally diverse range of traits and associations, from controlling the circulation of blood or women's menstrual cycles; to symbolizing boys' transition from youth to manhood; to hermaphroditism.[15] Regardless of its varying attributes from group to group, notes folklorist and encyclopedist Anthony Mercatante, "Throughout these tribes there is a belief that the serpent will devour human beings who approach its home unless they are medicine men."[16] But how, exactly, does a rainbow become a dragon?

Blust asserts that the phenomenon of the dragon, in general, is "one of the supremely instructive examples of convergent evolution in the symbolic life of the mind."[17] To exhibit this virtual universality, Blust presents a table exhibiting how the sets of traits of the dragon compare among six major and discrete geographical regions: Europe, the Near East, India, the Far East, Mesoamerica, and North America. Of the twenty-six traits or attributes listed—from "giver/withholder of rain" to "encircles the world"—the dragons of the Far East (19), Europe (18), and North America (13) are found on the upper bound of representation. Conversely, the dragons of India (9), Mesoamerica (9), and the Near East (8), exhibit fewer examples of these recorded common traits.[18] Blust at first rather definitively disagrees with the kind of "biological explanations for the idea of the dragon" presented by, for example, David E. Jones in his "Dragon Complex" hypothesis.[19] In its stead Blust contends that the myth arose from natural yet inanimate, non-biological phenomena—and especially those related to water. "By far the most common view," Blust notes, "is that the rainbow is a giant snake which either drinks water from the Earth and sprays it over the sky (thus causing it to rain), or that drinks rain from the sky (thus causing it to stop)."[20] He provides various examples of dragons (or approximations thereof) from throughout the world and notes that many of these "rainbow serpents" are dwellers and guardians of not just any bodies of water but especially of sacred bodies of water, including waterfalls, where rainbows regularly occur due to the constant presence of droplets in the air.

Though Blust's postulate is potentially compelling, it may not be as mutually exclusive from Jones (and others) as he suggests: both the water-rainbow and the chimerical-predator properties *together* are likely to have merged during humans' early evolutionary history to become what we know today as the multifarious manifestations of "dragon." Though it is unclear which of these two interpretations by ancient humans may have emerged first, such a determination is irrelevant and, furthermore, highly unknowable. Despite his earlier statement, even Blust must eventually concede this point. "All that really matters," he writes, "is that the cold-blooded serpent, which is clearly inspired by the shape and color of the rainbow itself, be symbolically hybridized with a warm-blooded animal, hence a mammal or a bird (or some combination of the two)."[21]

The origin stories of many Aboriginal peoples of Australia hold a particular connection with totemic reptiles, whether as the rain-bringing rainbow serpent or a lizard implicated in their very creation as a people. The Arandan, or Arrernte, people of the Northern Territory, for example, revere a creator-lizard named *Mangwer-kunger-kunja*. This figure, according to legend, is responsible for bestowing sacred totemic objects as well as more practical items like the boomerang, essential for

The Rainbow Serpent is a sacred motif in the cosmology of the Aboriginal peoples of Australia. These two massive, standalone boulders at Karlu Karlu, Northern Territory are known as the Devil's Marbles in English, but to the Kaytete, Warumungu, Warlpiri, and Alyawarra they are the Rainbow Serpent's Eggs (Benny Marty/Shutterstock.com).

hunting and thus the people's very survival.[22] Hans Mol further explains the importance of totems to Aboriginal peoples:

> Australian totems are not fundamentally concerned with subsistence, but with the delineation of a variety of intricately interwoven wholes: tribes, moieties [i.e., kinship groups], clans, sexes, individuals. These intertwining identities showed considerable social organization and emerged initially probably because each of them assisted the survival of tribes over those which did not have them.[23]

Though the Rainbow Serpent is auspicious for these reasons, like many conceptions of the dragon in Far Eastern cultures, in Aboriginal Australia it is also mercurial. "On several occasions over the years," writes anthropologist Philip A. Clarke, "Aboriginal people have said to me that they feared Rainbow Serpent spirits living at a particular remote waterhole, the presence of waterlilies seen as evidence that the water was deep enough for them."[24] Not only is the totem a bringer of life, it is just as often a harbinger of death.

4

North America, Central/South America, and Cross-cultural/ Parts In-between

North America

Cherokee (*Tsalagi*): *uktena* (ᎤᎦᏖᎾ)
Hopi: *taaho*
Inuit (*Inuktitut*): *pulateriaarsuk* (ᐳᓚᑌᕆᐋᕐᓱᒃ)

Chippewa (*Ojibwe*): *manitou*
Sioux (*Lakota*): *unhcegila*
Mohawk (*Kanien 'kéha*): *onyare*
Navajo (*Diné*): *na 'ashǫ́ 'iitsoh*

Defining the parameters of "indigeneity" is to tread through a landscape littered with semantic mines and pitfalls. Is indigeneity always a marker relative to some other, colonizing or invading force? Is it a gauge of relative technological level? Merriam-Webster defines *indigenous*, firstly, as "produced, growing, living, or occurring natively or naturally in a particular region or environment." The secondary definition is: "of or relating to the earliest known inhabitants of a place and especially of a place that was colonized by a now-dominant group."[1] The first interpretation offers little help in a world of nuance and shifting context, much less in regard to political machinations. But the latter is the more pragmatic interpretation of this state of being as it most often occurs: by the metric of known tenure. By this standard, indigenous peoples have unequivocal chronological and territorial seniority over the non-indigenous. However, history has shown that the former groups have often lacked recourse against the forces that spawn from the latter's imperial projects or otherwise state-level operations—the very means by which the non-indigenous arrive in new lands have often been correlated with technological and other strategic advantages (e.g., the coastal Portuguese and their precocious developments in seafaring). Furthermore, the potential for large-scale violence by such inherently resource-extracting, imperial states (whether composed of settlers, merchants, or both) upon indigenous groups—themselves virtually always more sustainable in their relationships to the land and natural resources in question—is inextricable from the historical record, and especially that of the last 500 years. This violence, at first physical and, often, epidemiological in nature, later manifests itself into pervasive cultural, political, economic, and linguistic patterns and modes of dominance that have exterminated, subjugated, and/or marginalized indigenous peoples and their cultures around the world. To be *non*-indigenous by this reckoning, then, is most often to be colonial-imperial, or otherwise advancing or aspiring towards such a state.

But cultural or physical erasures are seldom total. Many indigenous people-groups have, against all odds, steadfastly maintained or reclaimed their languages, folkways, and other cultural touchstones. In this sense, indigeneity may be defined by not only survival but defiance to the *forces majeures* of the military-industrial complexes of non-indigenous, imperial technocracies. Many contemporary indigenous groups, though often existentially threatened amid their surrounding post- or neo-colonial societies (e.g., the United States, Canada, Mexico, Brazil), continue to maintain many of their traditional values and practices. In fact, the overall population of those identifying as Native peoples in the United States and Canada is growing[2] along with concerted revitalization projects to revive, teach, and spread their traditional languages and other core traditions such as the culinary arts, oral storytelling, music, and dance. Meanwhile, in certain regions of Mexico, Bolivia, Brazil, Peru, and Paraguay, for example, large populations of Indigenous peoples have effectively *always* maintained both substantial numbers and meaningful contact with their traditional folkways, despite centuries of encroachment.

Thus, we arrive at examples of pertinent Indigenous or Native American folklore and material cultures, often highly disrupted but nevertheless resilient amidst the attempts by the agents of empire to enforce eminent domain and thus supplant said cultures and the peoples that embody them. As we will see, certain trends arise surrounding dragon (or dragon-like) lore that follow these same complex fault lines between tradition and assimilation. But no people-group's history, and especially not from the perspective of a colonizing power, can be fully understood without plumbing the depths of the oldest and most resonant stories that it has told both about and to itself.

In the Algonquian (also sometimes called Algic) cultural sphere, which corresponds to a family of languages once widely spoken in coastal New England, the Great Lakes region, the central Mississippi Valley, and well into the plains of Canada, perhaps the most potentially dragon-like class of mythological entity is known as *manitou* ("MAN-it-too"). Though connotations of the word vary depending on language, dialect, and period, a manitou is generally conceived as a spirit, god, or otherwise a supernaturally mighty creature.[3] In the pre-contact, pre–Christian Native American context, such ambiguity or malleability was commonplace. "In the traditional belief systems of the Algonquian peoples," writes Miami University (Ohio) scholar of Algonquian studies David J. Costa, "'manitous' generally denote any number of various powerful spirits or supernatural beings, potentially good or evil."[4] A common type of manitou, to which we will return shortly, is often referred to by Native American experts as an "underwater panther"—*araamipinšia* in the Miami-Illinois language, which is now functionally extinct.

Originating among the Kaskaskias and Peorias, two tribes among the Miami-Illinois-speaking peoples of central Algonquians, a man-eating *manitou* lives on to the present day in the form of a large petroglyph in what is now the southwestern corner of the State of Illinois, just north of the city of St. Louis, Missouri. Painted upon the limestone bluffs above the Mississippi River, near the modern-day town of Alton, Illinois, is the image of the famous monster, popularly known as the Piasa Bird ("PIE-a-saw"). It is an undoubtedly fiendish chimera of a creature, with a long, fishtail-tipped but otherwise scorpion-like tail; a pair of deer antlers; scales covering its body; four raptor talons; red wings veined with white; and a maned or bearded face, leonine but also somewhat humanoid. Yet it must be said that this well-known riverside attraction is most certainly not the original depiction of what has been named and marketed (inaccurately, as we will see) as a "Piasa."[5]

Before unpacking its nomenclature, some background is in order. The monster's image was first documented in the historical record over 350 years ago, by the French explorer and Jesuit priest Jacques Marquette in the summer of 1673. His account is as follows:

> When skirting some rocks, which by their height and length inspired awe, we saw upon one of them two painted monsters which at first made us afraid, and upon which the boldest

"The Piasa Bird" is found on the cliffs above the Mississippi River near Alton, Illinois. Photographed here in 2018, the image has been recreated in the modern era from drawings and descriptions dating back to the seventeenth century (Logan Bush/Shutterstock.com).

savages dare not long rest their eyes. They are as large as a calf; they have horns on their heads like those of deer, a horrible look, red eyes, a beard like a tiger's a face somewhat like a man's, a body covered with scales, and so long a tail that it winds all around the body, passing above the head and going back between the legs, ending in a fish's tail. Green, red, and black are the three colors composing the picture.[6]

One hundred thirty-one years (and one American Revolution) later, in 1804, one of these paintings was also briefly described and sketched by the American explorers Captain Meriwether Lewis and Lieutenant William Clark in the journals to their famous expedition through what are now known as the Midwest and Pacific Northwest.[7] No mention is made of any wings in either Marquette's or Lewis/Clark's account; these were most certainly added later by more settled Euro-Americans in the area, likely inspired by the attributes of the traditional Western dragon. Furthermore, the last-remaining traces of the original petroglyphs were demolished in the middle of the nineteenth century.[8] And what of the manitou's popular moniker, the "Piasa Bird"? As Costa and others have pointed out, the confusion lies again in Euro-Americans' misunderstanding of Native language and folklore, along with the more universal tendency of a dominating culture to repurpose a foreign and subaltern narrative in either its own or an otherwise novel, fabricated image. But how this process emerged takes some archeological and linguistic unraveling.[9]

First, the so-called "Piasa" should more accurately be *páyiihsaki*. And the error here is deeper still, for *páyiihsaki* describes not a dragonesque manitou but instead a kind of malevolent dwarf found in Miami-Illinois folklore. Costa elucidates the correct source through his translation of a tale recounted by a native Peoria speaker about a trickster named Wissakatchakwa (or *Wiihsakacaakwa*). The tale's raconteur, a man named George Finley (1858–1932), was one of the last fluent speakers of the Peoria dialect of the Miami-Illinois language. In his "sacred story" (*aalhsoohkaakana*) he told of how Wissakatchakwa and a Frenchman, while traveling by canoe to a trading post, were captured by a seven-headed manitou. To escape its watery cave, Wissakatchakwa used gunpowder to explode the monster while it was sleeping. "Then, after he blew him up, the water boiled up for many years."[10] (It should be noted, of course, that the presence of both a Frenchman and gunpowder date this telling to no earlier than the Peorias' first contact with French explorers around the mid- to late seventeenth century.) Once the water cooled, Wissakatchakwa took possession of the cave and refurbished it so he could live there comfortably. However, a pair of *páyiihsaki* (malevolent dwarves) then appeared and bullied Wissakatchakwa into giving up his new home to them. "And so the dwarves became its owners. You can still see the footprints of the dwarves quite clearly there."[11] This last comment explains how several local topographical features first came to be called "Piasa," including a creek, a trail, an unincorporated community, and, by association or proximity many centuries later, the nearby famous cliffside monster, especially in its modern, somewhat reimagined Euro-American manifestation. Echoing the *páyiihsaki* tale, a common practice among the local Kaskaskias and Peorias was, indeed, to leave oddly shaped "footprints" from these malevolent dwarves in the riverside stone.

Presently, a local high school calls its athletic teams the Piasa Birds and a new (founded in 2020) collegiate summer baseball team in the Prospect League is known as the River Dragons.[12] Few in the area may be aware, however, that "Piasa" more accurately describes a dwarf than a dragon or bird. Regardless of its name, the figure's resonance as a popular mythological presence is still felt to this day, as attested by an Alton native whose family has been long resident in the town. The local children, he told me, were and still are warned by adults that the Piasa Bird exclusively hunts and eats *them*.[13]

There remains one other element which appears to relate to *why*, in a practical sense, the image of the manitou or *araamipinšia* was placed so prominently on these bluffs above the Mississippi River. "While conversing about these monsters," Father Marquette continued in his 1673 journal,

> sailing quietly in clear and calm water, we heard the noise of a rapid, into which we were about to run. I have seen nothing more dreadful. An accumulation of large and entire trees, branches, and floating islands, was issuing from the mouth of the river Pekistanouï [Missouri], with such impetuosity that we could not without great danger risk passing through it. So great was the agitation that the water was very muddy, and could not become clear.[14]

Though the twenty-mile stretch of the Mississippi in question may have itself been relatively tranquil (which here runs generally west to east instead of north to south, and along which the "Piasa Birds" were found on the cliffs of the north bank), entering the mouth of the Missouri River was fraught with danger for Marquette and his tiny band of Frenchmen. Little did they realize: the monsters were there to warn them. This is as true as it ever was: "I would go up the Missouri [in a small boat]," my informant told me, "and my dad was always very strongly urging me to be careful because of the riptides and the undercurrents."[15]

Central/South America

Aymara: *asiru*
Aztec (*Nahuatl*): *Quetzalcóatl*
Maya (*Yucatec*): *Kukulkán*

Inca (*Quechua*): *Amaru*
Tupi-Guaraní (*Tupinambá*): *mbóia*

In the Nahuatl language of Mexico, sometimes called Aztec after the empire with which it is associated, the word *cóatl* or *cohuātl* means "serpent" or "snake." (Incidentally, the word can also mean "twin.") *Cóatl* is the second component of the name of the plumed serpent of Aztec mythology and religion, *Quetzalcóatl*—the first element referring to the splendid "plumage" (*quetzalli*) also known in the form of the appositely named and endemic *quetzal* bird (*Pharomachrus mocinno*) of the trogon family (*Trogonidae*). Thus, the primary Aztec deity Quetzalcóatl is commonly portrayed as a splendidly plumed serpent. "[Quetzalcóatl's] cult probably grew from

Despite centuries of Hispanicization, the Aztec god Quetzalcoatl remains a powerful totem in Mexican culture, as seen here in a large ornament on La Plaza Mayor, also known as Zócalo, Mexico City, the epicenter of both the Aztec and Spanish iterations of the metropolis (Luxbox/Shutterstock.com).

that of an ancient Mesoamerican sky god," writes encyclopedist Charles Phillips, "a dragon who was worshiped as a fertility and agricultural deity because of his ability to deliver fresh winds and life-giving rains."[16] In this sense, we immediately see the parallels between Amerindian/Indigenous American dragon tropes and those of the Far East, such as in China, Japan, and Korea, where both auspiciousness and associations with rain predominate.

Approximately 800 miles (1,300 km) away from the Aztec capital of Tenochtitlán (today's Mexico City), the Maya people of the Yucatan Peninsula (today's southeastern Mexico, Guatemala, Belize, and Honduras) worshiped their own plumed-serpent deity. Theirs was named *Kukulcán*, the god of wind, light, and waters, with *kuk* being the Maya's own word for the *quetzal* bird. In addition to its elemental associations, Kukulcán was also endowed with other elemental characteristics, such as those relating to the sun and thunder.[17] As in all mythologies, the Maya's shared sense of personal agency and morality filtered into their gods and monsters. "The Maya have a sense of a human universe," political anthropologist and Maya expert Simon Martin explains, "not simply an architecture made out of dangerous, predatory beasts."[18] Interestingly, the hybrid nature of monstrous creatures among the Maya includes a wide array of attributes identifiable with beasts endemic to the region, including not only big cats (such as the jaguar), serpents (various snakes and other reptiles), and birds of prey (such as the American harpy eagle),

Statue of the plumed-serpent god Kukulkán at the ballcourt of the Maya temple of Chichén Itzá, Yucatán, Mexico (Daniela Constantinescu/Shutterstock.com).

but also centipedes, bull sharks, crocodiles, bats, and cormorants.[19] These monstrous figures are represented not only in oral folklore, but also in the illustrated texts of the Maya, which, unlike virtually all other pre–Columbian societies in the Americas, boasted of a completely functional, logosyllabic system of writing—part-syllabic, part-ideographic—one not unlike the hieroglyphs of the ancient Egyptians.

Dating back to at least 200 BCE, the Maya writing system included approximately 850 distinct characters or glyphs (a much smaller subset of this number was used on a regular basis) and was often carved into buildings and statuary or painted onto pottery. In such cases many texts have been well preserved into the modern era. However, due to the disdain and vandalism of early Spanish priests, who deemed Maya books heretical and condemned virtually all of them to the flames, only four manuscript codices written have survived until today. These were all made of accordion-folded, fig-bark pages. One of these four manuscripts, and the most well preserved, is known as the Dresden Codex. Its name derives from its having been rediscovered—and still being housed—in that city in Germany, in what is now the Saxon State Library. "The Dresden," as it is more familiarly called, dates to the eleventh or twelfth century CE, making it one of the oldest extant books created in the Americas. It is mostly astronomical in its subject matter and is thought to be a copy of an even older text, one dating between the 5th and 9th centuries CE. (The classical period of Maya history is usually dated between about 250 and 900 CE.)

While Maya astronomical data are remarkably accurate in minutiae and

expansive in their overall scope, these achievements have by now been well documented and analyzed elsewhere. Fairly recently, a great deal of attention and speculation was dedicated to such matters in mainstream news media leading up to the
"deadline" of December 21, 2012, when the Maya "Long Count" calendar turned over
to a new era or cycle. Some claimed that this shift portended the end of days, though
such interpretations mostly belied a complete misunderstanding of the Maya system of measuring time. For example, the Dresden, claimed Hans Henrik of the site
holybooks.com in a blog post of December 17, 2012, is one of "a short list of books
you might want to study during your last week on planet Earth."[20] (Not surprisingly, when nothing particularly apocalyptic occurred on or around this date, the
doomsayers were either silent or had already moved on to their next set of prognostications.) But of interest here are the mythological aspects, and especially those
deities and/or monsters that illustrate the extant Maya textual corpus in significant ways, whether incorporated into astronomical treatises or otherwise. One such
representation is that of the dragon-like creature on the final page of the Dresden
Codex.

It bears repeating that due to the Spanish colonization of the Maya cultural
area starting in the mid-sixteenth century, the exact meanings of extant Maya texts
had lain forgotten for at least three-hundred years. Predominantly the domain of
an elite scribal class, the Spanish snuffed out the precious skills of Maya reading
and writing by burning untold amounts of written documents or otherwise by mur-
dering those few who were literate. Of course, the introduction of the Spanish language and the Catholic religion also hastened the demise. By 1600, the glyphs were
effectively dead as a living script; several Maya languages began to be written in the
Latin script if they were written at all. Otherwise, Spanish predominated. As was
the case of the Arabs and their salvaging of great swaths of Greco-Roman scientific knowledge during the Medieval Era (detailed in Chapter 2), it took the perspective and resources of an outside culture to revitalize an otherwise defunct system
of knowledge. In the case of the Maya script, starting in earnest around the 1830s,
it was a mix of American, British, French, German, and Russian scholars (among
those of a small handful of other non–Hispanic nationalities) who were ultimately
responsible for solving the mystery of Maya writing. It was not until the twentieth
century that the system was mostly deciphered by this international cast of mostly
professional academics. As a result of this decades-long effort, which mostly cul-
minated in the 1980s, we now know for certain the logosyllabic nature of the Maya
script and approximately 85 percent of the extant Maya glyphs can be read with
certainty.[21]

As was established by German librarian and scholar Ernst Förstemann (1822–
1906) after his careful study of the extremely rare Maya book in his care at the Royal
Public Library of Dresden, much of the Dresden Codex was calendrical in nature.
"One can only guess," mused fellow Maya scholar Michael D. Coe almost ninety
years after Förstemann's death, "how long he had been puttering there before he

became intrigued with the strange codex that his predecessor Goetze had brought back from Vienna in the previous century, and how long before he thought of doing something about it."[22] As a result of his near-exclusive, uninterrupted access to the text itself, along with what were clearly uncanny skills of analysis and deduction, Förstemann was also the first non–Maya to decipher the glyph signifying "zero" (a seashell), as well as the vigesimal (base-20) Maya system of numerals in general. Förstemann began publishing in earnest on the subject in 1880 and, with these foundational discoveries firmly in place, unequivocally led the vanguard of the next century's advancements towards decipherment.

That brings us back to the "sky dragon" of the text's final page (usually enumerated as page 74). Förstemann surmised that, due to the otherwise calendric nature of the book, and its placement and the very end, that this image was not only prophetic but apocalyptic. Though much has been learned of the Maya and their writing since Förstemann's time, the current scholarly consensus is that he was right all along. The unmistakably reptilian figure, first identified as "God D" before his true name could be fully deciphered, is now known as Itzamná, a supreme deity of the Maya pantheon. (Tellingly, *itzam* is the word for the caiman, one of the crocodilian species endemic to the region, as well as a word for lizard or fish, depending on the Maya language.[23]) Itzamná looms large in the Maya pantheon, as he is both the god of creation and the inventor of writing. The Maya also apparently considered him the first priest. On page 74 of the Dresden is shown the destruction of the universe by floodwaters issuing from Itzamná's mouth and appendages, as well as from the pottery of the "old creator goddess." This goddess also wears a live snake upon her head. Meanwhile, God L (full name still unknown), one of whose principal attributes is war, launches darts downwards. The clear perspective of the image is that this scene occurs in the sky, a portending of doom from above the human realm.

In 1992, when his book *Breaking the Maya Code* was published, Michael D. Coe was wise to include in an epilogue a mention of the Maya's calendric "deadline" of or around December 23, 2012. (December 21 was the date later popularized leading up to the "event" itself.) Coe concludes with his translation of the following prophecy, taken from the Maya *Book of Chilam Balam of Tizimin*:

> Then the sky is divided
> Then the land is raised,
> And then there begins
> The Book of the 13 Gods [the Long Count Calendar].
> Then occurs
> The great flooding of the Earth
> Then arises
> The great Itzam Cab Ain [a manifestation of Itzamná].
> The ending of the word,
> The fold of the Katun [a unit of time equal to 19.713 years]:
> That is a flood
> Which will be the ending of
> the word of Katun.[24]

Perhaps the ancient Maya author of these words believed and meant them literally; perhaps he meant them figuratively. Perhaps he just wished to tell a compelling story. We surely cannot know for sure. What we do know, of course, is that the Earth did not cease to exist in the middle of December 2012. Rather than despair of our unknown future, perhaps we would do better to dwell on the awesome foresight and precision of the Maya Long Count Calendar itself, as it not only completed thirteen cycles (each one composed of 394.26 tropical years) at this precise time in 2012, but it is also so thoroughly designed that it can be extended back to August 13 (or 11, depending on the calculation) of the year 3114 BCE in the Western calendar. According to Maya cosmogony, this was the exact day on which the world first came into being.

Cross-Cultural/ Parts In-between

Afrikaans: *draak*
Armenian: *vishap*
   (վիշապ)

Digital recreation of the final page of the Dresden Codex, the most complete text of extant Maya literature (Pete Hermes Furian/Shutterstock.com).

Georgian: *drak'oni* (დრაკონი)   Romani (Kalderash): *aždaja/hala/*
Haitian Creole: *dragon*   *šerkano/zmajo*
Maltese: *dragun*   Yiddish: *shlang* (שלאנג)
Pennsylvania Dutch: *droch*

There are many ways in which a language may develop over time, and only in cases of true isolation (as on remote islands) does this process *not* include contact with other languages. Though the normalizing phenomenon of *Sprachbund* is common, its occurrence implies a certain—though by no means always stable—equilibrium of power between speaker-groups, such as in the Balkans region of southeastern Europe, or in areas of contact between (some of) the Indo-European and the Dravidian languages of India. In other cases, the power differential between two groups may be vast, whereby one physically, politically, economically, and/or ideologically dominates another to the extent that the latter is essentially transformed. As French linguist Claude Hagège writes, "The domination of some over others and the state of jeopardy into which dominated languages fall can be explained by the insufficient means available for resisting pressure from the dominating languages."[25] Without a sustained defense strategy, whether military, legal, cultural, societal, or otherwise, a less privileged language is almost always likely to yield to—and often be replaced by—its more powerful neighbor. Such cases have been the norm in the 500+ years of exchange between the colonizing European nations and, especially, the people-groups that those Europeans encountered in the Americas.

The linguistic outcomes of this lopsided power dynamic—in many ways best framed either under the sub-subfield of creolistics, or that of "contact linguistics" (both of which lie within the subfield of sociolinguistics)—are an essential component of what is more broadly known as the Columbian Exchange. Most notably, creole languages exist (or once existed) in locations such as the Cape Verde Islands, Haiti, Colombia (i.e., Palenquero), Suriname (e.g., Sranan), the American South (i.e., Louisiana for French creoles and the coastal Carolinas/Georgia for English creoles), Jamaica, and elsewhere in the English-speaking Caribbean. These are all areas, not coincidentally, where Europeans enslaved Sub-Saharan Africans in plantation-based colonies, virtually always after first exterminating or otherwise greatly diminishing the indigenous Amerindian populations that were once prevalent there.[26] There also exist what some linguists consider "semi-creoles," a category in which South Africa's Afrikaans, as well as vernacular Brazilian Portuguese and African American Vernacular English (AAVE), may be included.[27]

The second type represented in this miscellaneous section are those cases I have opted to term "crossroads languages": Armenian, Georgian, and Maltese. These are languages that, primarily due to the locations of their traditional homelands, have absorbed large amounts of lexical and other linguistic components from the various empires, popular religions, and other sources of input that have crossed through—or perhaps over—them. As contrasted with creole languages, however, which represent scenarios of major societal and thus linguistic upheaval, in most cases the underlying grammars of these crossroads languages have not been significantly restructured.

Finally in this miscellaneous grouping are the diasporic or "wanderer" languages of Pennsylvania Dutch (still widely spoken by Amish, Mennonite, and other Germanic Anabaptist communities in the Americas); Yiddish (or "Judeo-German," nowadays most spoken in New York City, and specifically in the borough of Brooklyn); and Romani, once more commonly known under the generic term "Gypsy," though this is now considered not only inaccurate but also quite offensive. Romani is spoken in a wide range of modern dialects, primarily in Eastern and Central Europe, though fluent speakers exist throughout the Western world and beyond. All such wanderer languages are fascinating and distinct for their development by means of, to a large degree, their speakers' diffusions over wide geographic areas. In the case of Pennsylvania Dutch, these Protestant Christians fled from sectarian persecution in west-central Europe between the sixteenth and eighteenth centuries and eventually settled as far west as the sweeping Midlands of what are now the United States and Canada. As for Yiddish, Ashkenazi Jews, anciently originating in the Levant (Israel-Palestine and environs), had settled during the Middle Ages in various locations throughout Europe only to see a massive proportion of speakers or their descendants be murdered or exiled *en masse* by the Nazis during the 1930s and early '40s. These refugees' and survivors' re-settlement in New York City, already a center of global Jewish life, represents the Yiddish language's largest cohort of modern speakers. And in the case of Romani, Indic-speaking nomads—possibly an itinerant warrior class—originating in what is now northern India and Pakistan, migrated over several centuries to various locations throughout Europe (as well as the lands Europeans colonized). In many cases, the Roma's insular culture and reputation, often viewed as liabilities by outsiders, have served as rather strong preservatives for their language.

Considering the migrations of all these "wandering" speaker-groups throughout both time and space, another term for these languages might also be "stateless" (though of course thousands of "stateless" languages exist if we consider those hundreds if not thousands of minority languages without official recognition that are spoken within the borders of all 193 member-states of the United Nations). It should be noted that all three of the above "wanderer" languages (or dialects thereof) have, since at least the seventeenth century, also spread throughout the New World and beyond, alongside (or perhaps more accurately, embedded within) the same European colonial powers and their successor states that were ultimately responsible for the creation of this section's creole (or semi-creole) representatives.

It is difficult to choose one or even a handful of examples to represent what the dragon looks like in such exceptional or "miscellaneous" socio-cultural contexts. And though it is tempting to describe how all nine of this section's ethnolinguistic cultures perceive the draconic or otherwise monstrous in their respective mythological imaginaries, one particularly fascinating example of the wanderer type will hopefully suffice: Romani (and more specifically, one dialect thereof).

There are at least twenty-seven spoken dialects of the Romani language, according to subject expert Yaron Matras and his *Romlex* (Romani Lexical Database).[28] These dialects are represented in significant populations in countries as widespread as Germany, Russia, Bulgaria, North Macedonia, Greece, Turkey, Hungary, Romania, and generally throughout the nations of eastern and southeastern Europe. Though Roma people (also known as Roms) can be found in western Europe as well (e.g., Spain, the UK, Norway), in these countries they tend to have lost Romani as a first language and instead may infuse their speech—whatever the local majority language may be—with words of Romani origin, especially when conversing with other Roms. But the most remarkable trait of the Roma is this ethno-linguistic group's ultimate geographic origin, the definitive knowledge of which was quite murky until relatively recently: northern India.[29] To linguists, Romani is classified under Indo-Aryan, the easternmost subset of the Indo-European family which also includes Kurdish, Farsi, Hindi, Gujarati, and many others. However, the Romani dialects have experienced extensive divergence from their origins due to exposure

The Roma people are remarkable for maintaining their Indic language and other distinct traditions despite their centuries of transnational migration, though absorption of external elements has taken place to varying degrees. Their folklore is likewise a synthesis of indigenous and borrowed influences. Here, Romani participants of the International Roma Day in Uzhhorod, Ukraine, April 7, 2017, don national costumes while standing near a cart decorated with the flags of Ukraine, the European Union, and the Roma diaspora (Yanosh Yemesh/Shutterstock.com).

to the wide array of majority languages of the lands in which they have made their homes. Researchers have conclusively determined that the Roma began to migrate out of the Indian subcontinent in the Middle Ages, around 1100 CE.[30]

Not surprising for a group that has maintained such a relatively distinct identity amidst so many centuries of migration and proximity to, at times, hostile majority populations, Romani folklore is uniquely tied to its people's lived experiences. Dragons play into this modality quite strongly, as shown by ethnographer H.E. Wedeck in his *Dictionary of Gypsy Life and Lore*. He notes under the heading "COLLEGE OF SORCERY" that the Roms of Romania,[31] also represented by the Kalderash dialect listed above, tell tales of a school in Salamanca, Spain "deep down in the mountains, where the secrets of nature[,] the language of animals, and all magic spells were taught by the devil in person...."

> Only ten scholars were admitted at a time, and when the course had been completed, nine students were dismissed to their homes, but the tenth was detained by the professor in payment. Henceforth, mounted on a dragon, he became the devil's aide-de-camp, and assisted him in preparing thunderbolts and in managing storms and tempests.[32]

The dragon's lair was said to be a small but extremely deep lake in the mountains of Transylvania (central Romania), near the present-day city of Sibiu (formerly also known by its Saxon [Germanic] name, Hermannstadt). In this "cauldron," the dragon "brewed" thunder.[33] It is likely that the tale's inclusion of the Spanish city of Salamanca—whose university was founded in 1218 CE—speaks to the locale's renown as a preeminent center of not only conventional higher learning (especially in the Late Medieval and Early Modern eras), but also of the occult and even purported Satanism. Such hyperbole may have originated from extended kinsfolk as they meandered as far west as Spain and then back again to the more established Roma cultural areas in Romania and its immediate environs.

Another Romani tale of Romanian/Central European, recorded by French medievalist and philologist Claude Lecouteux (b. 1943), himself building upon the earlier writings of German ethnologist Heinrich Adalbert von Wlislocki (1856–1907), has its dragon living in a castle made of iron on the "Mountain of Glass." There, the dragon or *ušáp* (from the common Romani word *sap*, "snake" or "serpent") serves as a kind of prison guard, sometimes over kidnapped young maidens among whom he may choose his future bride. "Despite his name," Lecouteux notes, "the dragon is quite close to being a human being: he speaks, has feelings, and experiences fear. He sometimes has the features of an ogre, and he possesses the ability to metamorphose into other beings."[34] In this sense, the dragon approaches ever closer to the human psyche in a form that is hybrid in nature, split between animal and human.

Of the most dynamic phenomena common among such "wanderer" or "stateless" languages as Romani, Yiddish, or Pennsylvania Dutch are the grammatical and lexical transformations they undergo under the influences of their neighbors. This is readily apparent in the various words for "dragon" in the Kalderash Romani dialect:

aždaja, *hala*, *šerkano*, and *zmajo*. For starters, we see the originally Persian word *ajedha/* اژدها—via Turkish *ejderha*—clearly echoed in Kalderash *aždaja*. Indeed, the Romani language (or rather, the Romani dialect continuum) at large was influenced early on in its gradual westward migration by an extended proximity to (if not embeddedness in) the sphere of not only Byzantine Greek, but also that language's imperial rival and successor, Ottoman Turkish. Characteristically, the Roma took such winds of change in stride. The second word, *hala*, interestingly, is derived from the Hungarian for "fish," displaying considerable semantic drift. The third, *šerkano*, is also from Hungarian—*sárkány* ("dragon")—and thus is also cognate with Slovak *šarkan*. In both Hungarian and Slovak the respective words can also refer to a toy kite; the other principal "dragon" word in Slovak is the Greek-derived *drak*. And, finally, the southern Slavic complex (namely, the mostly mutually intelligible languages of Bosnian, Croatian, Serbian, and Montenegrin) is the obvious source of Kalderash *zmajo* (or *zmejo*, *zmêvo*), most likely via Serbian due to the higher concentration of Roma among that national population. The Romani suffix *-o* is the only distinguishing marker from the word's origin as *zmaj* (see the *Europe* section of Chapter 2). Surprisingly, however, the Romanian "dragon" (*balaur*, also discussed in Chapter 6) does not appear to be reflected whatsoever in Kalderash, despite Romanian being the principal contact language for the latter.

PART II

East and West

5

The (Anti-)Christian Dragon

When I looked for good, then evil came unto me: and when I waited for light, there came darkness. My bowels boiled, and rested not: the days of affliction prevented me. I went mourning without the sun: I stood up and I cried in the congregation. I am a brother to dragons, and a companion to owls.[1]

And there appeared another wonder in heaven; and behold a great red dragon, having seven heads and ten horns, and seven crowns upon his heads. And his tail drew the third part of the stars of heaven, and did cast them to the earth: and the dragon stood before the woman which was ready to be delivered, for to devour her child as soon as it was born.[2]

Christianity, even from its earliest origins as the cultus surrounding the divinity and teachings of Jesus of Nazareth, had the makings of a transcultural, transnational phenomenon.

Forged within Judaea, at the time a distant and tenuous province of the Roman Empire, Christianity first emerged as a radical sect of Judaism. The parent tradition was already ancient, and the status quo of its rigid requirements of textualism, ritual, and pedigree would not allow for the Messiah to be confirmed in the deified personage of the Galilean carpenter. But the Christian scripture itself included and built upon that of Judaism, or *Tanakh* (תָּנָ״ךְ), later to be called the Old Testament by the Christians. Through its evangelists and converts, themselves mostly ethnic Jews at first, the new faith-movement was then exported to the imperial metropole—to the city of Rome itself—where its mettle would be violently tested for approximately two hundred years. But persist and grow it did, its doctrines and parables whispered in dank catacombs by marginalized and disaffected people, the forgotten or maligned of Roman society. There, in Rome, the cultus of Christ also partially syncretized with Greco-Roman polytheism and mystery religions (such as the Persian-derived Mithraism), priming it for its eventual replacement of these contributing influences and other traditional pagan rites. By the forces of personal charisma and the countervailing effects of Rome's precipitously accelerating political decline, Christianity then rose from its lowly, secret warren to become the exalted faith of the Roman emperors themselves.

The new religion then spread rapidly out of Italy and into the rest of Europe, quickly overtaking and supplanting other local pagan/animist traditions. In some cases, this took place only within a generation or two. Eventually, once practically every corner of Europe had been officially Christianized—whether by the sword, societal compulsion, or both, by around 1400 CE—it was carried via commerce, conquest, and colonialism to the rest of the globe starting around 1500. Indeed it served as an impetus for all three: a banner under which to plant colonial settlements and, with marked consistency, to commit atrocities against Indigenous peoples, whether those individuals were autochthonous to (primarily) the Americas or otherwise enslaved and trafficked from Africa.

In the form of either the embellished or otherwise entirely fictionalized lives of saints, the dragons of Christian lore have also traveled thousands of miles over hundreds of years to accrue their fantastical and allegorical attributes. This chapter aims to gather the many far-flung threads of this dragon-lore in worldwide Christian metaculture and thereby weave a cohesive overview. The focus begins with Christianity's source literature (the Bible itself, including passages found in both its canonical and apocryphal books) and then progresses to the visual arts (especially painting and sculpture) and to the legends and folklore that inspired new works, themselves to be absorbed into the canon.

Dragons in the Bible

As exemplified by the two passages in epigraph above, from the Old and New Testaments, respectively, dragons are frequently referenced throughout the Bible. It should be quickly noted, however, that a comparative analysis of the original biblical texts alongside their many translations reveals a plethora of creative and/or strategic choices by those who commissioned and/or executed them.

In the King James Version of the Christian Bible of 1611 (KJV), for example, which comprises the first complete translation from the original Hebrew/Aramaic (Old Testament) and Greek (New Testament) into early modern English, the word "dragon" appears a total of forty-six times. However, it is by no means definitive, nor even likely, that "large, ferocious avian-mammalian-reptilian hybrid"—in other words, the standard Western conception of the dragon—was the intent of the Old Testament's original Hebrew and/or Aramaic texts. Writing for the *Catholic Encyclopedia* in the early twentieth century, Franco-American priest and scholar Charles Léon Souvay elaborated that

> Of the fabulous dragon fancied by the ancients, represented as a monstrous winged serpent, with a crested head and enormous claws, and regarded as very powerful and ferocious, no mention whatever is to be found in the [Hebrew] Bible. The word dragon, consequently, should really be blotted out of our Bibles, except perhaps Is[aiah], xiv, 29 and xxx, 6, where the *draco fimbriatus* [the real animal otherwise known as the fringed flying dragon or the crested gliding dragon] is possibly spoken of.[3]

Nevertheless, the translation committees commissioned by King James I of England (IV of Scotland; 1566–1625, r. 1603–1625) very intentionally chose to immortalize the various ambiguous creatures referenced, especially in the Old Testament, as "dragon."

In the Old Testament, or Hebrew Bible, the two principal Hebrew terms for what is usually translated in English to "dragon" are as follows. First, there is *tannin* (תַּנִּין, fifteen instances, including its plural form), a term often, though not always, referring to large whalelike or otherwise generically amphibian or reptilian beasts rather than the more terrestrial class of monster connoted by *behemoth* (בהמות, "beasts" or "animals").[4] Then there is *tan* (תַן, fourteen instances, all of which are found in the plural form). *Tan* is also a sinister and foreboding creature whose name, much like *tannin*, ultimately derives from the Proto-Semitic verb stem *tanan* (תנן), speculatively meaning "to elongate" or "to stretch (out)."[5] Though the semantic drift between *tannin* and *tan* as generic but distinct classes of creature would become considerable over time, the commonality between them lies along the shared line of "predator" or "marauder." They are both creatures that may make themselves more threatening by elongating or stretching themselves out, as in preparation to attack.

A more practical reading of the *tan* of Job 30:29, however, and one that comports with ancient Israel's desert biome, would be "jackal," the medium-sized canid still extant in the region, commonly known in English as the golden jackal (*Canis aureus*). Another candidate would perhaps be the African wolf (*Canis lupaster*).[6] In fact, "jackal" is the Modern Hebrew meaning of *tan/tannim* (*-im* being the plural suffix for this masculine noun).[7] But herein lies the confusion—or perhaps better yet, the intentional conflation and simplification—by King James' translators: The word *tannim* ("jackals") is remarkably close to the *singular* for that other marauding animal, *tannin* (plural *tanninim*), otherwise known as the Nile crocodile (*Crocodylus niloticus*). The latter is the specific usage of the word in *Modern* Hebrew: "crocodile(s)," usually referring to the family of large reptiles in general but certainly also to the Nile species best known in the region. In a highly figurative text such as the Hebrew Bible, the connotation of monstrousness and awe of the creature is the intention. To wit, Psalm 74:13: "Thou didst divide the sea by thy strength: thou brakest the heads of the **dragons** [*tanninim*] in the waters" (originally, "אַתָּה פוֹרַרְתָּ בְעָזְּךָ יָם שִׁבַּרְתָּ רָאשֵׁי תַנִּינִים עַל־הַמָּיִם׃").

Despite the obvious major differences between jackals and crocodiles, it is quite likely that King James' translators conflated the two malevolent, out-stretching beasts of the Levant/Egypt—clearly both familiar and yet still rather mysterious to ancient Levantines in distinct ways—in order to manufacture what my informant, a native Hebrew speaker, wryly refers to as "the Broadway version" of ancient scripture.[8] King James' seventeenth-century English-speaking scholars of Hebrew and Aramaic clearly (and correctly) anticipated that few Bible-reading or -listening Christians in the Britain of their day would have the foggiest idea of what either jackals or crocodiles were, and much less what they were meant to symbolize. Evolutionarily speaking, a golden jackal is not wholly dissimilar to a red fox, a species well known in Britain, but the quiet slinkiness of the latter simply does not carry the

The golden jackal (*Canis aureus*) may not be reptilian whatsoever, but in the English translation of the Christian Bible commissioned by King James I, the species became a "dragon" for poetic effect (and perhaps by mistake) (Zoya El/Shutterstock.com).

same psycho-spiritual weight as the haunting, howling presence of the former. Crocodiles were, furthermore, completely unknown to most Europeans of the era as well. However, due to dragons' long pedigree and resonance in both the pre- and post–Christian lore of Britain and the greater Indo-European *Sprachbund*, such monsters were immediately familiar to early-modern English speakers. Thus did "dragon" more adequately capture the original sense of eerie or uncanny entities that not only inhabit desolate landscapes but also symbolize estrangement or disconnection from God/godliness.

As for the "owls" of the KJV, these supposed counterparts to dragons were not originally from that order of bird whatsoever. Although species of owl are indeed found in the Levant (and virtually everywhere else on Earth), in Job 30:29 the foreboding creatures were instead יענה (*ya'ănâh*), "ostriches." (These tall, desert-dwelling birds were once common in the general region in question but are now limited to the African continent.) The art of translation (never an exact science), especially in a socio-religious context with strong political undertones as had the entire KJV project, is not and cannot be a simple exercise in mapping each word of the source to its exact equivalent in the target language; there are precious few "exact equivalents" to begin with. Be that as it may, and especially from the perspective of our interconnected present, jackals and ostriches do seem a far cry from dragons and owls. For better or for worse these bold choices were made and linger with us in the English-speaking world (and beyond) to this day.

The engraved image of a king, representing the social contract, himself composed of many other men, serves as the frontispiece to Thomas Hobbes' 1651 *Leviathan*. However, the notion expressed was based on a faulty etymology, then widely accepted, of the Hebrew word itself. This reproduction was published in the French *Magasin Pittoresque*, 1852 (Morphart Creation/Shutterstock.com).

The marine counterpart to the terrestrial *behemoth* is *leviathan* (לִוְיָתָן). Besides its biblical instances, which are often used interchangeably with *tannin*,[9] the term was further popularized in the English-speaking world as a metaphor for the social contract among humans in each society by English philosopher Thomas Hobbes in his 1651 political treatise of the same name. The notion among philologists at the time—now considered erroneous—was that the two components of the word were *lavah*, to couple, and *Thannin*, a serpent or dragon. The intended sense was something like "the beast composed of many smaller beasts," hence Hobbes' thesis-metaphor for the "monstrous" nature of the body politic.[10] But four decades before *Leviathan* was ever published, King James's Bible had left in ten transliterated but otherwise unchanged instances of this term from the original Hebrew. With a proper name, the connotation was that this is not just any monster, but rather a specific and particularly malevolent individual. The creature is even given a proper name in various books of the Old Testament: Rahab.[11]

When we move on to the New Testament, the textual picture surrounding our quarry comes into even sharper focus. As for the red dragon in the second passage in epigraph (Revelation 12:3–4), since the language in which the entire New Testament was written was not Hebrew but Greek it is not altogether surprising that our familiar *drakōn* (δράκων) is in fact the original. Found most frequently in the Book of Revelations (Chapters 12, 13, 16, and 20), this specific term is the source of every single instance of "dragon" in the entirety of the New Testament of the KJV. What's clear by such homogeneity is that the large serpent of Greek tradition was, by the first century of the Christian Era, regularly found in this specific allegorical garb (dragon = Satan/evil), as will be detailed both below and in the following chapter.

***

It will be essential, especially in this chapter, to anticipate the inevitability of semantic shifts of language over time. Additionally, a consideration of how these shifts correlate to those of popular mythology and religion will be salient. In the case of the dragon, as we have already begun to establish in the previous three chapters, such an archetypal chimera must also be malleable over time and space, transmuting between its reptilian, mammalian, avian, and other components. But despite this eternal shapeshifting, a core of essential, near-universal meaning for "dragon" remains. This is perhaps most emblematic in a little-known but remarkable tale about the baby Jesus and his own brush with dragon-smiting.

The non-canonical *Gospel of Pseudo-Matthew* was compiled in Latin in the eighth or ninth century CE. Like the similarly non-canonical *Gospel of Thomas*, detailed further below, it concerns events from the infancy and childhood of Christ. In *Ps.-Matthew*, we learn that the baby (or perhaps toddler) Jesus is on a journey with his parents Mary and Joseph and a small group of other children. Taking a rest from their journey in a cave, Jesus sits on Mary's lap as Joseph lingers nearby with the others. "And lo!" the story goes,

> suddenly a great number of dragons [*dracones*] came out of the cave. Upon seeing them, the children cried out in the extremity of their terror. Jesus climbed down from his mother's lap and stood on his feet before the dragons. They worshipped him and withdrew from them. And then the utterance of the prophet David was fulfilled: he said, "Dragons of the earth praise the Lord, dragons and all from the abyss."[12] Little baby Jesus, walking about in front of them, commanded them to harm no one.[13]

Though such gospels concerning the thirty or so years between Jesus' birth and his prime adulthood were omitted from the canonical Bible, the existence of such a story whatsoever speaks volumes to the potency of the dragon as a foe of all things good and pure. Baby Jesus, in his power and glory, makes short work of the marauding pests. "'Do not be concerned for me on the ground that I am a little baby,'" he—quite eloquently for a baby ... or toddler—tells the terrified Mary, Joseph, and their four young companions. "'For I always have been and I continue to be perfect. All the beasts of the wilderness become tame before me.'"[14] Dragons are no match for a messiah. Even an infant one.

Going Medieval

In a twelfth-century Latin bestiary, composed by monks at the Abbey of Revesby in Lincolnshire, England, the following is included under the entry *Dragon* [*Draco*]:

> The Devil, who is the most enormous of all reptiles, is like [the] dragon. He is often borne into the air from his den, and the air round him blazes, for the Devil in raising himself from the lower regions translates himself into an angel of light and misleads the foolish with false hopes of glory and worldly bliss.[15]

Here we also see the common medieval motif of the dragon as hoarder and guardian of treasure (i.e., "glory and worldly bliss") but, more importantly, as akin to Satan himself, if not one and the same. Notably, the manuscript's modern–English translator and editor, T.H. White (also the author of the fantasy novel that was adapted by Disney into the 1963 animated film *The Sword in the Stone*[16]) offers this comment in footnote: "'Dragon' was simply the medieval word for a large reptile, and the more one regards it as not being a joke from fairy stories, the more interesting the following pages [of the bestiary] may prove to be."[17] This is the correct assessment: a naturalistic, ontological allowance that snakes and lizards (and perhaps even worms) could easily be perceived as larval or juvenile or otherwise miniature iterations of dragons and, furthermore, be wielded allegorically in a way accessible to most people.

The discussion of the transition from classical (pagan) Greco-Roman to Christian representations of both dragons and dragon-slaying heroes is not without its share of debate. As Daniel Ogden contends, "The Christian tradition of saintly dragon slayers grows directly out of the classical one, whilst incorporating, of course, an infusion of serpent symbolism from the Old and New Testaments."[18] Such "serpent symbolism" is found through the Bible but is most potent in the case of the Serpent of the Garden of Eden of Genesis 3, as discussed at length in this book's introduction.

Folklorists Jane Garry and Hasan El-Shamy confirm that the dragon-slaying motif of Christian hagiography "harkens back to the Greek myth of Perseus and Andromeda."[19] This view is further qualified by professor of Islamic theology Sara Kuehn:

> It has ... been suggested that the dragon-slaying iconography grew out of the tradition of associating the saints with ancient Greek mythologies [...] However, this theory is based on the assumption that the story of a Christian saint rescuing a princess or maiden from a dragon was ancient, whereas it dates back no earlier than the eleventh century...[20]

The repurposing of pre–Christian legends to a Christian context was the innovation, though the dragon-slaying motif itself is much, much older. Jonathan D. Evans is unequivocal that St. George's tale is not only a "thinly veiled retelling of the Perseus legend," but also of ancient myths of the Near East wherein gods slay sea monsters, such as in the battle between Marduk and Tiamat in Babylonian legend.[21] If we delve

Dragons captured the medieval European imagination, as both expressed in, and propagated by, illuminated manuscripts. Illustrations such as those found in this English bestiary of the mid-thirteenth century (*c.* 1260) often doubled as Christian allegorical messaging: the mythical peridexion tree on the left provides a flock of goodly doves refuge from draconic perdition (© The British Library Board, Harley 3244, ff.58v–59).

even further into the Indo-European tradition of oral folklore, we arrive at what can decisively be classified as ATU Type 300, or, "The Dragon Slayer," a motif which will be discussed further below.

A valiant hero defeating a dragon is not a trope that was conjured out of thin air. As Ogden clarifies, "The most famous Christian dragon slayer of them all, St. George, did not acquire his dragon until the twelfth century CE, but his dragon story is of a variety broadly established for other saints as early as the third century CE."[22] This overlay of classical and/or pre–Christian dragon/dragon-slayer motifs (e.g., Haracles/Hercules, Perseus) onto existing Christian hagiography, despite the former's great antiquity, was applied to saints many centuries *ex post facto* and in some cases, such as St. George's, almost a millennium after the historical or otherwise purported lifetime of the principal actor. Then again, as we will see, other saints were recorded as having fought dragons soon after their legends emerged in the early years of the Church's establishment and expansion. As this genre of devotional literature developed, so did its motifs and patterns coalesce and expand, especially as later appendations to prove godliness prior to saints' martyrdoms within their received narratives. These appended dragon fights would, ultimately, supersede in the public consciousness the torturous death sequences which made them martyrs in the first place.

Besides that of St. George, also included in this genre are the legends of Saints Margaret (also called Marina), Martha, Thomas, Philip, Silvester, Caluppan, and Victoria,[23] among others.[24] As pertains to their inclusion in frequently copied medieval manuscripts, these stories served the purpose of promoting godliness and virtue by juxtaposition with the compelling and unambiguously malign figure of the dragon as the manifestation of evil and, moreover, paganism. By the height of the medieval era in which they were often popularized in manuscripts, the lives and deeds of these holy men and women were already well-shrouded in the mists of antiquity.[25] It is thus not surprising that a mythological creature would feature so prominently to fully enshrine the mystique and wonder surrounding the earliest heroes of the Christian faith. The physical or existential threat posed by such a menacing and predatory creature as a dragon serves as a potent and useful metaphor for the spiritual threat posed by the devil and his lures towards the commission of all varieties of sin, especially the sins of paganism or apostasy. The mighty, "good-hating dragon"[26] was, simply put, the most allegorically transparent and convenient vehicle for such an evil presence.

The Cultus of St. George the Dragonslayer

The renowned American folklorist Stith Thompson (1885–1976), among his many other accolades, lends his surname to the trio of scholars recognized in the Aarne-Thompson-Uther Index (ATU). This literary tool, which was first established by Finnish scholar Antti Aarne (1867–1925), translated into English and developed by Stith Thompson, and further extended by the contemporary German folklorist and literary scholar Hans-Jörg Uther (b. 1944), provides a framework for cataloging and referencing the documented motifs of folktales throughout the ethno-linguistically defined cultures of the world.

Type 300 of the ATU Index is "The Dragon Slayer." More specifically, this type is classified under the following schema:

> II. Ordinary Folktales;
> 300–749. A. Tales of Magic;
> 300–399. Supernatural Adversaries.

Italian Renaissance master Raphael's depiction of St. George and the Dragon, *c.* 1505. The work, now housed at the National Gallery of Art, Washington, D.C., was commissioned by the Court of Urbino and intended as a gift to England's Henry VII. The painting would remain in England until 1651. It was bought in 1931 by American industrialist Andrew Mellon (Everett Collection/Shutterstock.com).

In his 1946 book *The Folktale* Thompson attests that there are at least 1,100 known examples of this type.[27] But more poignantly, he demystifies this motif alongside another to which it is inextricably tied, one known as "The Two Brothers" (ATU

Type 303), the full details of which are summarized in Chapter 2 (*Europe*). More relevant is that the latter is a much longer tale which contains the entirety of the former. "[I]t is necessary to study the two tales together," Thompson writes, "if one is to secure an accurate picture of their mutual relationships, and of the history of the two stories, both when they are merged together and when they exist separately."[28] Though "The Dragon Slayer" is of course of greater relevance in our present study, this type's regular embeddedness in the more extensive narrative elucidates much about the worldwide popularity of the cultus of St. George.

The "Dragon Slayer" tale was already well known before it was adapted as a Christian morality tale appended to one of standard Christian martyrdom. (It also presents an intriguing question that cannot be answered by the extant literature: If George is but one of "The Two Brothers," who is the other? Did he ever have a name?) The central core of "The Dragon Slayer" motif (also called "Dragon Rescue" by Thompson and others) is nearly identical—minus the specific names of "George" and that of the kingdom he liberates from the dragon's scourge—to the most common versions of the St. George the Dragonslayer legend. There are elaborations in Thompson's telling of the generic version that do not appear in the later Christian hagiographic version (such as information on the background and origin of the slayer himself), but the essence is unmistakably similar. "The king promises that whoever saves her [the king's daughter, the princess, from the jaws of the dragon]," Thompson relates, "shall have her hand and half his kingdom."[29] As we will see, though revisions were made to produce the early–Christian, highly propagandistic version that came to be known as St. George's legend, this originally pagan folk-motif has enjoyed not only prevalence among many Indo-European peoples (and the Basques, as detailed in Chapter 2) and the creole cultures catalyzed therefrom,[30] but also boasts an antiquity that far predates the introduction of Christianity into Europe.

In general, the establishment and propagation of much of the extant Christian hagiographic dragon lore into modernity and popular European culture(s) can be traced to one foundational text: *The Golden Legend* (*Legenda Aurea*). The *Legend* was first compiled in the mid- to late thirteenth century by Jacobus de Voragine (1228–1298), a Genovese archbishop. The text was further popularized in England when it was printed by William Caxton, that country's first movable-type printer, in 1483.[31] During the late medieval era, however, de Voragine's manuscript was responsible for fixing the St. George dragon legend, which then was incorporated into the saint's popular veneration in countries as varied as Catalonia, Georgia, Malta, Lithuania, and Ethiopia, among others.

The (possibly) historical George[32] (d. April 23, 303 CE, traditionally) did not himself originate in any area that today reveres him on an ethnic or national(istic) level. Rather, he was likely born and martyred in a historical region of what is now Muslim Turkey, then a Hellenized region known as Cappadocia. During George's purported lifetime, from the late third to the very early fourth centuries CE, this east-central region of Asia Minor (or Anatolia) was still under Roman rule. The area was populated at the time by a significant number of ethnic Greeks (or otherwise culturally Hellenized and Greek-speaking peoples), of which George was most likely one as well. His mother, so the story goes, was a Christian from Israel-Palestine—hence, it stands to reason, his own intense and unequivocal devotion to the still-new religion. Though centuries after his death George's dragon-slaying escapade would be commonly set in distant Libya, this geographical feature of his legend is most likely the result of a copyist's error that was subsequently passed down as the saint's legend proliferated throughout the world.[33]

In George's time (i.e., before 324 CE, when Christianity became enshrined in the Roman Empire by Constantine the Great), openly professing the radical new faith was not only dangerous and illegal, but often deadly. Such conflict often led to the martyrdom of many who would go on to be the most venerated saints of early Christendom. And while George's martyrdom (by beheading, according to legend) figures broadly in his hagiography, his famous encounter with a dragon is the tale that his far-flung cultus most reveres and represents in various works to this day. Pop-culturally speaking, there is no George without a dragon.

So what and how do we know about Georgius (the Latin version of his name), the dragon-slaying hero of Cappadocia? According to most versions of the legend he was a young soldier in the Roman emperor Diocletian's service, which is likely enough given the saint's purported lifetime. While ostensibly on leave from (or possibly en route to) his military service, George happened by a walled city-kingdom variously referred to as Gylena, Silene, Silena, Lasia (among other names), located either in Libya, Asia Minor, or the Levant, depending on the version. At the edge of a swampy lake outside the city George came across a forlorn, unaccompanied young woman. She was, in fact, the princess of the nearby city, she told George, forced to offer herself as food to the pestilential dragon who dwelled in the lake's waters. Tragically, the city folk had already attempted to sate the dragon and prevent any future attacks by first feeding it their livestock. But the dragon's hunger was insatiable. Once all the city's animals had been devoured, the names of the local children were drawn by lots and they were sent to their doom, one by one. The princess' father, the king, had tried to protect his daughter from such a cruel fate by dint of his royal standing. But faced with his subjects' resentment and ire over such nepotism, even his own beloved heir was eventually selected as tribute and ordered to sacrifice herself to the beast.

Alban Butler (1711–1773), an English Catholic priest and writer, attempted to reconcile the fantastical dragon lore registered and popularized by Jacobus de Voragine with that of the famous saint's still-potent cultus, then as now. "Saint George is usually painted on horseback, and tilting at a dragon, under his feet," wrote Butler, "but this representation is no more than an emblematic figure, purporting, that, by his faith and christian [*sic*] fortitude, he conquered the devil, called the dragon in the Apocalypse."[34] During the Enlightenment neither a literal dragon nor a superhuman saint was fully plausible to an educated, discerning Christian such as Butler. "Indeed," contends Sherry L. Reames in her study of the *Legend*, "there have been few periods when the typical man of learning had less sympathy with hagiography ... than the later seventeenth and eighteenth centuries."[35] But even in that era of intellectual flowering could an allegorical dragon still be useful for the purposes of religious instruction among the faithful. Unlike in Butler's day, medieval predecessors like de Voragine (and his readers) were as readily credulous of the early Christian saints' purported campaigns against actual, literal dragons as they were morally and fervently opposed to the perceived scourges of paganism, heathenism, or otherwise any ascribed sinfulness that such monstrous creatures represented. In such an older worldview, characterized by incomplete scientific understanding and the concomitant potent superstitions, the literal and the figurative were rarely decoupled.

As the legend continues, George, hearing the princess' plight as she awaited her doom beside the dragon's lake, understood the situation to be one of a religious (i.e., magical), and not animalistic, nature: the dragon would not harm her, nor anyone, should she accept Christ as her savior. The princess, however, was unconvinced by such hubris: "'You are a brave knight,' she replied. 'But do not perish with me. It is enough that I die, for you cannot save me, you would only die with me.'"[36] Unbeknownst to them while they were speaking, the noxious dragon had emerged from the lake and advanced towards the two youths. Suddenly spotting it, George sprang into action....

> Brandishing his lance and commending himself to God, he dealt the beast such a deadly wound that he threw it to the ground. He called to the princess: "Throw your girdle round the dragon's neck! Do not be afraid, child!" She did as he told her and, and the dragon followed her around as meekly as a puppy.[37]

Accompanied by the princess, George then led the subdued creature—the "deadly wound" was more of a severe blow or gash and not quite so deadly after all—back to the city. George presented the dragon to the citizens as proof of the power of his faith over evil. "'Only believe in Christ and be baptized, every one of you, and I will slay your dragon!'" he crowed.[38] And so they did: the people of Silene were all baptized right there and then. George then fulfilled his promise to the king and his subjects by swiftly killing the dragon with his sword. Though various depictions have the dragon as about the same size as a large dog, other versions state that several ox carts were required to carry the monster's corpse out of the city, to be unceremoniously dumped in a field.[39]

The sequence in this version presents somewhat of a departure from the archetypal image of the knight piercing the dragon's throat with a spear while on horseback, a distinction which de Voragine himself acknowledges as well: "We read in some sources ... that when the dragon was rushing towards the girl to devour her, George actually armed himself with a cross, and then attacked and killed the dragon."[40] But to his credit, de Voragine's version adds the element of drawn-out degradation and humiliation to the dragon—recall that it is the embodiment of paganism, of course synonymous with immorality—in lieu of its swift execution. Such a sequence furthers the story's (and that of de Voragine's entire book) objective of Christian propaganda through compelling dramatizations.

The other episode of St. George's life as told by de Voragine is that of his martyrdom—part two (of only two) of his legend, as it were. And though it takes place in the narrative *after* the dragon-slaying sequence, this part of George's legend was the original and possibly centuries older; it is typical of early–Christian martyrdom accounts. Since it does not directly involve dragons, I will briefly summarize: Emperors Diocletian and Maximian have ordered all Christians to convert back to paganism or be slain. George, being a pious Christian from a noble Christian family, refuses. Diocletian's local prefect, Dacian, brutally and extensively tortures George, who remains steadfast in his piety and does not submit whatsoever. George prays to God, who promptly smites the local pagan temple (and its priests) to ashes. Dacian's wife second-guesses her husband's methods and is forthwith beaten to death with scourges for her insolence and sympathy to the Christian cause. George, despite defying several attempts on his life, finally, is beheaded.

The martyrdom story is of importance, of course, but the appended dragon tale from earlier in his life reinforces his entire hagiography; saintliness is typically not conferred by martyrdom alone, even for possibly legendary figures. And while it's unclear why decapitation would end George's bodily life but not so by such brutal methods as the rack, iron hooks, branding, evisceration, poison, the breaking (or "Catherine") wheel,[41] or submersion in a cauldron of molten lead, what's expressed is that, according to his legend, the soldier was not only good and noble but saintly. The act of dragon-slaying (including the conversion of an entire city's population in one fell swoop in its aftermath) provides a backstory that explicitly shows George's life-long exemplary character when otherwise such an attribute would be confined to his courage under torture. Symbolically, the two episodes are inextricably linked and produce a synergy that powers St. George's trans-national and -cultural appeal up to the present.

To this day, when April 23[42] comes around, St. George and his slaying of the dragon are still celebrated in several countries and cities throughout the world. But the nature of each observance has also absorbed various other elements, depending on the locale. On a secondary level, the symbolism of the dragon-slaying motif has developed from one of triumph over Greco-Roman paganism/general evil to also include military and cultural conquest over Islam. But, as western Europe has become generally more secular over the last century, so too has this trend seeped into the symbolism of the saint and his day. The English spend April 23 celebrating not only the religious underlay, but moreover their ethnic identity writ large.

Not surprisingly, the anti–Islamic element was grafted onto the St. George legend because of the Crusades, that protracted medieval conflict between Christian (Catholic) Europeans and Seljuk Turks and other Islamic groups over control of the mutually sacred Holy Land (Palestine). Once the smoke had cleared by the end of

Much lesser known than his defeat of the dragon is St. George's martyrdom, here depicted by Flemish painter Michiel Coxie (1588) (Renata Sedmakova/Shutterstock.com).

the thirteenth century, the politics of what we today refer to as the Middle East had been profoundly transformed. Decades later, embodied by a new manifestation of St. George the Crusader, a fourteenth-century English king would invoke this potent narrative towards his consolidation of power.

Of Edward III of England (reigned 1327–1377) the British historian Ian Mortimer writes, "For the last two hundred years he has been portrayed in popular history books as a rapacious, adulterous warmonger. Yet it is fair to say that he did more than any other individual to create the English nation as we know it today."[43] How he achieved this feat is due in no small part to an astute deployment of nationalistic branding and marketing. Not long after Edward had ascended to the English throne, at the age of eighteen, the young king made use of the already familiar image of the dragon-slaying St. George—"the most cosmopolitan of all patron saints," according to Mortimer. Since George was already well known from his appearance in de Voragine's popular *Golden Legend* of the previous century, his legend was easily conjured to rally troops as Edward consolidated power not only in England but also in Scotland and France. George the Dragonslayer was the king's personal patron saint but quickly became intertwined with the entire nation that he ruled: the English themselves, in their own imagining, became the brave, resolute Christian knights at arms against any foes that might defy them. "[Edward's] increasingly regular use of St George in his war-cries, banners and religion," Mortimer continues, "was just one part of an integrated strategy which made England the most powerful nation in Europe by 1350."[44] Success—often, though not always—breeds more success; what had been a repurposed symbol during this moment of English ascendency remained so as a good-luck charm, a heraldic device (namely, St. George's Cross), the national flag on which that device later appeared, and in general as a mascot of the English and Englishness throughout the subsequent centuries; in sum, as a powerful totem.

Starting with the Crusades of the twelfth and thirteenth centuries, when the figure took on strong political undertones, the English have fostered a strong reverence for St. George. As seen in this parade for Ollerton, Nottinghamshire's St. George's Day celebrations in 2018, this affinity continues to the present today (Ian Francis/Shutterstock.com).

This further transformation of the saint into an English hero, through a baptism of war and nationalism, was such that to this day the figure of St. George is understood to be as quintessentially English as it/he is Portuguese, Georgian, Maltese, Ethiopian, or any number of other national or ethnic groups that continue to celebrate the legend of the brave, dragon-slaying, and ultimately ill-fated Christian soldier. The red cross of St. George[45] thus features as the principal device on an almost dizzying array of national and municipal flags: of England, the United Kingdom (and its many [post-]colonial derivatives), and the Republic of Georgia; and of the cities of London (where the municipal coat of arms also includes a pair of dragons, as also referenced in this book's introduction), Montreal, Genoa, and Barcelona. The saint's familiar dragon-slaying motif also appears in detail on the flag of the City of Moscow as well as that of the erstwhile Russian Empire.[46]

Other saints of Late Antiquity also feature dragons in their hagiographies, though none has remained as symbolically potent as that of George. Nevertheless, other such examples of lore are interesting for their creative interpretations of the common theme of Christianity versus the Other (traditionally paganism but later also Islam) or, more individually, piety versus profligacy, the latter of course embodied by what else but a noxious, bloodthirsty dragon.

St. Margaret

St. Margaret, or Marina (feast day: July 20), much like George, was persecuted for her devout Christian faith. She was a beautiful young maiden, Jacobus de Voragine tells us, so much so that the Roman prefect of her city lusted after her upon first sight. He demanded that she be brought to him to be either his wife ("'if she is freeborn'") or his concubine ("'if she is a slave girl'").[47] Since Margaret's father was a "priest of the idols," according to Alban Butler[48]—Margaret had been converted to Christianity by her nanny as a child—she could expect neither assistance nor support from her biological family. She was thus kidnapped and brought to the amorous prefect, whose name was Olybrius. Unsurprisingly, Margaret spurned Olybrius' advances and was thus put to torture. Like George, various cruel attempts to kill the pious youth at first failed. But after rounds of being beaten and having "her flesh … raked with iron combs until the bones were laid bare and the blood gushed from her body as if from the purest spring"[49] (and somehow not succumbing to such injuries), she was then given respite in a prison cell. There, she prayed to God to learn who or what was behind her persecution.

Here de Voragine presents *two* magical conjurations, both mentioned somewhat hesitantly, hedging against the medieval reader's disbelief, so it seems: (1) A fierce dragon appears and charges towards Margaret but is repelled and obliviated with a sign of the cross. And (2) a dragon appears and then succeeds in devouring her but is soon burst asunder when Margaret makes the sign of the cross while inside its stomach. "But this story of the dragon devouring the virgin, then bursting apart, is considered apocryphal and of no historical value," de Voragine hastens to note.[50] Is the first encounter with a dragon (whereby it is neutralized by a cross, recall) *not* to be considered apocryphal, then? With such commentary it's unclear exactly to what degree de Voragine would have his readers believe not only in literal dragons but furthermore in their spontaneous manifestations. (Notwithstanding is the likelihood of a human being surviving the effects of both a dragon's maw *and* its digestive tract.) Regardless of the disclaimer, the image of the virgin St. Margaret bursting through the dragon's body, intact and radiant, is one commonly found in illuminated medieval manuscripts inspired by the legends contained in *The Golden Legend*. When an allegorical tale is poignant enough to suspend disbelief, or otherwise to inspire religious devotion, its tropes are often preserved in popular mythology (coterminous with the Christian religion in this case). Such tropes have persisted for centuries or longer, and especially when ensconced in various derivative media such as paintings, heraldry, and vexillography, which will be elaborated in Chapter 12.

St. Margaret (or Marina) of Antioch's legend famously maintains that the chaste Christian youth burst through the stomach and back of a great dragon when she began to pray. Here, in a stained-glass depiction in the Cathedral of St. Bavo, Ghent, Belgium, the dragon appears less like a marauding predator and more like a pesky house pet (jorisvo/Shutterstock.com).

In this more typical depiction, in a book of hours of *c*. 1465, the mechanics of St. Margaret's delivery from the dragon are made expressly graphic (© The British Library Board, Harley MS 2974).

Writing about five centuries after de Voragine, Alban Butler omitted any mention whatsoever of either of St. Margaret's encounters with the dragon in his *Lives of the Fathers, Martyrs, and Other Principal Saints*. By the eighteenth century, in England at least, such fantastical elements were no longer practical for the purposes of proselytizing potential converts or preaching to the devout—virtually the entire population of his country had been Christian for centuries, if not a millennium. But even more realistically, it is likely that by then Margaret's two strange dragon episodes were seen as what they are and always have been: whimsical asides for the purpose of dramatic effect, and simply not central to a "serious" contemplation of her hagiography.

St. Martha

St. Martha's legend is notable for a few reasons, not least of which because it bridges a narrative gap between the origins of Jesus Christ's cultus in the Near/Middle East and Christianity's eventual adoption throughout virtually all of western Europe.

As a sister to the more well-known biblical figures Lazarus and Mary Magdalene, Martha (feast day: July 29) fills out this trio of siblings

St. Martha of Bethany, the sister of both Mary Magdalene and Lazarus, supposedly traveled to what is now southern France after the death of Jesus Christ. There, before converting the local populace to Christianity, Martha defeated the dragon known as the Tarasque. The moment before she smites the beast is captured in this stained-glass panel in the Church of Antibes, France, wherein an unlucky victim has already fallen prey (jorisvo/Shutterstock.com).

of royal descent who all, according to scripture, came to follow Christ through their various blessed encounters with him. Martha was renowned for having been such a gracious host to the Messiah when he still walked the mortal plane. All three siblings then carried on Jesus' message after his death as his missionaries, or at least were ascribed such accomplishments by later Christian authors.

De Voragine's account of Martha of Bethany (or Magdalum, another of the family's seats, hence her sister Mary's epithet, "Magdalene," to distinguish her from the Virgin Mother) not only includes details of her bout with a very distinctive dragon, but also some fascinating notes on the saint's life not found elsewhere. One such embellishment is Christ's posthumous announcement to Martha, one day during her waning years, that she would die exactly one year hence.[51] But more germanely, after Martha had been banished from the Holy Land after Christ's death, the first miracle she encountered was to arrive unscathed at Marseille, on the southern coast of France, despite being put on a boat by her enemies "with no oars, sails, rudders or provisions."[52] It was shortly after safely landing intact—as the crow flies, over 2,700 miles (4,345 km) from her origin—and then quickly converting the local pagan populace, that her dragon emerged. "[H]alf-beast, half-fish, larger than an ox, longer than a horse," is how de Voragine described it, "with sword-like teeth as sharp as horns and flanks impenetrable as twin shields."[53] This monster was the offspring of the well-known biblical Leviathan and a terrestrial creature called Onachus. The latter was himself[54] endowed with the curious trait of shooting its dung like an arrow at a distance of up to an acre.[55] This hybrid monster of notable parentage, specifically referred to as a "dragon" by de Voragine, dwelled on the banks of confluence of the Rivers Rhône and Durance near where Martha had made landfall.

Martha caught the beast *in flagrante delicto* on the riverbank as it was eating a man whole. Such was Martha's godliness that all it took was a sprinkle of holy water as she held up a cross: "The beast was at once defeated, and stood there as meek as a lamb while St Martha tied it up with her girdle, and the people pelted it with stones and spears and killed it."[56] The dragon was, in Latin, called "'Tarasconus,'" de Voragine tells us, "and that is why, in commemoration of this miracle, the place is still called Tarascon (it had formerly been known as 'Nerluc,' i.e., the 'black place,' because the forest there was dark and shadowy)."[57] Nowadays, the locals know this mythical creature as *Tarasque*.

Martha then settled down to a life of intensely ascetic worship for the rest of her days. Fittingly, the current coat of arms of Tarascon features as its lower device a six-legged, spike-backed, yellow dragonoid monster on a field of azure (indicating the rivers, of course). The creature feasts on a man in a white toga, only his lower torso and legs dangling from its gaping maw.

Statue of St. Martha's draconic foe, the Tarasque, in Tarasacon, Provence-Alpes-Côte d'Azur, France. The creature is also depicted *in flagrante delicto* on the flag and coat of arms of the commune (municipality) (David Vioque/Shutterstock.com).

Other Christian Saints

As mentioned above, other Christian saints associated with dragons include Thomas, Philip, Silvester, and Caluppan. In this section, each of these four will be briefly considered, along with the lesser-known saints Barlaam and Josaphat.

Saint Thomas (feast day: July 3) was one of Jesus' Twelve Apostles. He is commonly known by his sobriquet "Doubting" for having doubted that Jesus had been resurrected, at least according to the Gospel of John. The Saint Thomas Christians, an ethno-religious group of southern India (in modern-day Kerala State), maintain that Thomas arrived as an evangelist in that country around 52 CE and was martyred there twenty years later, in what is now the state of Tamil Nadu. His dragon encounter, attested in the apocryphal (non-canonical) *Acts of Thomas* (*c.* 220–40 CE), likewise relates to his travels in India.

While walking down a path "to where the Lord had commanded,"[58] Thomas encountered the corpse of a handsome young man. Thomas intuited and then announced to a group of his followers that the man's death was not caused by some accident or disease, but rather by Satan in the form of a large snake or dragon (*drakōn* in the text's original Greek). The dragon then indeed appeared and, able to speak "[i]n a booming voice,"[59] confessed, or rather boasted of, his murder motive:

There is a beautiful woman in the village opposite. As she paused by me I saw her and fell in love with her. I followed her and kept watch over her. I found this young man kissing her. He also had sex with her and did other shameful things with her. [...] Because I did not wish to upset this woman, I did not kill him there and then, but waited for him to pass by in the evening, and I struck him and killed him then, not least because he had the effrontery to do this on the day of the Lord.[60]

Though Ogden explains that a non-human creature's romantic infatuation with a human is a common motif in classical Greco-Roman lore,[61] the rationale of the dragon in this case is particularly frenetic in a Christian reimagining. The monster appears to be, in rapid sequence, hopelessly romantic, prudishly jealous, righteously indignant, murderous (though not as a means of predation), and, rather counterintuitively, highly reverent towards the Judeo-Christian "Lord" (the dragon's word) and His precepts. Further, in the confrontation with Thomas we learn from the talking dragon a few details regarding the creature's own origins: "I am a reptile of reptile race, a harmful creature born of a harmful creature. [...] I am the one who entered Paradise through the fence and said to Eve everything my father [Satan] commanded me to say to her."[62] This is, then, the Serpent of Eden, or at least a new manifestation of the same.

Thomas disregarded the dragon's indictment of the lustful (and now deceased) man and instead ordered the beast to undo its crime by sucking out the fatal poison it had administered, presumably through its fangs. The dragon, powerless before such a man of God, obeyed. As it sucked, the dead young man in turn came back to life, rose, and threw himself at the feet of his savior. The dragon, now ballooned up with its own poison, promptly exploded. "And in the place in which its venom was spilled there opened a great chasm, and the dragon was swallowed down."[63] This method of dragon extermination is thus akin to that employed by St. Margaret— though seemingly much preferable, as it did not require first being swallowed whole to achieve, as she was.

In de Voragine's *Golden Legend*, the author recounts St. Thomas the Apostle's other saintly adventures in India, including his work as an architect in constructing a local king's palace.[64] However, there is no other mention of a dragon among them.

One fascinating, though somewhat tangential, connection to Thomas is the pair of legendary saints Barlaam and Josaphat, also known as Bilawhar and Budhasaf (*Ioasaph* in Greek). These two bear the distinction of being the only figures in extant Christian hagiography to be directly linked to the legends and precepts of Buddhism. In summary, according to the Greek (via Georgian, via Manichean/Persian) text that was popularized throughout Europe and the Middle East during the Middle Ages,[65] after St. Thomas' campaign of evangelization and mass conversions in India, that country, officially at least, lapsed back to paganism. However, embers of Christianity still burned clandestinely among certain circles, among which was the son of a local king, Prince Josaphat (the Latinized version of the name). At this early point in the narrative, the parallels between this pious and world-renouncing prince and the young Siddhartha Gautama, or Shakyamuni, later known as the

One of Jesus' twelve apostles, "Doubting" St. Thomas is purported to have traveled after Jesus' death to what is now Kerala, southern India, where he established Christianity in the mid first century AD. *Santhome* Church, or St. Thomas Cathedral Basilica, in Chennai (Madras), Tamil Nadu, was originally built in 1523 by the Portuguese over the supposed tomb of St. Thomas (Satish Parashar/Shutterstock.com).

Buddha (*c.* sixth to fifth century BCE or *c.* fifth to fourth century BCE), are abundantly clear.[66] With the guidance of his elderly teacher, the itinerant ascetic Barlaam, Josaphat escapes the designs of his violently anti–Christian father, King Abenner, to proceed to a life of Christian virtue. It is in one of Barlaam's lessons to the neophyte Christian Josaphat, in the form of a fable or parable, that an interesting dragon tale emerges.

"These men that have foolishly alienated themselves from a good and kind master," the old monk begins,

> to seek the service of so harsh and savage a lord ... that always grasp after bodily enjoyments but suffer their souls to waste with hunger ... these I consider to be like a man flying before the face of a rampant unicorn [μονόκερος, though the creature is an elephant in the older Georgian version[67]], who, unable to endure the beast's cry, and its terrible bellowing, to avoid being devoured, ran away at full speed.[68]

Yet the unicorn quickly became the least of the man's problems. While "flying" from the crazed beast, he suddenly fell into a deep pit or chasm. As he fell, he reached out and clung to a tree growing from the side of the pit. He also somehow found a foothold on the pit's earthen wall. Greatly relieved, he believed for the moment that he would be able to climb out to safety, a particularly urgent task considering that at the bottom of the pit was a dragon, "breathing fire, fearful for eye to see, exceeding fierce and grim, with terrible wide jaws, all agape to swallow him."[69] Just then, however, "he looked and descried two mice, the one white, the other black, that never ceased to gnaw the root of the tree whereon he hung...."[70] Not to be outdone, four asps had also poked out of the pit's wall near his feet. But it was then that the man saw it: a trickle of delicious honey dripping from the branches of the tree he clung to. "Yea, he forgat, without care," continues Barlaam, "all those sights of awe and terror, and his whole mind hung on the sweetness of that tiny drop of honey." Though the narrative progresses no further—Barlaam appears to become sidetracked as he explicitly deciphers for Josaphat each one of the parable's metaphors—the moral is clear: Do not become distracted by temptations of the flesh. Especially not in the face of "the fiery cruel dragon [who] betokeneth the maw of hell that is hungry to receive those who choose present pleasures rather than future blessings."[71]

Might we interpret any more specific details in *Barlaam and Josaphat* as having originated in the legends surrounding the life of the Buddha? Though it may be tempting to draw a parallel between the fleeing, falling man's tree of the former narrative and the sacred Bodhi Tree of the latter—or between the pit-dragon and the *naga* (great serpent[72]) known as Muchalinda, for that matter—such direct transfers appear unlikely. It is better to content ourselves in the knowledge that such a fascinatingly cross-cultural and polyreligious text as this has survived whatsoever to the present day.

Saint Philip (feast day: May 3), like Thomas also one of Jesus' Twelve Apostles, has had attributed to him not so much a dragon tale as an entire dragon saga. In another case of non-canonical *Acts*, probably written in the mid- to late fourth century CE, the anonymous author or authors detail the adventures of Philip along with fellow apostle Bartholomew and Philip's sister, Mariamne. The three are dispatched by Jesus after his resurrection to preach his gospel in foreign lands such as Greece and Phrygia, a region in what is now southwestern Turkey. But, more urgently, they must contend with a series of dragons, their serpentine minions, and, finally, the mighty Echidna ("She-Viper") of Greek mythology, often depicted as a woman with snakes instead of legs. In this sense, and though Ogden disputes the existence of a direct point of contact, we may read this legend as one of the more explicitly confrontational between the adherents to the old pagan rites and creeds of the era and the wandering missionaries who sought to convert and transform them into pious Christians.[73]

Saint Sylvester (or Silvester; feast day: December 31) holds the rare distinction among dragon-adjacent saints of also having been an actual, historically attested pope. As the thirty-third Bishop of Rome, Silvester I reigned over the Holy See from 314 to 335 CE (the year of his death), a highly significant period for the young Western Church and its popular adoption. As papal scholar Claudio Rendina notes, "One could say that Sylvester was simply a figurehead for [Roman Emperor] Constantine who, in fact, made full use of him."[74] Sylvester was, after all, the first pope whose spiritual authority was fully recognized by the Roman state; Constantine the Great's

St. (Pope) Sylvester (r. 314–335 AD) was remarkable primarily for his role as the pope who, as legend has it, baptized Roman emperor Constantine the Great. In fact, the episode never took place but was invented much later, in the eighth century. Though entirely fictional (Constantine was not baptized until right before his death, in 337), the moment holds important significance for the historiography of the Catholic Church. This fresco by Ludovico Gimignani (1688) is found on the main apse of the Basilica of Saint Sylvester the First, Rome, Italy (Renata Sedmakova/Shutterstock.com).

Edict of Milan in 313 (under Pope Miltiades, also known as Melchiades), which had decriminalized Christianity (and all other religious cults) throughout the Empire, had preceded Sylvester's election to the papacy by one year. Notable events of Sylvester's twenty-one-year reign would include the foundational Council of Nicaea (325), the re-founding of the city of Byzantium (now Istanbul) as Constantinople (330), and the Church's response to, and the long-lasting political effects of, the Arian heresy.[75] Yet Pope Sylvester himself, Rendina tells us, "carried little weight in the theological disputes of the age."[76]

Sylvester's dragon-smiting lore, like George's and, clearly, akin to virtually all other saints,' is a naked allegory for the victory, whether real or revisionist, of early Christianity over paganism. The principal distinction between Sylvester and most others in this league, however, lies in the lofty status that Sylvester maintained as pope during a time of newfound preeminence only shortly after a period when Christianity had been a movement of paupers and outcasts. And while George—according to legend, at least—was martyred as an unflinching, salt-of-the-earth devotee to Christ, Sylvester died, ostensibly, peacefully and of natural causes in a pope's finery, under the protection of the most powerful man in the

Roman Empire, Emperor Constantine the Great. Why, then, was another dragon necessary?

Both the allegorical and propagandistic uses of such a malevolent beast were particularly irresistible during Christianity's red-letter century: the fourth CE, when the new faith began to reach a critical mass of tolerance, if not yet widespread adherence. Specific to St. Sylvester's legend, which was first propagated in the early fifth century,[77] was his defeat of the Dragon of Rome. This noxious fiend dwelled, not surprisingly, in a pit not far from the still-active pagan temple of Vesta in the Forum. In one version of the *Acts of Silvester* (Latin, *c.* 500 CE), pagan Romans afflicted by the pestilential breath of the dragon beseech the heroic pope to "make it desist from killing the human race even for just one year, so that we may believe that your Christ possesses the virtue of divinity."[78] Though Sylvester first scolds these Romans for their fair-weather proposition, he nevertheless acquiesces. With the instruction of the ghost of St. Peter, he descends to the dragon pit. He then chains and locks up the bronze door to the beast's chamber, all while invoking the name of Jesus Christ. He buries the key. Two years pass with no sign (or smell) of the dragon. Finally convinced, those who had previously paid sacrifices to or otherwise worshiped the beast "prostrated themselves before St. Silvester, put their faith in Christ and were baptized."[79] Thus was an otherwise forgettable pontiff—though one gifted by association—raised to the high, epic standard of the Age of Constantine.

Saint Caluppan (or Callupan), according to the sixth-century CE legend chronicled by Gregory of Tours, was a hermit who lived in what is today south-central France. By any standard, he is an obscure figure. Nevertheless, his legend is of note due to its inclusion of what can only be called what it is: a farting dragon.

In brief, Caluppan sought spiritual refuge from the sinful world by living in a cave. Despite his attempts at ascetic devotion, though, he was constantly disturbed by snakes that dropped onto his head from above and tried to strangle him. Caluppan succeeded in mostly ignoring these pests until one day a pair of larger, more dragon-like beasts entered his sanctuary. One he subdued by making the sign of the cross and then accusing it of being the Serpent of the Garden of Eden itself (ostensibly these dragons were capable of both understanding human language and feeling shame). Rather anticlimactically, "the dragon [*draco*] was confounded by the virtuous power of the sign and in response abased itself and sank to the earth."[80] Much mischief was in store from the other creature, however, which had meanwhile been wrapping itself around Caluppan's legs. Snapping to attention, the hermit quickly prayed the dragon off him. "But the snake, after retreating as far as the threshold of the little chamber, emitted a loud noise through its lower part and filled the room up with such a stench that it could be believed to be nothing other than the Devil."[81] Rude and uncouth, yes. But it makes for one of the more memorable saintly dragon tales. The escapade also creatively reinterprets the anatomical source of dragons' infamously noxious emissions: venomous gas or vapors, and not fire, is often the deadliest trait of classically derived Western dragons.

6

Dragons in Western Folklore and Literature from Prehistory to 1900

Though all the crannies of the world we filled
with Elves and Goblins, though we dared to build
Gods and their houses out of dark and light,
and sowed the seeds of dragons—'twas our right
(used or misused). That right has not decayed:
we make still by the law in which we're made.[1]

In the countless centuries of our species' existence leading up to the Industrial Revolution of the late eighteenth century (*c.* 1760), which first began in England and then quickly spread to the rest of Europe and its colonies, most humans around the world were illiterate. Throughout the eons, it was not through the writing and reading of books, but rather memorized or improvised oral storytelling that the creative prowess and imagination of the masses were captured and disseminated. Though tales of dragons and other monsters were in many cases recorded for posterity by rare (and usually highly privileged) scribes and authors in literate societies starting around 3000 BCE, most of these works would have been spoken in caves or around fires or during feasts to entertain, moralize, or instill awe in listeners. It took a special admixture of technology, economic initiative, and various other cues and supports to motivate scribes to take down or embellish the oral folktales of their respective traditions, not the least of which was their given society's standardized script or other system of writing itself (not to mention the media on which such things were written). And, especially in the cases of the oldest literate civilizations, such as the Egyptians and the Assyrians, it is thanks to these enterprising individuals that we have any record of the worldview and mythologies of many of our distant forebears.

In a 1936 essay, J.R.R. Tolkien, who refers to the dragon in the Anglo-Saxon epic poem *Beowulf* simply as the eponymous protagonist's "bane,"[2] the soon-to-be published author of *The Hobbit* attempted to view the creature through the eyes of the ancient, anonymous poet himself. To channel an individual transitioning between the oral and written traditions, as it were. "He esteemed dragons," Tolkien wrote, "as rare as they are dire, as some still do. He liked them—as a poet, not as a sober zoologist; and he had good reason."[3] To a sixth- or seventh-century CE Anglo-Saxon, perhaps only a few generations into his own clan's settlement on the still predominantly Celtic island of Britain, such a mystical vision of the dragon held the potential to deeply enthrall an audience. This vision also likely invoked the poet's Continental Germanic ancestors' renown for, at least rhetorically, conquering all comers, including such uncanny monsters as Grendel, his nameless mother, and that quintessential final boss, the dragon. "Whatever may be his origins," Tolkien continued, "in fact or invention, the dragon in legend is a potent creation of men's imagination, richer in significance than his barrow in gold."[4] It is no coincidence that Tolkien's essay was written and presented to the British Academy not long before the author would become famous for his own literary creations, among them the hobbit Bilbo Baggins and that brave hobbit's bane, the mighty dragon Smaug. Like the Beowulf poet, Tolkien also clearly esteemed dragons, and the extent of this great esteem and its massive pop-cultural impacts will be explored in depth in Chapter 7.

One broader point to consider throughout this chapter, and as a continuation of the previous, is the semantic confluence between "European" and "Christian" cultures and traditions. These two classifications, depending on the time and place, may be one and the same or mutually exclusive, even within a culture that has been Christianized for centuries, if not over a millennium. As we will see, the resulting cultures of Christian(ized) Europe often appear as reconfigurations which only very imperfectly override original or pre–Christian modes. Or, to put in terms more immediately modern: as old hardware running new, and sometimes buggy, software.

In the form of the "Christo-European" or "Euro-Christian" dragon writ large we may track the peripatetic movements of this ethno-religious complex from its mythologically/spiritually Semitic origins in the Levant, to its Greco-Roman intellectual overlays and fusions, as well as to those of Germanic, Celtic, and other (mostly, but not exclusively) pagan Indo-European origins. By as early as 1100 CE, especially in Western Europe, this variegated cultural complex would be processed through the nexus of the virtually all-powerful Roman Catholic Church and the Latin language, Europe's putative pan-continental lingua franca. As a result of such far-flung influences, the mythologist Jonathan D. Evans surmises, "The dragon-lore embedded in the medieval literature … is *not* coherent: it springs from sources as diverse as medieval European geography, ancient Semitic and Hellenistic cosmology and cosmogony, Roman mythology and popular legend, Latin hagiography, and Germanic legend and folklore."[5] Nevertheless, the dragon's utility as an allegorical foe tracks closely with the various Christo-European cultures' evolutions from what had been cases of ethnolinguistic fragmentation to a smaller number of consolidated and (eventually, in several cases) imperial powers. As some of these European nation-states coalesced around their ethnolinguistic affinities, and then launched into commercial and/or seafaring empires, so too did their common breed of dragon—a chimera of chimeras—follow them throughout the world.

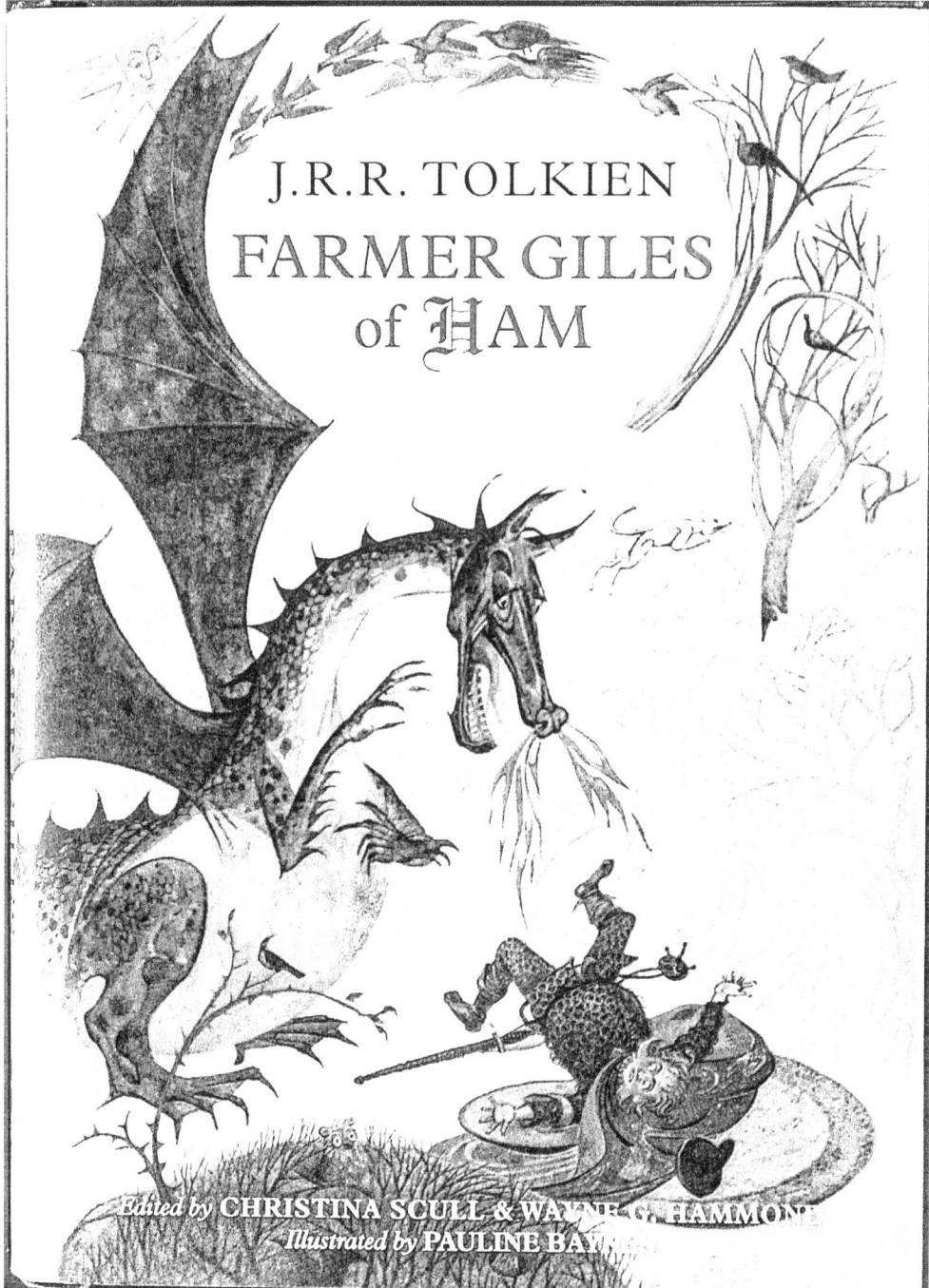

J.R.R. Tolkien wrote *Farmer Giles of Ham* around the same time he published *The Hobbit*, in 1937, but the former was not published until 1949. The story features the cowardly dragon Chrysophylax, himself less akin to the vicious Smaug and more so to those semi-puerile dragons of Kenneth Grahame and Edith Nesbit of decades earlier. The edition shown here was published in 2014 by HarperCollins (Oscar Peralta Anechina/Shutterstock.com).

Greek and Roman

As Phil Senter et al. have argued, the dragon of classical Greco-Roman lore is more akin to a large (but not uncannily large) constricting snake than, say, a massive, tripartite monster à la David E. Jones. "That Homer uses the term *drakōn* in reference to a snake," Senter writes, "is consistent with the other passages which tell us that drakōn is small enough to fit beneath an altar (2.314), is able to climb a tree (2.312–14), eats small birds (2.314), can be carried by an eagle (12.200–203)," etc.[6] Further, as corroborated by the writings of Aristotle, the ancient Greek conception of the "sharp-sighted one" was not just any snake, but specifically the Aesculapian snake, *Zamenis longissimus*.[7] This extant species can grow up to over six-and-a-half feet in length and is among the largest snakes in Europe. It is also the basis for the Staff or Rod of Aesculapius (or Asclepius), the Greek god of medicine whose symbol still regularly represents the medical and pharmaceutical professions in the West and beyond to this day.[8] (The snake is named for the god, himself a son of Apollo and a mortal woman. Several myths connect the deity with snakes, but one in particular maintains that Aesculapius was rewarded by a snake for some kindness given, in the form of healing or medical knowledge.) Its relatively large size notwithstanding, this species of snake is a far cry from most conceptions of "dragon," at least by modern Western standards. And though it preys on small birds and mammals, *Z. longissimus* is not even venomous. But for how long, and why, did the Greeks really keep their dragons to such relatively minuscule proportions?

The ancient or classical Greeks are renowned to this day, especially in the West, for their historically precocious levels of achievement in what would later be known as scientific logic and reasoning. The early adoption of an adapted phonetic alphabet to best capture their spoken language—an event influenced in large part by the Greeks' proximity to the Egyptians, Hebrews (and other Jewish peoples), Phoenicians (who had first developed a phonetic alphabet), and other literate cultures—gave them a distinct advantage among Europeans in recording their literature and, later, their science and philosophy. Yet, as a people-group, most ancient Greeks were just as prone to mythology, spirituality, and magical thinking as any other. Furthermore, and as in virtually all pre-modern societies, only a very select few individuals, virtually always males of the elite, were even permitted to learn how to read, much less to write. All things oral thus continued to predominate for centuries, including the epics which would eventually be transcribed by Homer.

The Greeks' pantheon of gods, monsters, and other fantastical creatures was elaborate, vividly represented in oral folklore and the visual arts, and tenaciously maintained by bards as a wellspring of wisdom, morality, and entertainment. This tradition continued even as early Greek philosophers, historians, and mathematicians began to establish rationalist modes of thought and epistemology—a rudimentary or preliminary version of what would eventually become the scientific method and furthermore rationalist modes of thought. These two realms—the mythological/

The Aesculapian snake (*Zamenis longissimus*), common throughout the Mediterranean basin, is named for the Greek god of medicine. The basic association is that snakes possess powers of immortality and healing (Marco Maggesi/Shutterstock.com).

The Rod or Staff of Aesculapius, often confused with the staff wreathed with dual, winged snakes known as a *caduceus*, was traditionally and is still regularly used to represent the fields of medicine and pharmacy. This engraving is found on a headstone, probably of a physician or pharmacist, who died in Munich, Germany, 1902 (FooTToo/Shutterstock.com).

The *ouroboros* symbol was borrowed by the Greeks from ancient Egyptian lore. The imagery comports with many traditional cultures' beliefs that snakes were immortal. This composite door knocker is in Troyes, France (ArTDi101/Shutterstock.com).

allegorical and the rationalist/scientific—were not mutually exclusive to the classical Greek mind: they often circled back on one another, not unlike the *ouroboros*, or serpent/dragon eating its own tail, itself originally an Egyptian deity that was later introduced into Greek lore and symbolism.

Elements of Greek or Hellenic culture spread far and wide throughout the classical world, including its mythology and folklore. Thanks to the military conquests initiated by Alexander the Great, King of Macedon (356–323 BCE), this sphere reached as far from the Greek homeland as present-day Afghanistan and Pakistan, on the cusp of what is today India. (Legends persisted even through the Middle Ages that Alexander was not the biological son of Philip II of Macedon, but of Zeus, or his Egyptian counterpart A[m]mon, sometimes portrayed in manuscript illustrations as a dragon or large serpent found bedded with the ruler's mother Olympias.)[9] But, as in many cases of colonization, such imperialistic overlays normally did not extinguish all or even most indigenous practices now within Alexander's empire, resulting in a common process of dynamic syncretization with reverberations felt even today.

Later, when the ascendant Romans incorporated Greek philosophy, science, literature, and other elements into their own imperial and cosmopolitan milieu, so too came Greek narrative modes and their overarching cosmogony and cosmology. The prestige of these established cultural totems—especially in the form of the Greek language—as well as Greek breakthroughs in mathematics, science, and philosophy, ensured their virtually wholesale incorporation into the gestalt of the new hegemonic power structure of Rome. (Though not unprecedented, this pattern runs contrary to the typical exchange—namely, from the conquering to the conquered—that otherwise occurs in cases of imperial conquest.) Thus did *drakōn* become *draco*, as seen in the constellation as well as the many myths surrounding the creature. As the Romans themselves spread throughout the Mediterranean basin and beyond, so clashed and blended their innovations in technology (and especially in civil engineering projects such as roads and aqueducts), laws, and military might with the folkways of the many indigenous groups—predominantly fellow Indo-Europeans, but not exclusively—they encountered outside of the Italian peninsula, and particularly with those of Germanic and Celtic stocks. Though the Roman Empire would fall by the end of the fifth century CE, the influence of the Latin language—and the Western or Catholic variety of Christianity (and, later, the scholarly output transmitted through that language)—would loom large for centuries on end. By about the year 1500, when the era of western European transcontinental expansion and colonization had begun in earnest, the mold was set for the heirs of Rome—whether genetic, cultural, or both—to in turn overlay their imprint like a palimpsest, a new layer of text often written in blood, sideways, as it were, upon various peoples across the globe.

In the wake of Greco-Roman hegemony, before that tradition's heirs could coalesce into distinct empires of their own, there remained those myths and legends that classical-era peoples had wrought and spread, both in writing and in oral folklore. In particular, the pantheon of Greek titans, gods, half-gods, mortals, and monsters loomed large. The advantage that the Hellenic tradition wielded, as mentioned above, was defined by an early and sustained focus on efficiently documenting its narratives, values, and, furthermore, its knowledge of the cosmos, in written language. To this extent, for centuries the Greeks were at the vanguard of their Indo-European extended kin-group, successfully capturing and disseminating what may have also been embedded in the numerous ancient oral tales and cosmologies of other ethno-linguistic groups—but, because the latter were predominantly illiterate nations, such content was also highly susceptible to loss amidst conquest or other cultural upheavals. Thus do the precociously literate Greeks lay claim to the oldest extant written examples of the common folk-motif known as ATU Type 300, "The Dragon Slayer" (also discussed in Chapter 2). And no more brilliantly does this motif come to life than in the Greek myth of Perseus and Andromeda.

Perseus, the son of a princess named Danae and the grandson of Acrisius, king of Argos, a city-state in the Peloponnese peninsula of southern Greece, has grown up to be a strapping young man. He lives with his mother not in Argos, however, but on the island of Seriphos (or Serifos), an actual Greek island in the Aegean Sea. Danae and Perseus had not come on their own volition to what is their seemingly idyllic island home: years ago, King Acrisius, Danae's father, and Perseus' grandfather, fearing the prognostications of the Oracle of Delphi that Acrisius' daughter's son would kill him, had banished the pair to the sea in a wooden chest, soon after

Perseus was born. Little did King Acrisius know, however, that Perseus' father was Zeus. The chief deity of the Greek pantheon, merely upon seeing her, had become besotted with, and then impregnated, the beautiful and cloistered Danae. (He happened to do this rather covertly, in the form of a golden rain.) In their hour of need on the turbulent high seas, Zeus interceded to save his infant child and "lover" from oblivion by calling on Poseidon, his fellow god, and the lord of the seas, to blow the castaway wooden chest all the way to Seriphos. The mother and son were then rescued by a kindly islander and allowed to live and thrive far away from the dangers of Argos.

Compared with St. George's legend, which was thoroughly investigated in the previous chapter, Perseus' dragon-slaying narrative is the more sophisticated, by far. For the common St. George-versus-the-Dragon legend, ATU Type 300 was transformed from what had been in pre–Christian, Greek hands a highly humanistic drama into a rather blunt, propagandistic morality tale in its new hagiographic dressing. Indeed, in classic(al) Greek tragic style, lust and legacy emerge as the principal catalysts for upheaval in Perseus' adventures, themes that often eschew simplistic or binary interpretations.

Unfortunately for her, the ruler of the isle of Seriphos, King Polydectes, has also found himself smitten with the supremely pulchritudinous Danae. To remove a major obstacle to his romantic conquest, the king sends the youth Perseus on what he believes will be a fatal fool's errand: to not only kill the serpent-headed monster Medusa, but also to bring back her head, petrifying eyes and all. Though daunting, of course Perseus succeeds in his task—he is the son of Zeus, after all, and can furthermore rely on the assistance of several other deities. A tip from Athena leads Perseus to use a polished shield to keep Medusa in view while also avoiding her deadly gaze. Perseus walks backward, draws his adamantine sword, and cuts off her head, which he then preserves in a sack.

It is after this point that the parallels with St. George's dragon-slaying legend—as well as with that of St. Margaret, explored in the previous chapter—begin to become rather unmistakable. Like George, Perseus is a soldier (of sorts) returning from battle when he finds a young woman in shackles (whether figurative or literal, depending on the telling), awaiting her own annihilation at the claws and teeth of a dragon (or something similar). In the Classical Greek version, the maiden in question, Andromeda, finds herself on a cliff by the sea, while, as we have seen, St. George's princess is banished to the shore of a lake. The difference is moot: both princesses have been placed as close as possible to the lair of a poisonous, ravenous, evil, and, moreover, marine (or at least amphibious) monster (in Greek, κῆτος/kētos, rather than drakōn). The distinction between the Christian and classical versions lies in the former's insistence that paganism, or rather, the mere absence of Christianity, is the root cause of most crises. The Greeks, on the other hand, knew that humans and their interpersonal conflicts with each other, or with the mercurial gods (read: with nature itself), were usually to blame.

The *kētos*, or sea monster, that the mythological Greek Perseus slew to save the princess Andromeda is often portrayed as a dragon with fins or other piscine qualities. This relief carving of the scene is found on the city fountain of Friesach, Austria (Sonja Mair/Shutterstock.com).

To wit, Poseidon, once the kindly savior of Perseus and Danae, has now grown wrathful upon hearing a rumor that Andromeda's mother, Cassiopeia, queen of Aethiopia,[10] has claimed that her human daughter is more beautiful than Poseidon's "god" daughters. But it was not Poseidon himself who had chained Andromeda to the cliff as a sacrifice—it was a posse of anxious and traumatized subjects of King Cephus and Queen Cassiopeia of Aethiopia. After Poseidon's vengeful inundation of Aethiopia's coastal settlements after taking such offense, and as a ferocious sea-dragon had picked off any survivors, the common folk then rebelled, captured Andromeda, and offered her up to appease the angry sea-god over her mother's insouciance. With most depictions of the shackled Andromeda as completely naked, there is a sexual element to this sacrifice as well: should the dragon not feast upon her flesh, Poseidon may likely take her as his concubine.

Perseus, naturally, saves the day. He rescues Andromeda from the clutches of the heinous *kētos*, though perhaps not as directly as we might assume a hero of this caliber might. Failing to slay the creature by pelting it with rocks, Perseus meets it head on, its poisonous, steaming breath (again, not yet fire in the Western tradition) fouling the air between them. The young man's hubris is ill-gauged, however, and the charging dragon swiftly swallows Perseus whole. Prefiguring St. Margaret's method of escape (detailed in the previous chapter), "Perseus drew his adamantine sword—diamond-edged—and cut his way out, killing it from the inside out. Then with mighty strokes he cut off the monster's head."[11] And with one more mighty sword stroke, Princess Andromeda is freed from her chains.

Suffice it to say, Perseus' story does not end here. The Delphic prophecy that Perseus will kill his grandfather, King Acrisius, is indeed fulfilled, though, in true ancient Greek style, rather ironically. And there is even a rather happy ending for the story's three main heroes, Perseus, Andromeda, and Danae. But the parallels and departures between this dragon fight and St. George's are of course of most interest. As a caveat, Ogden warns that such textual comparisons may be misleading: "It is often held that the tale of Perseus and his *kētos* eventually inspired the famous tale of St George and his dragon, but in fact the early versions of the St George story have far more in common rather with the Hesione[12] tradition."[13] Regardless, the bridge between the pre- and post–Christian usages of dragon and dragon-slaying allegory, as shown both here and in the previous chapter, was built piecemeal of various odds and ends, and over many centuries. Ultimately that bridge reached the modern West as it transmitted the dragon in a form unequivocally equated with evil.

Germanic

The meaning of the Anglo-Saxon (Old English) word *aglæca* is a point of much intrigue, and some contention, among scholars of the medieval epic poem *Beowulf*. The noun[14] went extinct long before it could transmute into anything recognizable to modern English speakers. But its general sense is related to its root *ege* ("fear"), itself related to the word that eventually became our "awe." In the context of the original language of *Beowulf*, *aglæca* is usually translated as "formidable one," or "awe-inspiring (thing or person)."[15] But what's most intriguing of all is that this word is used to describe or modify not only the poem's three principal monsters—Grendel, Grendel's nameless mother, and the nameless dragon—but also the legendary warrior-hero Beowulf himself.

Personally, I prefer the older, more literal meaning of the word "awesome": "[one or something] characterized by or eliciting awe." This connotation, of course, long predates the word's semantic drift into the contemporary (and particularly American) colloquial meaning of "excellent" or "exceptional," often in the form of an interjection. Though shades of both meanings will apply here, the former is particularly apt. Regarding all four principal supernatural beings in *Beowulf*, whether hero or villain, human or monster, we understand that each is uncanny, mighty, and, what's more, well-matched: three supervillains versus, at various moments, a superhero. They are all exceptional, too, if not always *excellent*: Grendel and the other monsters are unambiguously evil, the poet makes quite clear. But whether we love or loathe them, they are worthy of awe. Only with a grip as awesome as Beowulf's could the Geatish hero's Danish allies ever contend with a gigantic, monstrous descendent of the biblical Cain such as Grendel (or his vengeful mother, a being often described in modern translations as a "sea-wolf," though this designation remains controversial[16,17]).

According to the story, fifty years after Beowulf has slain the two monstrous *aglæca*, mother and son, the Danes ask their awesome savior to come out of old-age retirement to face an even more awesome foe: a dragon. In the original, the creature is called a *wyrm* ("worm") or *fyr-draca* ("fire dragon" or "drake," the latter being an archaic English word also derived from the Greek *drakōn*). As medievalist and scholar of Anglo-Saxon language and culture Simon Roper explains, "The word *wyrm* could describe a snake, a worm, a maggot, or it could describe a folkloric creature resembling one of those things, like a serpent." Though certain larger creatures such as bears and whales were rarely encountered by people in Old England, they were understood to be real (which of course they were and still are).[18] Therefore, if a mammal or a "fish" could exist in both minimal and maximal forms, so too could a garden-variety worm or snake, to the ancient mind, have a fearsome, gigantic analog in the form of a dragon. Stories like *Beowulf* both emerged from and reinforced such a taxonomic scheme. The anthropologist Cecil H. Brown identified such larval dragons, common in mythologies throughout the world, as *wugs*, a novel portmanteau of "worm" and "bug."[19]

Beowulf is an Anglo-Saxon (Old English) interpretation of an otherwise pan–Germanic mode of epic verse. Estimated to have been composed between 750 and 950 CE, the tale itself hearkens to the oral traditions of various continental Germanic tribes (e.g., Danes, Geats [also known as Goths], Swedes) and their vision of a mostly allegorical, primordial heroic age. In *Beowulf* there are strong hints of the native Germanic pagan religion, though much of this influence was either suppressed or expurgated by later Christian scribes, including the two that are purported to have produced the only extant manuscript of *Beowulf*. Contemporary Anglo-Saxons, otherwise separated from their extended Germanic kinfolk by the North Sea, first orally performed and then manually transcribed such tales as *Beowulf* with the knowledge and awe that they were themselves linked to the deeds and conquests of their ancient kinfolk on the mainland. Though the 3,182-line prose poem was written onto vellum around 1000 CE,[20] the story itself most certainly had a long oral tradition that is now entirely lost to us.[21] But what remains is a document that provides copious insights into how the Anglo-Saxons understood the cosmos in terms of both monsters and men.

In the 2007 CGI feature film *Beowulf*, several points of ambiguity of the original poem are clarified for the sake of narrative cohesion. Certain plot details are also simply altered altogether. For one, Beowulf no longer simply slays Grendel's mother; in true Hollywood fashion he instead has a passionate love affair with her in her human form (both voiced by and physically modeled on actor Angelina Jolie). And the result of that tryst in her mere (or, in this version, a murky and mystical subterranean cave-lair)? A dragon. Decades later in the story, we find that Beowulf's nameless, illegitimate son and final foe is also an *aglæca*—a shapeshifter who alternates between the forms of a golden man and a gigantic, destructive golden dragon. (It should be noted that, in the original text, however, the dragon is female and does not appear to be related to the Grendel family whatsoever.)

In the film, King Beowulf's seduction is a repeat of a deed of the previous king, Hrothgar (voiced by Sir Anthony Hopkins). For both men were these sexual encounters life-altering mistakes. Hrothgar, in his youth, had mated with the "sea-wolf" in her irresistibly beautiful human form, making him Grendel's biological father. (This, it should be reiterated, is artistic license and, like the dragon's paternity, also does not find a parallel in the original text.) Having had no

The only extant copy of the Anglo-Saxon prose poem *Beowulf* is found in a manuscript version which dates to the early eleventh century CE (© The British Library Board, Cotton Vitellius A. XV, f.132).

children with his much-younger queen, Wealhtheow, Hrothgar is cursed by the knowledge that his only offspring is the hideous, man-eating giant Grendel[22] that so benights his people. Beowulf, in this version, suffers a similar fate to Hrothgar when he too succumbs to the seductions of Grendel's mother, impregnating her. She promises Beowulf that as long as the royal "golden dragonhorn" chalice of Fafnir, previously in Hrothgar's possession, should remain in her lair's treasure hoard, she will leave Heorot, the seat of Hrothgar's kingdom, in peace. But she demands an additional term: that Beowulf give her a son to replace Grendel, whom Beowulf has already killed in hand-to-hand (and naked) combat. This portrayal hints that

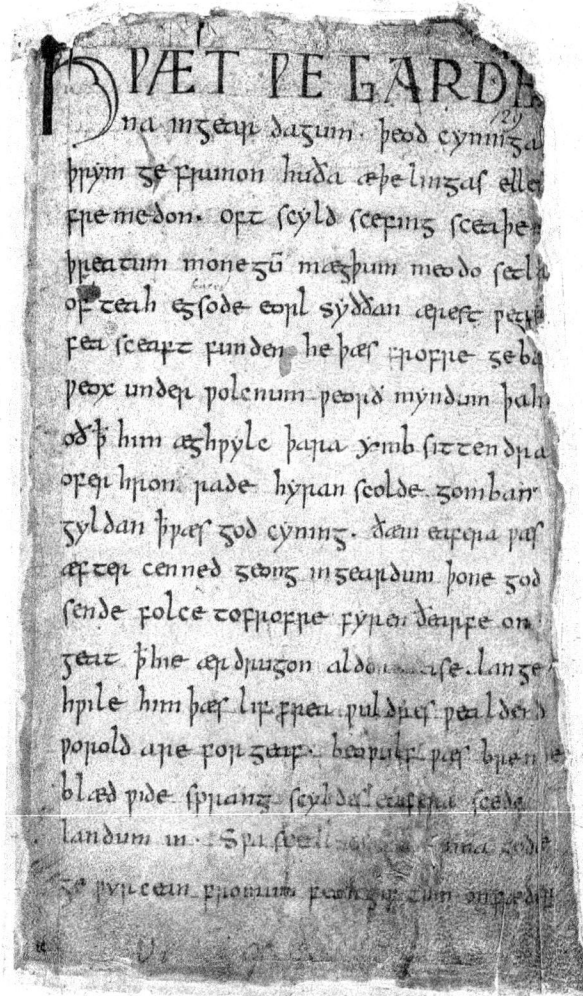

perhaps the dragon Fafnir of old mainland–Germanic folklore, "the prince of all dragons,"[23] archnemesis of the hero Sigurd (his name in Old Norse/Icelandic; Siegfried in the German version), is also a spawn of the shapeshifting sea-wolf otherwise known as Grendel's mother. Regardless, in the film version at least, she is more literally a "mother of dragons" than Queen Daenerys Targaryen, the official holder of that august though figurative epithet in George R.R. Martin's *A Song of Ice and Fire* novels (and their television adaptations).[24]

Interestingly, Sigemund (or Sigmund), the legendary father of Sigurd from the same Germanic legendary cycle, is mentioned in the text of the original *Beowulf,* though Sigurd is not, as shown in this modern translation:

> The scop [oral storyteller] had opinions, and he shared them:
> compare/contrast. Stories he'd heard
> About another warrior, Sigemund. Verses detailing
> that man's hidden past, stealth acts, dark secrets
> spat only into his kinsman's ear [...]
>
> "After he died, Sigemund was shaped
> into story-glory for his crowning kill,
> cutting through the hide of a hoard-holder,
> a dragon whose cave he'd crawled inside,
> outrageously alone...["][25]

In this and other tellings of his legend, Sigemund's dragon is nameless. But like his son Sigurd's bane (Fafnir, who was once a human and only became a dragon once he was morally corrupted) and Beowulf's bane (also nameless), the sins of greed and pride are almost always embodied in these Germanic dragons, traits highlighted further when pitted against such valiant and selfless human heroes. The reference to one hero within the tale of another reinforces the well-established tradition of the Germanic dragonslayer, though it is unclear whether one necessarily predates the other in real time. Since the *Beowulf* manuscript, as we have seen, exists in only one extant copy, it is possible to read the poem as an Anglo-Saxon reinterpretation of much older, mainland–Germanic heroic lore, most of which long predates Christian influence and modes of thought.

Following his late-twentieth-century translation of *Beowulf,* Howell D. Chickering, Jr., assesses the essence of the *Beowulf* dragon:

> [Its] nature ... is something else again. One would like to say, "Dragons will be dragons," and be done with it. No serpent in Western literature means well. But whether we should also understand the dragon as a Christian symbol for the general evil in the world, or as the Devil who appears as serpent and Leviathan in the Bible, has been a matter of considerable controversy.[26]

But why not both? What remains of Germanic mythology in its oldest documentation is representative of the transitional period from paganism to Christianity (*c.* 500–1000 CE) and thus serves as a composite of two distinct religio-cultural worldviews. And a dragon is indeed a behemoth in the sense that we have seen: a small serpent (or worm) must, by the old taxonomy, have a logical analog on the macro

A marauding dragon adorns the façade of Munich, Germany's town hall (Torruzzlo/Shutterstock.com).

scale. Once a creature of any kind attains such a massive size, according to this same schema, it must also pose both an existential threat (through predation) and one of a more psychological or even spiritual nature to an individual human person and, by extension, to human society.

In his own translation of the poem, the Irish poet and translator Seamus Heaney offers that "…the dragon has a wonderful inevitability about him and a unique glamour. It is not that the other monsters are lacking in presence and aura; it is more that they remain, for all their power to terrorize, creatures of the physical world."[27] Yet, as Heaney continues, the dragon is also "a figure of real oneiric power."[28] Like Chickering's assessment, these descriptors are at first glance contradictory—that the dragon is both material and dreamlike. Is it, then, the dragon's unique magic to transcend such binary limitations? Both Chickering and Heaney signal that the very purpose of a mythological creature is just that. Heaney: "…he [the dragon] lodges himself in the imagination as *wyrd* rather than *wyrm*, more a destiny than a set of reptilian vertebrae."[29] This metaphysical interpretation indeed correlates with the placement of the dragon at the ending of *Beowulf* as the Geatish warrior's third and final adversary—the one that takes the hero's life just as the hero takes its own. Such a mighty superhero, if he is to maintain this status forever through folklore and legend, is fated to die only at the fangs and claws of a worthy, monstrous foe. But—as is over-whelmingly the case in dragon-lore—not before he kills it first. Thus have they both lived and died as *aglæca*.

As Joseph Campbell surmises of legendary Germanic heroes' relationships with their draconic counterparts,

> [The hero] may kill the dragon power, as Siegfried does when he kills the dragon. But then he tastes the dragon blood, that is to say, he has to assimilate that power. And when Siegfried has killed the dragon and tasted the blood, he hears the song of nature; he has transcended his humanity, you know, and reassociated himself with the powers of nature, which are the pow-ers of our life, from which our mind removes us.[30]

The slaying of the Germanic dragon, then, is a return to the primordial, the heroic, and the essential through a baptism by dragonfire. The dragonslayer is the ultimate warrior, in such control of his physical strength and cunning that he matches and then subsumes into his very being the qualities of the mighty beasts he has slain, inoculating himself against the evil that such unholy or otherwise inhuman crea-tures may (re)present. He does so even as the vicious combat with the dragon, in some cases, results in his losing his own life just as he finishes off the monster. To hold fast to that power, even for a few fleeting moments of waking life, is worth many factors more than the boundless, glistening acreage of the dragon's hoard itself.

Celtic

Though it has been significantly filtered through the prisms of Germanic (Anglo-Saxon and then English) and Romance (Norman or otherwise French) lan-guages and cultures, what is commonly known as the Arthurian Cycle is both ulti-mately and essentially of Celtic origin. The original principal elements date to the earliest centuries of the so-called Dark Ages (*c.* 400–600 CE) and, it has been argued, can be traced to an even earlier, pre–Roman epoch, when the Celts and their druidic priestly class reigned unopposed throughout the island of Britain.

The name Arthur itself is derived from the word "bear" (*arth*) in what is in English known as the Welsh language (natively, *Cymraeg*) but once was the com-mon Celtic language of most of Britain. (King Arthur is also, interestingly, referred to throughout the original literature as not the "Bear," but the "*Boar* of Corn-wall."[31]) Prior to the Anglo-Saxon invasions of the fifth and sixth centuries CE, the ethno-linguistic character of Britain was Brythonic-Celtic,[32] with some late–Latin influence from the Roman settlements on the island starting with Rome's conquest in 43 CE. The ruins of Tintagel Castle—where King Arthur, son of Uther Pendragon, was conceived, according to legend—are to be found on the once (and still, to a lim-ited degree) culturally Celtic peninsula of Cornwall, for many centuries now con-sidered an integral part of the Home Country England but once its own distinct kingdom. Monuments and sites linked to the legends of Arthur and his entourage

(Merlin, Guinevere, Lancelot, Gawain, etc.) are to be found throughout England, Cornwall, Wales, and, in what is now the Republic of France, Brittany. Sites of interest also include Dinas Emrys in Gwynedd, northwest Wales; Cadbury, in Somerset, southwest England, near Cornwall; the forest of Broceliande in Brittany; and several others.[33]

If our only basis of reference for Arthurian legend was the 1975 cult comedy *Monty Python and the Holy Grail*, we'd be forgiven for an incomplete—if not wholly farcical—understanding of the hero Arthur, "the King of the Britons." Comedian Graham Chapman plays the role perfectly straight, as a proper and earnest Englishman, speaking eloquently in Received Pronunciation, as he seeks the Holy Grail. Then again, that's the joke: How does one "accurately" portray a slew of cobbled-together, disputed, and ancient legends? Better to just have fun with it, as the comedy troupe clearly did. The result is a spoof of a far-bygone era and, furthermore, of our modern, befuddled, and often overwrought perceptions thereof, including still-prevalent notions of British, or rather "Anglo-Saxon," exceptionalism.

The "Britons" whom Arthur represented and ruled, to reiterate, were the Celtic indigenes of the Island of Britain, those previously predominant inhabitants who for the better part of four centuries also commingled with the Roman colonists in their midst.[34] These Britons had predated the Germanic "English" on Britain as the dominant culture by at least a millennium and a half, though likely much longer. Though today we understand the demonym "Briton" to most immediately approximate "Englishman/woman/person," and then only secondarily "any native or citizen of the United Kingdom," prior to the fifth century CE most British islanders were ethnically, culturally, and linguistically Celtic. Arthur and Merlin, though largely fictitious or at most semi-historical figures, would thus have been of this stock. Ironically, the Anglo-Saxons (i.e., the proto–English), were viewed by these ancient Britons as barbaric invaders and sworn enemies. Though by no means a perfect analogy, modern Britons' (and especially English popular culture's) appropriation of Arthur and his Knights of the Round Table as national superheroes is not wholly dissimilar to European-descended or white Americans' (ab)use of Native American figures or personae as sports mascots (see also Chapter 12).

We inherit much of Arthurian lore thanks to one scholar and cleric of the twelfth century, Geoffrey of Monmouth (c. 1095–c. 1155). Though it is unclear whether Geoffrey was himself linguistically and/or ethnically Welsh,[35] as an educated Catholic ecclesiastic he of course wrote in Latin. Geoffrey claimed that he had drawn his source from a book in "the British tongue" (i.e., Welsh),[36] but it was in the lingua franca of Western Christendom that Geoffrey produced his highly popular and frequently copied manuscript, *De gestis Britonum* (or *Historia Regum Britanniae*), usually rendered in English as *The History of the Kings of Britain*. The book was first published around the year 1138 and then quickly became a sensation throughout Europe. Regardless of his ethnic or linguistic identity, as Arthurian scholar Geoffrey Ashe notes, Geoffrey of Monmouth "believed … that the ancestral

Britons had been a great people, with wise and powerful rulers, among whom the renowned king Arthur was supreme."[37] In the power vacuum left by the departing Romans in the late fifth century, Britain was for the proceeding centuries up for grabs—either the Celts' or the Germanics' for the taking as the dominant power—a theme integral to both the *History* and most, if not all, of the subsequent Arthurian literature.

Though a few dragons figure into the traditional Welsh folktales known collectively as the *Mabinogion*,[38] it is in Geoffrey's *History* that we gain a fruitful sense of the Celtic conception of the dragon. Such a motif is therein employed as an allegory for the Welsh-Saxon conflict in Britain that Geoffrey's book embodies. It is also through the *History* that the eternal wizard Merlin first began to capture the popular imagination of western Europe at large, spearheading what is now almost 1,000 years of the character's appearances in literature, cinema, and other mass media.

Geoffrey introduces Merlin early in his saga, amid the power struggle for the fate and spirit of Britain. An opportunistic Celtic overlord or chief, Vortigern, has betrayed his countrymen and allied himself with the ostensibly ascendent Saxons. The indigenous Celts have at this point largely converted to Christianity; the still-pagan Saxons are "the heathen," and are represented as likewise brutish and menacing. But despite their assumed Christian piety, the Celts still openly maintain a syncretic relationship to the animistic, druidic practices of their forebears. In the pursuit of control over his realm, Vortigern has attempted several times to raise a tower for himself on a site known as Dinas Emrys. Every time his crew begins to build, however, the ground sinks in, imploding any construction and forcing his workmen to start from scratch. Vexed, Vortigern seeks counsel from a group of local druids. "Find a fatherless boy," the old mystics ascertain. The child's blood should be shed upon the tower's foundations … and his dead body buried at its base. This is the only way to keep the earth from caving in on itself, they assure the desperate Vortigern.

That boy, found in a local village, is named Merlin.[39] Merlin's father's identity is unknown, though the story goes that it had been an incubus, or demon, who had sired him. Merlin's mother, on the other hand, is a kindly mortal, and of noble lineage. Merlin is duly brought to Dinas Emrys. Before he can be brutally sacrificed by Vortigern and his minions, however, he speaks: "Tell your magicians to appear in front of me," he declares, "and I will prove that they have lied."[40] The reason for the construction's troubles is immediately clear to him. The workmen should dig down to the base of the foundation, where they will find a pond or small lake. The water, he continues, should be drained. All this being done, the crew then encounters two large, egg-shaped stones. They break them open and find that in each is a dragon, one white and one red. Small at first, the two monsters quickly grow as they simultaneously fight—they had been trying to attack each other before their liberation, causing the tremors that had ruined all prior attempts at setting the tower's

According to Arthurian legend as popularized by Geoffrey of Monmouth, as a young boy the wizard Merlin used his clairvoyance to guide a local warlord to the source of his architectural woes. Two dragons, one white and one red, were found fighting for dominance deep below the earth. The metaphor for Germanic (white) versus Celtic (red) competition would not have been lost on Geoffrey's contemporary (thirteenth century) readers (© The British Library Board, Cotton Claudius B. VII, f.224).

masonry. Though the white dragon at first routs the red dragon to the edge of the drained pool, the red quickly fights back, putting the white to chase....

As we saw in Chapter 1, the red dragon defiantly and perpetually stands for Wales, then as now. Clearly, the white dragon represents England or, since at this point that entity has not yet coalesced into a sovereign nation-state, the Germanic-speaking Saxons and their several burgeoning kingdoms on Britain. This lore is, in fact, the very origin of the red dragon (*Y Ddraig Goch*) of the Welsh flag. The suspense lies in Geoffrey's allegorical framing: Though this conflict may have already been several centuries in progress by Geoffrey's time (in the mid-twelfth century), the result of the battle for the soul of Britain was not yet a foregone conclusion in the hearts of minds of the subaltern Welsh[41]—or rather, the "true" Britons. They may always rise again, Geoffrey intimates through the oraculations of the boy Merlin:

> The race that is oppressed shall prevail in the end, for it will resist the savagery of the invaders.
> The Boar of Cornwall [i.e., Arthur] shall bring relief from these invaders, for it will trample their necks beneath its feet.[42]

And, in 1485, with the emergence of the Tudor dynasty, this revanchist vision at least nominally came to fruition. Of Welsh origin, King Henry VII's succession to the throne heralded a unification of the Saxons and Britons, if not exactly a decisive

The City of London's coat of arms features the traditional white dragons of the English people; their wings are inlaid with the red St. George's Cross. The motto translates as "Lord, guide us" (Fotokon/Shutterstock.com).

victory on behalf of the latter. That king's son, Henry VIII, further consolidated British power both domestically and on the world stage. As did his daughter, Queen Elizabeth I. The penultimate sovereign, Queen Elizabeth II, and her son, the current monarch King Charles III, the former Prince of Wales, are direct descendants of this line (hence Her Majesty's well-documented fondness for Welsh Corgis, among other Welsh or otherwise Celtic royal accouterments). Such a prophetic fable reminded Geoffrey's medieval readers of the enchantment and glory of the Celtic Britain that once was, and could perhaps still be again. The red dragon rampant (on its hind legs) in the heraldic crests and badges of the Tudors makes this political undercurrent abundantly clear. And the white or silver dragons of the City of London's coat of arms remind us that the cultural and symbolic landscape of Great Britain remains nuanced.

Other European Dragons

Dracula is more than just the proper name given to the world's most famous vampire. Within the name itself is embedded a phrase in the Romanian language meaning, in one interpretation at least, "the devil's son."[43] But the story only begins there.

The Romanian word *drac* is, as in many languages around the world, derived from Greek *drakōn* via Latin *draco*. A more common word for "dragon" in vernacular Romanian, however, is *balaur*, likely originating in Dacian, the region's little-documented and extinct pre–Roman language.[44] *Drac* became a synonym for the devil in a process wholly predictable given the dragon's close or selfsame associations with Satan in the Judeo-Christian context. But the exogenous meaning of *drac* can still be recalled, and especially so in earlier centuries, to invoke the mythological reptilian in a more versatile guise.

The historical Dracula, Prince Vlad III "The Impaler" (*Tepes* in Romanian), Voivode[45] of Wallachia (*c.* 1430–1476), was so called because his father, Vlad II, had carried the epithet "the Dragon," or *Dracul*. Vlad II Dracul was a member of the Order of the Dragon, an Orthodox Christian fraternity, founded in 1408 by the king and queen of Hungary and Croatia, Sigismund and Barbara. The monarchs had adopted the iconography of St. George the Dragonslayer in their ongoing campaign against the Muslim Ottoman Turks, who were then actively encroaching on the region. "[F]rom 1408 to 1437," writes Romanian historian Constantin Rezachevici, "the Order of the Dragon became the most important noble political association in Hungary."[46] Vlad II, as an inductee to the order (in 1431), a voivode, and furthermore as a vassal to King Sigismund, took on the mantle of the dragon as he directly engaged in combat with the Ottomans. The symbolic power of the evil creature of Euro-Christian lore, otherwise an allegorical manifestation of Satan, was thus reflected against a foreign threat of equal parts religious, political, and existential

Before Bram Stoker's famous novel, *Dracula*, or "Son of the Dragon," was an epithet of Prince (Voivode) Vlad III "The Impaler" of Wallachia (d. *c.* 1476). The historical figure is revered to this day in Romania for his defense of Christianity (and early Romanian nationalism) against invading Muslim Turks. This statue stands in Bran, Romania (Gabi8o/Shutterstock.com).

antagonism, much as in the case of the Welsh red dragon vis-à-vis the invading Saxons. In such contexts, the wartime maxim of "the enemy of my enemy is my friend" becomes particularly germane.

When Vlad II and his eldest son Mircea died amidst political treachery in 1447, the heir to the Principality of Wallachia, Vlad III, assumed not only his father's crown but also a heightened policy of brutal vengeance against the Turks and their allies. It was after this point that Vlad III became not only "The Son of the Dragon," (*Draculea* in Old Romanian), but also *Tepes*, "The Impaler," due to his most infamous method of executing enemies. Through the influence of written accounts condemning the seemingly bloodthirsty prince in other regional languages, such as Turkish and Serbian, *Draculea* became *Dracula*.[47] By the time the historical figure and his legend reached Bram Stoker at the end of the nineteenth century, artistic license quickly took hold. The Anglo-Irish author re-envisioned the notorious warlord in his novel, first published in 1897, as the fantastical archvillain now known throughout global popular culture. Notably, this fictionalized version of Dracula was no longer an ethnic–Romanian (nor human) prince of Wallachia, but rather an immortal vampire who "sunlighted" as an ethnic Hungarian (Szekely) count of Transylvania.

But the etymological confusion remains: Is Dracula "The Son of the Dragon" or "The Son of the Devil"? And does it make a difference? As mentioned, in modern Romanian the common word for dragon is the non–Latinate *balaur* (though sometimes *dragon* is also used, showing a more recent re-borrowing from French; as is *zmeu*, cognate with the term in most of the neighboring Slavic languages). *Drac* is now synonymous with *diavol*, "devil." This development shows the gradual semantic drift of *draco* starting with its origin in the vulgar Latin spoken after the Roman emperor Trajan's conquest of the region then known as Dacia (early second century CE). By the fifteenth century (and Vlad III's lifetime), the Romanian language as we know it today had mostly taken shape. However, semantic drift was (and is, as in all natural spoken languages) ongoing. "For his son, Vlad Tepes," Rezachevici explains, "the name 'Dracula' became through affiliation an alternative, not only a nickname, with the side effect of increasing his bad reputation [among his enemies the Turks as well as any perceived usurpers], with its diabolical meaning, even though originally, in his father's days, 'Dracul' did not have a malevolent meaning." As in the Far East, "dragon" could be used as a totem of fungible or fluid intent. A dragon can be, aside from its evil and/or predatory aspects, also magical, lucky, awe-inspiring. If aligned with one's own values and motives as a sigil, it can even serve as a protective force against enemies, just as we saw in the case of the Welsh and *Y Ddraig Goch*, the mighty red dragon that still adorns their flag and keeps the Saxons at bay.

7

Dragons in Western Pop Culture and Literature from 1900 to Today

It may be that an inter-planetary dragon had been slain somewhere, or that this red fluid, in which were many corpuscles, came from something not altogether pleasant to contemplate, about the size of the Catskill Mountains, perhaps—but the present datum is that with this substance, larks, quail, ducks, and water hens, some of them alive, fell at Lyons and Grenoble and other places.[1]

There is an essential liability to the many myths and legends passed down to us from our ancient ancestors: They are often materially spotty, narratively inconsistent (if not logically preposterous), and stylistically or rhetorically opaque to us now. Furthermore, in many cases they may refer to conditions or concepts that, to us, are so archaic that they simply make little to no sense without additional context. When we receive these texts as the diligent work of a (usually) anonymous, centuries-dead author and/or scribe, we must recall that these tales or sagas are not just those written texts themselves, but quite regularly the documentation of even older oral folklore, first popularized long before widespread literacy was common to a given cultural tradition or society (which, in some cases, it still may not be). Such a consideration lays bare both the imperfections and the potentialities for transmutation and reinterpretation that occur when the spoken word is awkwardly, imperfectly reined in from the mouth and gestures of the raconteur or griot or shaman and, if or where writing may exist, conveyed into its first written version on the manuscript page or some other visual medium.

And then there are the myriad evolutions of language, of style, of the "average"—relatively speaking, by population—reader's expectations of pacing, exposition, length, delivery, etc., etc., themselves representing important market values. What would have a twelfth-century bishop in Rome, Italy expected and/or preferred to read? What about a twenty-first-century working single mother of two in Rome, Georgia? Furthermore, who is and who is *not*, broadly speaking, taught and/or encouraged to read whatsoever in a literate society? Surely, more persons can competently read now than ever before in history. Such shifts in educational standards and consumer markets are why there will always be a demand for new books and other media, and furthermore for any new takes on a perhaps well-trod story or story type. We are enchanted by a cast of dynamic characters, a cleverly innovative plot twist, and a new chance to reinterpret the world around us, especially if resonant with our own lived experiences. The seemingly endless parade of new translations of ancient works bears out this maxim of "everything old is new again" most demonstrably, in some cases even to the point of considerable commercial and critical success.

J.R.R. Tolkien: Professor, Author, Draconologist

Such is the case of the flood of Anglo-American high-fantasy fiction that began to coalesce and gain popularity in the 1920s and '30s with the novels and short stories of J.R.R. Tolkien, C.S. Lewis, Robert E. Howard, H.P. Lovecraft, and others. Though highly inventive, these authors did not create their mythoses out of thin air; they drew upon centuries if not millennia of existent lore. Where their true innovations lay was in the bridging of the gap between the ancient and the modern, the mist-shrouded and the crystalline. These authors' influence would be vast, providing many bases of reference for later high-fantasy universes portrayed in more recent franchises, such as Frank Herbert's *Dune*, Anne McCaffrey's *Dragonriders of Pern*, George R.R. Martin's *A Song of Ice and Fire*, and Christopher Paolini's *Inheritance Cycle*, among scores of others.

But the path towards such commercial and critical success was anything but clear when these transitional authors began their work in earnest. As will be detailed later in this chapter, the Disney-fueled tendency towards puerility in dragon lore, and the concomitant rise in books and other media created for and marketed specifically to children, first emerged around 1900 in the West. This puerility reached its apex as the predominant trend around the mid–1960s before gradually beginning to decline. Upon his first forays into fiction in the 1930s, J.R.R. Tolkien tasked himself with not only rejuvenating the predominantly Germanic dragon lore in which he was so immersed as a student and then philologist and professor of Anglo-Saxon and other languages at the University of Oxford, but also with combatting the countervailing rise in the underestimation of children's intelligence and preferences with infantile and asinine dreck. "A dragon is no idle fancy," Tolkien declared in his essay on the Beowulf legend, "The Monsters and the Critics" (1936), published shortly before *The Hobbit* of the following year.[2] In another paper, regarding the folklore and mythology of Finland, Tolkien further elaborated on his literary *modus operandi*: "These mythological ballads are full of that very primitive undergrowth that the literature of Europe has on the whole been steadily cutting and reducing for many centuries with different and earlier completeness among different people."[3] As a lover of both language and the literature that makes language come to life, whether orally or in written form, Tolkien vigorously channeled these seemingly esoteric passions into a vehicle that would be accessible to modern readers: the prose novel.

Though these readers would at first be mostly children, his later body of work would gain appeal among older age groups throughout the 1960s and '70s, and especially among teenagers and young adults.

Though several other dragons appear in the various works of Tolkien,[4] of greatest interest to us is his first, Smaug. This red-gold giant is variously monikered throughout *The Hobbit* as "The Chiefest and Greatest of Calamities," "Thief in the Shadows," "The Dreadful," and "The Worm of Dread."[5] (Compare these to the kennings, or compound epithets, of the otherwise nameless dragon in *Beowulf*: "sky-roamer,," "poison breather," "deep barrow-dweller," "ground-burner," "vile sky-winger," "old harrower of the dark.")[6] We do not learn much in *The Hobbit* about Smaug's background, but we can assume that he too originated in the Withered Heath, "where the great dragons bred."[7] The name Smaug itself, Tolkien's biographer Humphrey Carpenter notes, is etymologically sound, derived by the erudite linguaphile from the Germanic verb *smugan*, "to squeeze through a hole."[8] In his own words, Tolkien referred to this choice as "a low philological jest."[9] But even in jest, the parallel with the hackneyed biblical maxim seems apt: if it be easier for a camel to pass through the eye of a needle than a rich man to enter the Kingdom of Heaven, so too might the violent reign of an avaricious dragon be a lesson to us mortals on eschewing the trappings of greed. This mighty foe is of course the novel's principal

Smaug, the principal foe of *The Hobbit*, was a product of J.R.R. Tolkien's deep fascination with the dragon. This replica of the CGI version seen in the film trilogy of 2012–14 served as an installation at the 2014 San Diego Comic-Con, San Diego, California, USA (Lauren Elisabeth/Shutterstock.com).

antagonist, but also serves as a preternatural response to the excessive covetousness of the original dwarven inhabitants (and miners) of what has become Smaug's lair, the great mountain keep of Erebor. (Though not addressed in the book, it is feasible that it was the avaricious and *Edda*-inspired dwarves themselves who bestowed the name on the dragon after he seized their treasure.)

As in many traditional Germanic tales, the dragon is an allegory for the ruination—spiritual or otherwise—caused by such immense greed, a trope advanced in many literary dragons' own quasi-sexual obsessions with the precious hoards they co-opt. Upon these purloined troves dragons also often make their very nests, as seen in the final battle of *Beowulf*. "Greed is a real concern," writes medievalist Victoria Symons, "...reflecting heroic Scandinavian and Anglo-Saxon societies, the poem's human characters live and die by the generosity of their rulers. In standing against the dragon, Beowulf also stands against the greed it embodies."[10] The emphasis in *The Hobbit* is placed on not only such a parable against greed, but also on the transformation of the heroes themselves—Thorin Oakenshield and his brave band of dispossessed dwarves, along with the lone hobbit of the Shire, Bilbo Baggins, the unlikely and last-minute addition recruited specifically to extract the giant, priceless Arkenstone. Besides this party is a loose coalition of morally questionable men and elves who are similarly challenged to overcome their single-mindedness for material wealth. Through their ordeals and often violent conflicts, the imperfect heroes find common ground, collaborate, and emerge as kinder, nobler inhabitants of Middle-earth. These sentiments are also echoed in the book's latter-day live-action film adaptation, broken into three "prequel" installments of 2012, 2013, and 2014, respectively. "If more people valued home above gold," says Thorin Oakenshield (Richard Armitage) to Bilbo Baggins (Martin Freeman) at the conclusion of the third and final installment, *The Battle of the Five Armies*, "this world would be a merrier place."[11] All of the protagonists have contended with the dragon and its "dragon-sickness,"[12] greed and selfishness, as the roots and catalysts of turmoil (or, in the case of Bilbo Baggins, stagnation) in their lives—only after the riches of Erebor had become so extravagant as to be all-encompassing did this scourge arrive. The moral tone is thus set for Tolkien's subsequent trilogy of epic novels, *The Lord of the Rings* (1954–55; feature films in 2001, 2002, and 2003), featuring several direct or indirect descendants of the *Hobbit*'s cast who must contend with similar but larger-scale crises of conscience.

Though other, lesser-known works by Tolkien do include dragons (such as *Farmer Giles of Ham*, *The Silmarillion*, and *Unfinished Tales*), *The Lord of the Rings* does not present considerable treatment of them as principal figures. Nevertheless, dragons loom large for the author and philologist. "In the dragon-lore of Middle-earth," writes Jonathan D. Evans, "we see the dragon-lore of the Middle Ages of the external world disassembled, taken down to its elementary components, rationalized and reconstituted, then reassembled to fit the larger thematic purposes of Tolkien's grand narrative design."[13] With illustrious and foreboding names such as Chrysophylax, Glaumrung, Ancalagon the Black, and Scatha the Worm, the author sought an atmosphere of awe that drew from the long and gloried traditions of his beloved Germanic lore while also existing within his own separately constructed world, the magisterium of Middle-earth. As it developed over Tolkien's literary career, Evans explains, the notion is that his dragons are the products of "Morgoth's malevolent design,"[14] and thus represent components of a greater conflict between good and evil. Though never overt in his profession of religiosity through fiction, as a devout Roman Catholic this morality was nevertheless essential to Tolkien's worldview. "The Christian," Tolkien wrote, "may now perceive that all his bents and faculties have a purpose, which can be redeemed. So great is the bounty with which he has been treated that he may now, perhaps, fairly dare to guess that in Fantasy he may actually assist in the effoliation and multiple enrichment of creation."[15] Tolkien, ever the inventor of worlds himself, saw man as a busy creator subservient to but also made in the image of God, *the* Creator.

In a 1964 interview for the BBC, Tolkien ruminated on the resonance and meaning of dragons in general. "Smaug is … he's pure intelligent lizard," the author quipped to his interlocutor, contrasting his creation with the once-human dragon Fafnir of Germanic legend. "[Dragons] seem to be able to comprise human malice and bestiality together, and [a] sort of malicious wisdom and shrewdness … a terrifying creature."[16] But the continuum between the world of a fantastical time-out-of-time that a clever author might invent for us to dwell in temporarily and allegorically through fiction, and the real world in which we exist in our day-to-day lives is, to Tolkien, as significant a concern as any. This is also reflected in the very timeline of Middle-earth. As Evans concludes,

> To the extent that Middle-earth's Fourth Age [when the race of Men dominated] is analogous to the ancient epoch of our own world—and Tolkien himself made this explicit—then his fictionalized history of dragons is meant to connect seamlessly with the actual status of dragons in medieval literature, where they appear as facts about an earlier time in a world accessible only through the imagination in epic, elegy, legend, and folklore.[17]

Looking back at our own distant mytho-heroic ages, captured in their anonymous texts by scribes or scops throughout the world, we can perhaps readily relate to the human inhabitants of Lake-town (the erstwhile Esgaroth, so named by the former elven settlers) in *The Hobbit*. There, "some of the younger people in the town openly doubted the existence of any dragon in the mountain, and laughed at the greybeards and gammers who said that they had seen him flying in the sky in their young days."[18] Little did these youthful skeptics realize that the dragon Smaug was not only really there inside the mountain, but would soon upend their entire world when disturbed: "Some of the songs were old ones; but some of them were quite new and spoke confidently of the sudden death of the dragon and of cargoes of rich presents coming down the river to Lake-town."[19] Smaug's death was indeed imminent, but it would take the surefire arrow of their fellow man, Bard of Dale, to fell the beast first.

Kids' Stuff

In an article of 2003, Tina L. Hanlon surveyed the rise and proliferation of the dragon motif in contemporary children's literature. Though Hanlon never references Jorge Luis Borges and his assertion, in *The Book of Imaginary Beings* (1967), of the ascendent puerility of these once-feared monsters during the mid-twentieth century, she nevertheless arrives at the same conclusion. She does so more specifically from the more recent vantage of the aftermath of the moral (sometimes called "satanic") panics of the late 1970s and early '80s.[20] "The distrust and disapproval of fantasy throughout the history of children's literature," she writes, "kept alive by moralists and realists of the twentieth century, may account for the preponderance of picture books that remove dragons from their legendary contexts and strip them of their ancient powers."[21] Though Hanlon is correct in framing the trend along these more contemporary lines, as we'll also see reflected in the examples of dragons in other media besides literature (Chapter 9), the trend towards puerility began in earnest as early as the late nineteenth century with the rise of Western children's books in general. It was at this point that younger readers were first prioritized by publishers and marketers as a significant and lucrative target market.

Though it's difficult to pinpoint exactly when the puerile dragon was first established as a literary trope in the West, Kenneth Grahame's short story "The Reluctant Dragon," which is a chapter of his 1898 book *Dream Days*, appears to be as discrete a genesis as any. Born in Edinburgh, Scotland in 1859, Grahame is best known for his book *The Wind in the Willows* (1908), whence the woodland characters Toad, Mole, Badger, and company first originated. His earlier short story, however, is resonant to this day for its creative reimagining of the (St. George the) Dragonslayer motif (ATU Type 300) for a new era, one in which children should no longer be terrified of all dragons. In other words, Grahame solidified, if not introduced, the novel conception—to the Christian West, at least—that a dragon might be something other than Satan or evil incarnate. Though perhaps underappreciated in its day due to its "only" being a children's story, even in a spirit of irony and whimsy does such an inversion of the norm represent a sea change in the Western imaginary. In addition to Grahame, Hanlon also points to (or, more precisely, places blame on) the English author E. Nesbit (1858–1924) and her dragon stories for children, first published around the same time as Grahame's (1901) in *The Strand Magazine*. Hanlon holds the duo particularly responsible "for spawning generations of subservient dragons begging pathetically for affection from humans and for the chance to serve their masters and contribute to social progress by functioning as furnaces, water heaters, and beasts of burden."[22] Hanlon's obvious disdain for the trend notwithstanding, such a seemingly abrupt diversification of the semiotic bandwidth of "dragon" is, in fact, part and parcel with the already multifarious career of the monster.

What's most illustrative in this case is the correlation between the particulars

The modern puerilization of the dragon has extended even as far as the finance sector. Founded in 1937, St. George is a retail bank operating throughout Australia. This branch is in Perth, Western Australia (Rob Bayer/Shutterstock.com).

of global Anglo-American society (an admittedly broad term that nevertheless was still accurate enough given the homogeneity of the English-speaking regions of the world at this point in history) and the mainstream art and media that emerged from it. To wit, the year 1901, firmly within the so-called Progressive Era (1890s–1920s), included such landmark events as the death of Queen Victoria (r. 1837–1901) and geopolitical shifts such as the intensification of American imperialism (especially in locations such as the Caribbean, the Philippines, Hawai'i, and elsewhere in the Pacific), as well as the substantial growth of both the petroleum and motion-picture industries. It is thus not a coincidence that the once-fearsome dragon would in turn be reimagined as not only tame and/or domesticable, but furthermore as a malleable psychic commodity to the point of corporations' comfort with mass-marketing it to children. After Grahame and Nesbit, American author Ogden Nash's poem "Custard the Dragon" (1936) and the folk-pop hit "Puff, the Magic Dragon" (1963)—a product of a serendipitous collaboration between one-time poet Lenny Lipton and the singer-songwriter Peter Yarrow (of folk group Peter, Paul and Mary)[23]—served as conspicuous stepping-stones for the puerile dragon to wend its way through the remainder of the twentieth century. Amid such historic events as mentioned above was the constant of technological and ecological change, a correlation not lost on Hanlon whatsoever: "Perhaps recent stories about dragons defending nature rather than viciously ravaging the landscape," she writes, reflect not only the influence of ancient cultures that believed in good dragons (which are common in Asian folklore, for example), but also a drastic shift in Western society's view of the relationship between humanity and the natural world. Until the past few centuries, humans were at the mercy of wild, predatory beasts and destructive forces of nature they could not understand.[24]

Only when the Western world—and particularly the Anglo-American sphere, with its head start on the Industrial Revolution—had adequately convinced itself that it was (or at the very least *might be*) mightier than nature itself, generally around the year 1900, only then could its dreamers and bards envision a dragon as meek as a lapdog. And, more importantly, only at such a point would a growing mass of consumers with disposable cash in hand begin to be receptive to such an audacious conceit.

The Disneyfication of America … and the World

Since this chapter deals more explicitly with folklore and literature, the mass-market, audio-visual output that emerged from the Walt Disney Company, especially as such output relates to this book's quarry, is discussed at length instead in Chapter 9. What's of greater relevance at this juncture is the context in which the seemingly irresistible forces of Mickey Mouse and company first arose, coalesced, and then proliferated, leading to the company's status as a now century-old, publicly traded, multibillion-dollar media conglomerate. It is within this same context that we may best understand not only the puerilization of the dragon, but furthermore the resistance or backlash to that same trend. (This reversal has intensified in the media landscape of the late twentieth and early twenty-first centuries, but the puerile dragon, as we will see, has not been banished entirely.)

Walter Elias "Walt" Disney (1901–1966) and his older brother Roy Oliver Disney (1893–1971), along with their three other siblings, grew up mostly in rural Marceline, Missouri, with shorter stints in Chicago, the city where all five of the Disney children had been born. In 1919, Roy Disney, then in the United States Navy, contracted tuberculosis and was thus discharged from his military duties. To convalesce, Roy moved to arid southern California, reflecting a typical medical directive of the era, before the disease was brought under control by the middle of the twentieth century. In 1923, twenty-one-year-old Walt Disney left Kansas City, where he had relocated, to join his brother Roy in the Los Feliz neighborhood of Los Angeles; it was in Hollywood that Walt hoped to begin in earnest his career as a burgeoning cartoon animator and director.[25] The two brothers would work together as partners until Walt's death in 1966. With the contributions of another early collaborator, Ub Iwerks, by 1930 the now-globally recognizable characters of Mickey and Minnie Mouse had been designed and introduced in various cartoon shorts. By 1932, the Walt Disney Company had produced over one-hundred animated or live-action/animated short films. They had also won their first Academy Award, for the short *Flowers and Trees*. Disney's first feature-length film, *Snow White and the Seven Dwarfs* (based on the German fairy tale published by the Brothers Grimm in 1812), debuted in 1937. Adjusted for inflation, it is the highest-grossing animated film of all time (almost $2 billion).[26]

The effects of the new world of entertainment that Walt Disney and his associates crafted during the first half of the twentieth century have been unmistakably profound in both their breadth and depth. What the company succeeded in doing earlier and more explicitly than any of its competitors was to consistently mine the otherwise (mostly) untapped ore of predominantly European or Euro-American folklore, mythology, and literature, and repackage it as family-friendly, accessible, and, most importantly, entertaining fare. Simultaneously, as the company grew, Disney's content was created and marketed to appeal to the greatest common denominator across cultural and national boundaries. Though broader considerations of diversity and demographic representation have also become more visible priorities in the last two or three decades, the formula of distilling traditional (though culturally ever-expanding) folklore into mass-market entertainment nevertheless remains Disney's *modus operandi*. The result is not merely a brand but a virtually universally familiar juggernaut of internationally distributed films, television series, theme parks, publishing, and other lucrative properties. Currently, the company is worth nearly a quarter-trillion dollars in total assets.[27]

What Disney represents, then, is an unprecedentedly efficient and ubiquitous "dream factory," one whereby mythic storytelling meets American-style capitalism and hyper-consumerism. This was the engine through which innovations such as Grahame's puerile "Reluctant Dragon" could be most thoroughly processed, especially during the middle section of the twentieth century. With children strategically targeted as reliable proxies to separate increasingly solvent parents from their money during the massive economic boom that followed the Second World War in the United States and then, to a certain degree, in some other parts of the world, the tactic was cemented. If those smiling children of prosperity wanted a lion, a bear, or even a dragon that they could laugh at, cuddle, or dress up in baby clothes, then so be it. Disney was primed and ready to capitalize. It is no wonder then that, by the early 1980s, the original character debuted at Walt Disney World's Epcot Center in Orlando was none other than a cutesy, cat-sized purple dragon named Figment. By this time, when the unprecedented prosperity of the post-war boom had begun to peak, so too did the Western dragon reach its apex of puerility.

Harry Potter and the Return to Awe

Along with the publication of George R.R. Martin's adult-oriented, high-fantasy novel *A Game of Thrones* in 1996 (Part One of the *A Song of Ice and Fire* or *ASOIAF* series/franchise), the late 1990s saw in the form of *Harry Potter and the Philosopher's Stone* (1997)[28] the emergence of an analog marketed to (but certainly not *only* consumed by) children and young adults. The two highly popular medievalist-fantasy franchises—both would (or will soon, supposedly,[29] in the case of *ASOIAF*) comprise seven (or possibly eight) books—stand out for their treatment of dragons. Rejecting the puerility of much of the mid-twentieth century's fantasy content, both Harry Potter and *ASOIAF* represent a return to the pre–1900 paradigm of dragons as entities worthy of awe or fear, as opposed to adoration or cuddling (or coddling). Indeed, after almost a century of the puerilization or the otherwise popular perception of fantasy works as the province of the fey or geeky—with the possible exception of the works of J.R.R. Tolkien, starting in the 1960s—the Anglo-American (and, later, worldwide) interest in the fantastical and the medieval in literature and other media has returned with a vengeance. (Martin's particular treatment of dragons will be detailed in Chapter 10.)

To claim that Harry Potter is a worldwide, pop-cultural phenomenon would be a gross understatement. After the fourth installment of the novel series was published in 2000 (*Harry Potter and the Goblet of Fire*), the first of the feature films was released in late 2001, to massive commercial success. These two mediums together, plus theme parks, merchandise, and other properties, have resulted in a multi-billion-dollar franchise by the movie-series' conclusion in 2011. Indeed, creator J.K. Rowling has been richer than Queen Elizabeth II for nearly twenty years.[30]

What, exactly, is the appeal? "In addition to marketing children's franchises to adults," writes Maria Sachiko Cecire in *Re-enchanted: The Rise of Children's Fantasy Literature in the Twentieth Century*, "the first two decades of the twenty-first century have seen a surge of fantastical narratives targeted at adults that treat their 'childish' material as guidance for, not just escape from, everyday modern life."[31] As for that escape, perhaps this is because many of our lives have become both more technologically complex and more predictable. We get up, we go to work (in many cases, much of which is spent in front of a computer screen), we come home (if we still go into an office), we eat dinner, we watch television, and we go to bed. Repeat until death or retirement, whichever comes first. Stories set in worlds devoid of our technological trappings yet abundant in wonder and adventure appeal to moderns as an alternative to the safe yet monotonous routine. And as for our desire for "guidance," in this is implied a craving for simpler, less morally ambiguous times. There are distinct heroes and villains in *Harry Potter*, and we must pick a side. (To be fair, morality is a much more nuanced commodity in *ASOIAF*.) To be neutral in such a world, then, is to be practically irrelevant, if not ignorant to the point of wretchedness, as in Harry Potter's dreadful uncle, aunt, and cousin, with whom he lives in borderline-abusive languor, in a tiny "room" underneath the stairs, before his recruitment and escape to Hogwarts. This state of irrelevant or wretched commonness is accomplished adroitly through Rowling's presentation of the world of the boring, mundane "Muggles" (non-magical people) as existing right alongside the incredible (to the former) world of magical people, that of witches and wizards. To Muggles, who are portrayed as markedly more boorish than the magical, on average, the world of magic is mostly hidden in plain sight. For us as readers, then, a chance is presented that the magical, special world *may* turn out to be accessible if we are, after all, properly recognized as being special, too. Acceptance into an elite academy such as Hogwarts School of Witchcraft and Wizardry is the proof of one's specialness in this storyworld—not coincidentally reflecting the positive societal significance placed, in many circles, on acceptance to one of the real world's more prestigious preparatory high schools or universities. In the absence of an owl delivering a beautifully addressed invitation in the real world, however, immersing oneself in this literary world of magic may be the next best thing.

J.K. Rowling's use of dragons (Ministry of Magic Classification: XXXXX) in her "Wizarding World" is notable for a few reasons. For one, it is markedly feminist. "The female," explains the in-canon author "Newt Scamander" in the supplementary bestiary *Fantastic Beasts and Where to Find Them*, "is generally larger and more aggressive than the male, though neither should be approached by any but highly skilled and trained wizards."[32,33] Furthermore, Rowling presents ten types, "though," she notes, "these have been known to interbreed on occasion, producing rare hybrids."[34] These are: Antipodean Opaleye, Chinese Fireball (or Liondragon), Common Welsh Green, Hebridean Black, Hungarian Horntail, Norwegian Ridgeback, Peruvian Vipertooth, Romanian Longhorn, Swedish Short-Snout, and Ukrainian Ironbelly, the largest of them all.[35] Interestingly, and perhaps reflecting the artificial selection imposed by humans on domesticated dogs, cats, cattle, and other animals, these very physically distinct types are described as "breeds" rather than as separate species. Such a desired affinity with real animals seems even more plausible considering the similarity between Rowling's *Norwegian Ridgeback* and the Rhodesian ridgeback, a real dog breed. Biologically speaking—which of course is moot in a storyworld based on magic and fantasy rather than science—terminology such as "breed" would be consistent with the possibility of the animals interbreeding, as Rowling describes. At any rate, Rowling seems to hedge carefully between wild and domesticated as the status of the dragon in the Wizarding World—they *may be* at least semi-domesticated, though this is a task best left to wizards such as Hogwarts' gamekeeper Rubeus Hagrid or Charlie Weasley, older brother of Harry Potter's best friend Ron.

Also of note is that seven of the ten breeds in this bestiary are found in Europe (Wales, Scotland, Hungary, Norway, Romania, Sweden, Ukraine), clearly reflecting the author's Eurocentric bias. This has been a persistent observation, if not criticism, of Rowling's work, especially as the franchise reached global proportions by the early twenty-first century and, concurrently, as issues of diversity and representation have continued to receive heightened scrutiny. "The expectation of whiteness in Anglo-American cultural spaces is often invisible, even to those who might identify themselves as committed to diversity," writes Cecire.[36] Cecire further notes that this expectation is often starkly revealed in the negative reactions from anonymous or semi-anonymous social-media users when non-white actors are cast in roles not explicitly described in their source texts as being non-white.[37]

Statue of the Gringotts Dragon at the Wizarding World of Harry Potter, Universal Studios, Orlando, Florida, USA. The replica is capable of spewing fireballs (VIAVAL TOURS/Shutterstock.com).

Existing dragon lore—overwhelmingly though not exclusively of the Western variety—is intertwined with Rowling's own inventions throughout the creatures' section in *Fantastic Beasts*. For example, the Common Welsh Green's commonness is undoubtedly influenced by the prevalence of the dragon motif—though, as we have seen in Chapter 1 and elsewhere, the Welsh dragon is most frequently portrayed as red for a very intentional reason—in the Welsh national flag and in Arthurian/Welsh legend. "The only Oriental dragon," or the Chinese Fireball (Liondragon), is in its description and illustration reminiscent of the quasi-mammalian traditional Chinese or Eastern dragon: "…it has a fringe of golden spikes around its snub-snouted face and extremely protuberant eyes."[38] And as is consistent with Rowling's avowed feminist inclinations, Rowling writes of the Antipodean Opaleye that "[a] spate of kangaroo killings [in Australia] in the late 1970s were attributed to a male Opaleye ousted from his homeland [New Zealand] by a dominant female."[39]

Comparing *Fantastic Beasts* with another early-twentieth-century children's bestiary, *Dragonology: The Complete Book of Dragons*, written under the composite sobriquet of "Dr. Ernest Drake,"[40] the recent trend out of dragon puerility is drawn into further relief. The book begins with this foreword: "Of all the natural sciences, dragonology is perhaps the most rewarding, being at the same time one of the oldest and the least researched. Dragons have been studied since mankind's earliest days and yet, paradoxically, they are one of the least known of Earth's creatures."[41] As in Rowling's more generalized bestiary, the fantastical is presented as scientific, much as the bestiaries of the Middle Ages were presented when the fantastical and the scientific were, for all intents and purposes, one and the same. This blurring is an essential component to the maturation of children's literature into a medium that successfully combines whimsy and awe in equal parts. "So," the foreword concludes, "while many scientists believe that the vast majority of the world's flora and fauna are now understood, in the little-known field of dragonology the way lies open for exciting new discoveries."[42] With this opening message, the young reader is encouraged to enter and actively engage with yet another world of magic and adventure.

How Dr. Ernest Drake compares in his assessment of dragonkind to that of Mr. Newton ("Newt") Artemis Fido Scamander (b. 1897) is also worthy of mention. In the latter, as we have seen, the ten types of dragons are ostensibly all of one species. In *Dragonology*, however, they are clearly different species.[43] (Interestingly, the species in *Dragonology* also number ten, as in the breeds of *Fantastic Beasts*.) Drake's broadest level of classification is based on climate, whether forest (*knucker*, marsupial dragon), mountain (European dragon, Asian *lung*, Tibetan dragon), prairie & steppe (American *amphithere*, *lindworm*), arctic regions (frost dragon), desert & savanna (wyvern), and jungle (Mexican *amphithere*).[44] Tellingly, the other groupings in *Dragonology* are based on geography: Western, Eastern, and Other (including Africa, the Middle East, Australia/New Zealand, and the Americas). The first two classes follow the traditions of dragon lore on the East/West axis as highlighted throughout this book, though the Eurocentric bias (and rivalry with the "East") displayed by creating a miscellaneous category to capture such disparate locales/cultures as Africa and the Americas is unmistakable. Another notable Eurocentric device is *Dragonology*'s presentation of the runic script (specifically, a simplified, 22-character version of the Anglo-Saxon *Futhorc*), used until about the fifteenth century for various Germanic languages. This is given as "dragon script," implying not only the sentience but furthermore the literacy of the creatures. Dr. Drake: "They are the only creatures apart from humans who both speak and, when occasion demands, write."[45] This section also encourages the reader to translate various dragon riddles written in runes and presented as "language exercises."[46] As with several other cases in literature and other media, such uncanny similarities with human traits—spoken language, writing, cooking food with fire, etc.—are indicators of the dragon as a common manifestation of the human psyche itself.

I gifted *Dragonology* to my own three nephews a few years ago. On a recent visit, I was curious as to whether they had perceived its contents as fact or fiction, given its coy presentation as the former. Without any other cues, I asked them to tell me what they knew about dragons. My oldest nephew, about eight at the time, opened up *Dragonology* to explain to me what a two-legged wyvern was, distinguishing it from a standard four-legged Western dragon. His tone communicated to me that he considered this case much in the same way that he would explain to me what a rhinoceros or a blue whale is. Then again, I realized, it was also no different than if he were explaining to me who/what Jabba the Hutt or a Minion is. The average child, from a quite early age, understands on a basic level that the world of fantasy and stories may be separate from the world of the mundane, but that the distinction is moot. "Our ability to hold natural and unnatural narratives *in tension*, without the need to resolve contradictions completely or permanently," writes Canadian sociologist of religion Douglas E. Cowan, "is arguably the controlling facet of the mythic imagination. Indeed, this is the one aspect of what makes it 'mythic': there *are* dragons … and superheroes *do* fly."[47] Any representative of either class of being—factual or fictional—is, on a much more immediate level to a child, either stimulating to the imagination or not. And this convergence of the literal and the figurative is the essence of the inclination to storytelling—and furthermore meaning-making—that all modern humans have evolutionarily inherited and are overwhelmingly receptive to. This is the case not just in childhood but throughout our lives.

If the *Harry Potter* franchise, with its Latinate magic spells, Oxbridge-inspired scenery, and eldritch creatures and villains had not already borne such "childish material" over the threshold of not only acceptance but unequivocally massive global popularity, then Peter Jackson's muscular film adaptations of Tolkien's *The Lord of the Rings* trilogy (2001–3) and the graphic and violent brand of high-fantasy of HBO's *Game of Thrones* (2011–19) most certainly did. As stated in this book's introduction, this latter-day transition (or, perhaps, reversion to the status quo ante) required the suspension of disbelief that has accompanied quantum-leap advancements in CGI and other special effects. Nevertheless, the compelling and immersive storyworlds of all three franchises certainly should also be held to their own merits of world-building and dynamic character development. The richness of these magisteria is where children and adults alike clearly cannot resist escaping to, if indeed ratings and sales are the proof.

8

Dragons in Eastern Folklore, Literature, and Pop Culture

Because he sees with great clarity and cause and effects, he completes the six steps at the right time and mounts toward heaven on them at the right time, as though on six dragons.[1]

In an interview from early 2022, the dissident Chinese artist and activist Ai Weiwei (b. 1957) remarked on the West's perennial inability to grasp the nuances of Chinese culture and politics. "[It's] like a soccer school trying to understand how to play a chess game," Ai told Chris Harvey of the UK's *Telegraph*. "It's a completely different sort of system. You have too much confidence in your own ideology, or the kind of language you're using, but you don't understand the situation."[2] Truly, the process of accessing, much less assessing, the affairs of the Far East from the perspective of the West—much as it is in the reverse—often requires massive lifts in terms of study and, most essentially, meaningful personal exposure in order to approach anything close to unbiased or comprehensive analysis. And though the general East/West global dichotomy is not nearly as simple as one of black versus white, especially given the interconnected world in which we live, it nevertheless rings true that on the geopolitical stage these two major spheres regularly misconstrue each other's intentions and aspirations. One quality that the two polarities most certainly do share, however, is the goal (or maintenance) of hegemony in the zero-sum game of global economic domination, with the United States of America bearing the standard on one side and the People's Republic of China the other.

A considerable degree of humility, then, is not only appropriate but wholly necessary for attempting to bridge what often seems an unbridgeable chasm. Admitting this from the outset of any scholarly inquiry is imperative, lest glaring and perhaps even dangerous mistakes be made.[3] And especially in the present inquiry—wherein, as we have seen, there is not even full consensus as to whether the dragon of the West and the *lóng* of the East should even be in the same psycho-mythological order, much less genus or species—is it appropriate to tread gingerly to avoid the pitfalls of generalization or projection.

As an American and an unequivocally cultural "Westerner" with admittedly limited and brief interactions with the peoples and cultures of the Far East, I am nevertheless responsible for interpreting all the phenomena referenced in this book as fairly and as accurately as possible. Especially due to the inherent linguistic barriers, for the present chapter my sources are often consulted in translation and thus may be removed from their primary or even secondary states. As such, I am obliged to rely on works not merely in translation, but just as often on those of a highly editorialized nature. What's more, these sources are often filtered through the markedly Eurocentric prism of modern academic anthropology. Try as one might to swim upstream against these currents, sometimes the best one can do is tread water. But perhaps Ai Weiwei's own analogy presents an apt metaphor for our purposes than treading water, though one not exactly in the sense that he originally intended: Certainly, some students at a "soccer school" may at first be befuddled by the rules and techniques of chess. But I would argue that there must be many millions of chess-playing footballers—competent or better in both games—currently alive in the world. It is in such particularly versatile "players" that I place my trust and attention.

Feng Shui

"Dragon lines, or dragon currents," Mark O'Connell and Raje Aire explain of the traditional Chinese belief,

> which are thought to run through the land, consist of a negative yin current, symbolized by a white tiger, and a positive yang current, symbolized by the blue dragon. A yin countryside will have gently undulating feminine features, and a yang landscape will have sharp or mountainous male features.[4]

Yin and yang are the two most basic forces that govern the universe in traditional Chinese cosmology, and from them all other elements and entities emerge. Four creatures compose the guardians of the cardinal directions in this system of *feng shui* (literally, "wind-water"), also known as "Chinese geomancy": the Black Tortoise of the North; the Azure or Blue Dragon of the East; the Vermillion or Red Bird of the South; and the White Tiger of the West. Though the arrangement often varies, the association of each cardinal direction with a color is also prevalent in many Native American cultures.

It is no coincidence that one of the two elements composing the term *feng shui* should be water (*shui* 水). This essential substance, according to the classic text *Tao Te Ching* (attributed to the sage Lao Tzu, *c.* 400 BCE), "is the weakest and softest of things, yet overcomes the strongest and the hardest."[5] Such a contradictory set of attributes is also representative of the Chinese conception of the dragon, as seen in its "power of fluidity" and its renown as "the symbol of the infinite."[6] In most Far-Eastern cultures, the aqueous qualities or associations of the dragon are inexorable; the creature is beseeched and held in particular awe for its ability to deliver life-giving rains to planted crops. In many East Asian folktales, the dragon may live in a lair under the sea or other body of water. The rain, then, *is* the dragon: the beast signals the element's divinity as it accompanies it. Furthermore, as Ingersoll notes, dragons "have sometimes shown poor judgment in the matter of flooding rains and a careless use of lightning, yet in general they seem to mean well, and to be kind in answer to prayers for rain when the crops really need it."[7] In this regard the beneficence or auspiciousness of the monster may be its only recognized limitations or even slightly negative traits in the mythology of the Far East. Such a compromise is not only tolerated, however, but interpreted as a lesson to the wise: depending on context, excess can often be as much of a misfortune as deprivation. According to the Dutch philologist Marinus Willem de Visser (1876–1930), in his 1913 treatise *The Dragon in China and Japan*, "The appearance of *yellow* or *azure* dragons, often mentioned in the annals, was nearly always considered to be a very good omen. Only if they came untimely or on the wrong places they were harbingers of evil…."[8] Otherwise, the dragon, and especially the azure variety, is the welcome harbinger of the glorious, vibrant season of spring.[9]

In an article published in 1990, Michael Carr identified and analyzed over one hundred terms for dragon—*draconyms*, as he coined it—found in Chinese

The dragon in Chinese and other Far Eastern traditions is a highly auspicious creature, though it is respected and sometimes feared for its ability to bring or withhold rain, as well as other elements. A group of men in Taipei, Taiwan take part in a dragon dance at a parade on July 1, 2012 (123Nelson/Shutterstock.com).

literature.[10] Of these, Kenneth Dobson and Arthur Saniotis chose eight to highlight in their own analysis, all of which include the Chinese dragon suffix -*long*. These eight include *shenlong* ("god dragon"), *jialong* ("crocodile dragon"), *feilong* ("flying dragon"), and *zhulong* ("torch dragon"), among others.[11] *Zhulong*, "The Torch Dragon," is of particular interest due to its being among the most prominent and "demonstrably one of the most ancient in the world." It is thus also, according to the scholars, illustrative of the evolution of religious ideology due to its being so elemental in its functions: namely, to regulate light and darkness and therefore establish the most basic, binary infrastructure of the cosmos necessary before the emergence of humankind may proceed.[12] In this sense, *zhulong* is akin to other primordial draconic creatures of legend, especially Tiamat of the Babylonian *Enuma Elish*.[13]

What this wealth of lexical information collected by Carr confirms, beyond the obvious importance and ubiquity of the dragon to traditional Chinese culture, is that a significant appeal of the creature in the Chinese context is its malleability. It can be purposed and repurposed practically *ad infinitum*. Because of the dragon's beneficent connotations and associations in the Far East, such elaboration has a long tradition. In the societies of the West, however, the dragon has required a considerable degree of de-secularization and disassociation from Satan/evil/general malevolence for it to be similarly diversified and explored in the realms of fiction and allegory, as we will see in the following chapter.

Connecting the Dragon

The worldwide coronavirus pandemic of 2020–2022 began in the city of Wuhan, Hubei Province, China in December of 2019. Of that fact the scientific consensus appears to be quite certain. How exactly the novel virus emerged is still being interrogated as of the time of this writing. But the basic fact of a zoonotic origin in a wet market (one that contains fresh or perishable meat and produce) seems to be holding among epidemiologists and immunologists. Regardless of its source, once SARS-CoV-2, the novel virus that causes the respiratory disease Covid-19, escaped from Chinese territory, and quickly spread throughout the highly interconnected world, human societies and markets were and continue to be altered in historic ways. With such precipitous social and political upheavals in the pandemic's wake, popular culture and media, as ever, have closely followed suit.

In an article for *The New Yorker* published during the summer of 2020, China correspondent Peter Hessler recounted the method required of him as a resident of Chengdu, over 700 miles (1,162 km) from Wuhan, to confirm his children's health status, as well as his own with his employer. For the former did so by using the mobile text application WeChat to stay in constant communication with his fellow parents and their children's school. "I lived in fear of the dragon," he writes. "My mornings were a mess of fiddling with apps; one consisted of a daily form for the university on which I listed my temperature, location, and whether I had had contact with anyone from Hubei, the province that contains Wuhan, in the past fourteen days." He continues:

> If I missed the noon deadline, an overworked administrator sent a gently passive-aggressive reminder. Each day, my daughters had their temperature taken at least five times. This routine began at 6:30 a.m., when the class's WeChat parent group engaged in something called Jielong, or "Connect the Dragon." One parent would start the hashtag #Jielong, and list her child's name, student number, temperature in Celsius, and the words "Body is healthy."[14]

This seemingly banal usage exemplifies the figure of the long-bodied, serpentine, wingless Eastern dragon, the *lóng* (龍 [traditional] or 龙 [simplified]) and its ubiquity in the modern Chinese consciousness. Remarkably, this popular conception differs little from that of Chinese society of 2,000 years ago and more.[15] The creature's traditional auspiciousness and even divinity in China and other East Asian nations constitute its very essence. The *lóng* is an elemental being nearly synonymous with the phenomena of water, life, and fertility themselves. Humans may conjure the being to actively keep at bay or even obliterate negative, oppressive, or evil forces—such as a virus that causes a highly infectious and often deadly respiratory disease. The "dragon" created by those text messages, thereby reporting that all was well in a network of concerned parents, is supremely illustrative of the *lóng*'s perennially positive associations and overall significance. These parents' dragons signify community, health, collaboration, and perseverance.

By contrast, in the Western—or rather, non–Far Eastern—worldview, any virus and/or diseases resulting from viruses are much likelier to be represented *as* the fearsome dragon, rather than as the prevention or mitigation or adversary of the same. This distinction has been expressed in media originating in a diverse range of nation-states as Covid-19 has spread. Dragonesque monsters signifying the coronavirus were often depicted visually in graphics (memes) or videos, or otherwise in figurative language. For example, an animation of an Eastern or Chinese dragon, explicitly representing Covid-19, was shown flying towards the sky in a heavily edited video that went viral in India. (The implication was that the virus was thus purged from the Earth.)[16] In Iran, a green, bat-faced, tentacled dragonoid figure grappled with a public-health worker in an oil painting created and shared by artist Mikael Barati.[17] And, as one American physician on the frontlines of the pandemic reflected in a well-regarded medical journal,

> During the first months as an attending physician, transitioning from fellowship to independent practice, I felt I was chasing a horse; the horse was running, and I was running too. Before the holiday season, I thought I was finally reining in the horse and getting control; although we were still running, at least I was directing where we were going. At the beginning of this year, I felt that the horse and I were slowing down. A few weeks later, it was no longer a horse, it was a dragon (COVID-19), and this dragon had no intention of running with me.[18]

One mythological figure, two vastly different interpretations based on the cultural context, split most plainly along the axis of Far East/Greater West. Though it is plausible and even likely that the two major types of dragons ultimately derive from the same anthropological origins, regardless of human culture, what it has come to represent today has diverged into a distinct symbolic binary.

Dragon Babies

As also discussed in Chapter 3, dragon lore and specifically the popular perception of the dragon as a highly auspicious and beneficent being stretches back to prehistory in Japan, China, and elsewhere in East Asia. In this regard, little has changed whether in the People's Republic of China (PRC) or elsewhere throughout the world among ethnic Chinese. What has changed, and quite rapidly, however, is technology. And among such innovations have been novel and highly efficient methods of contraception and birth control, thus altering how we procreate and structure our families. Since about 1970, the dissemination of these new pharmaceuticals and procedures has allowed millions of people throughout the world to more strategically economize and plan for our futures on a household level. In addition to mass-produced condoms and vasectomy procedures for men, combined oral contraceptive pills have given women the power to safely halt their ovulation and thus, while regularly taking it, prevent pregnancy. Combined with massive decreases in infant mortality thanks to improved methods of pre- and neonatal care, the overall quality of life for countless families has improved because of these innovations, especially in the developing world. Nowhere has this been the case on a more institutional level than in the PRC, where, combined with many strict policies regulating marriage and childbirth, it is estimated (though not without considerable dispute) that several hundred million births have been averted.[19]

Of course, the one-child policy of China's Communist Party—which did not *prevent* as much as it *penalized* having more than one child, especially between 1980 and 2015[20]—has not been universally lauded as a success. Especially in the West the practice is still deplored by many China-hawks as draconian, cruel, and even immoral. It is true that "excess" population in the PRC has been mitigated somewhat, leading to a marked rise in general quality of life, but even an official state policy cannot regulate all human behaviors or habits, and especially not all sexual couplings. Millions of unwanted or "unofficial" babies, and especially girls (who are seen as less capable of caring for their parents in old age if instead, as is traditionally the case, their attention is drawn to their husbands' parents), were during those one-child-only years aborted, abandoned, killed, sold, or given up for adoption. Since the policy has been loosened over the last decade, many Chinese nationals have also become more outspoken on the unintended though, to many observers, retrospectively obvious consequences, including stark demographic imbalances of gender (too high a proportion of men) and age (too high a proportion of elderly people). According to many scholars, both factors are already affecting the social cohesion of the PRC and will continue to do so for the foreseeable future.[21]

Not all ethnic Chinese live inside the borders of the PRC, of course, and indeed many millions live elsewhere in Asia and beyond. In countries with large permanent Han or other ethnic–Chinese populations (e.g., Cantonese, Hokkien, Wu) such as Hong Kong, Singapore, Taiwan, and Malaysia, the one-child policy simply did not and does not apply. And since many Chinese families had left their ancestral home-lands in what is now the PRC precisely because of the upheavals precipitated by the communist revolution there, particularly in the 1950s, these overseas Chinese pop-ulations provide a useful control for understanding the impacts state-level policies may have had on otherwise relatively homogeneous groups.

In the absence of overt restrictions on childbearing for overseas (non–PRC) Chinese, such relative liberty has resulted in a markedly heightened number of eth-nic–Chinese babies that have been (and likely will continue to be) intentionally con-ceived so as to be born during a year of the Dragon—the fifth in the twelve-year cycle—of the Chinese or Eastern zodiac. The years for which we have reliable data for this phenomenon are 1976, 1988, 2000, and 2012.[22] This span, including additional years on its lower and upper bounds for added context, is highly conclusive in sub-stantiating this phenomenon, as we will see.

Whenever there is a choice for parents to make on behalf of their children, it is, of course, the more auspicious or otherwise more net-beneficial option that they will not only hypothetically prefer, but almost certainly actively pursue. "Luck" is by no means a scientific reckoning, but it is often the best we have at our disposal. To be sure, then, there is no substantial difference between overseas Chinese parents pre-ferring a Dragon year and Western parents preferring that their child *not* be born on any Friday the 13th, nor on February 29 of a leap year … nor on a nationally tragic and somber day (such as September 11 in the United States), nor furthermore on any inauspicious date, whether societally or personally significant. Similarly, some Western parents may actively endeavor that their child be born either in or out of a particular star sign (based on the old Egyptian and Babylonian-influenced Ptole-maic system) of the Western zodiac. That the Chinese zodiac is annual (and lunar) in focus, as opposed to the monthly (and solar, or tropical) Western zodiac, is also of essence: a year is clearly a much wider "landing pad" for a child to be born than is a month.

What's more, as noted by demographer Daniel Goodkind, another mitigating factor is the negative associations of the year-animal penultimate to (or, two before) the Dragon. This is because it is traditionally undesirable to have a daughter during a Tiger year, as these individuals are seen as prone to tempestuousness and thus may be difficult to "successfully" marry off. And since there is always a fifty-fifty chance that a live birth will be a daughter, such a risk, especially to many traditional-minded parents, may outweigh the benefits.[23] Of course, such an interpretation emerges from a particularly patriarchal and chauvinistic worldview typical to many traditional

As opposed to the Western, month-based (but non–Gregorian) astrological calendar, the Chinese zodiac operates on a twelve-year cycle. Each year is represented by a different animal and its unique set of qualities. The latest Dragon year began in early 2024 (Sunnydream/Shutterstock.com).

societies, but, as the statistics bear out, some old habits clearly die hard, even among otherwise socially progressive populations. Immediately prior to the Dragon year is that of the Rabbit, a creature known for its peacefulness and sincerity and, though generally preferable to the Tiger, is by no means as desirable as the powerful, charismatic, and furthermore lucky dragon. In fact, no other Chinese zodiac creature appears to come even close to such desirability based on both anecdotal and statistical evidence.[24]

The statistical data surrounding this phenomenon are indeed stunning and virtually impossible to dispute. In the "break-away" island province of Taiwan (Republic of China), for example, average total fertility rates (TFRs) significantly spiked over Tiger years as seen in the subsequent Dragon years of 1976, 1988, 2000, and 2012. In 2012 in particular, which more specifically was the Year of the *Water* Dragon (i.e., particularly associated with abundance and fertility), the uptick was even more drastically pronounced; a near-35 percent difference separated the birthrate of 2012 from the depths of the previous Tiger Year (2010).[25] When asked about this marked preference in the statistical data, several informants expressed their doubt as to its intentionality, also revealing the trend's relative novelty (especially since 1976). "One reason for this," Goodkind reports, "is that the Dragon Year preference is not grounded in any formal astrological principal […] In fact, Chinese astrology holds that the day and hour of birth, which cannot be timed nine months before, are far more important in determining the fate of a newborn child."[26] Nevertheless, since the populations in question now have a large degree of control over the birth year of their children thanks to modern methods of contraception, the choice is clear given the option: the Dragon trumps all other creatures in almost all ways. It is especially preferable over the nearby Tiger, considering the anxiety over the possibility of

As in the Eastern zodiac, the dragon is the only mythological creature found in the array of animal emoji used in most modern text-messaging applications (Carboxylase/Shutterstock. com).

unmarriageable daughters. What's more, the extreme drop-offs in average total fertility rates after Dragon years—the Snake follows the Dragon and is a significantly less auspicious creature in the menagerie of Chinese folklore—exemplify the high degree to which expecting overseas Chinese couples (or at least mothers) may intentionally aim for Dragon babies as opposed to other creatures in the Dragon's vicinity. In the brave new world of personal choice in which many now live, so too does perception often shift dramatically from what it once was. As a result, and since family-planning policies in the PRC have been relaxed in the past two decades, it now appears that this trend has spread back to its place of ultimate origin. The journalist Fong Mei reports that, especially since 2015, many couples now aim for a highly auspicious "phoenix-dragon" combo, or girl-boy twins.[27]

Statistics are one matter, but the real-world implications have been considerable: more babies born than average in a particular year means more resources than, on average, are necessary in the society where they live and mature. In Taiwan, reports my informant, who herself was born on that island in Dragon Year 1988, the result was a greater level of competition among her larger school cohort.[28] This is not surprising; a higher ratio of students to teachers means less individualized attention, which often equates to some students falling by the wayside when they might have otherwise thrived, or at least might have performed better. What's more, due to the correlation of intentionality and birth in a Dragon year, it is also likely that these Dragon children's parents may be more inclined towards expectations of high achievement on behalf of said children, thus heightening competition. And the general auspiciousness factor remains: my same informant, now many years resident in the United States and married, reported that if she and her husband have children, she strongly prefers that one be born in the current dragon year, which began on February 10, 2024.

The Golden Mountain

How East and Southeast Asian individuals and communities have been portrayed in Western literature and media is as complex as their lived experiences of immigration and assimilation in the West itself. Ethnic Chinese, and especially members of the Mandarin-speaking Han majority, began immigrating to the United States in considerable numbers starting around 1850. Since then, members of these groups have been subjected to historically notable levels of marginalization and discrimination, quite regularly to the point of verbal abuse, physical assault and other violence, and even public lynching. The Chinese Exclusion Act of 1882 indeed made this trend of discrimination federal law, effectively barring those of Chinese origin from becoming naturalized U.S. citizens. It wasn't until the passage of the Magnuson Act in 1943—nearly a full century after they had begun moving to the United States in earnest—that Chinese (and certain other categories of non-white, non–European) immigrants became eligible for American citizenship. Clearly a case of entrenched xenophobia and white-supremacist racism at its core, to this day individual Asian Americans—including some whose families may have been residents or citizens of the United States for generations—are still singled out by some non–Asians as "foreign" or otherwise culturally other. As the Korean American writer and novelist Min Jin Lee writes,

> For some, deep down, my ordinary Korean face—small, shallow-set eyes, round nose, high cheekbones, straight dark hair—reminds them of lost wars, prostitutes, spies, refugees, poverty, disease, cheap labor, academic competition, cheaters, sexual competition, oligarchs, toxic parenting, industrialization or a sex or pornography addiction.
> What feelings do such reminders arouse?
> Distrust, defeat, uncleanness, humiliation, sickness, death, terror, envy, anxiety and contempt.[29]

During the Covid-19 pandemic, such prejudice-fueled harassment—and, in some cases, physical violence extending to homicide—became particularly acute under the false assumption that Asians or Asian-descended people were inherently more likely to be carriers of the novel coronavirus, ostensibly because the virus was first identified in the city of Wuhan, China. But Min Jin Lee's references above to misplaced perceptions of "[d]istrust, defeat, uncleanness, humiliation, sickness, death, terror, envy, anxiety and contempt" unfortunately ring true as well. Members of out-groups have unfairly made Asians and Asian-Americans their scapegoats for a situation defined by great uncertainty and upheaval.

In the case of Chinese migration in the current era, *diaspora* may be a more accurate term than emigration or immigration, especially as the People's Republic of China has consolidated its power to the extent that it is second only to the United States in global-economic influence. As a result of various economic activities, including as workers and administrators of many state-run infrastructure projects in the Global South, Chinese nationals reside in virtually every corner of the globe, and in many cases only temporarily. This new global dynamic, achieved at an almost bewildering speed on the part of the once isolated and impoverished China, was precipitated by various events and factors in the aftermath of the Second World War.

The most momentous of these events was the consolidation of power by the Chinese Communist Party when, under the leadership of Chairman Mao Zedong (1893–1976), its adherents defeated the Chinese Nationalists in 1949. The latter fled the Chinese mainland and have operated their own democratic government from the island of Taiwan (Republic of China, or RoC, which the PRC still claims), with Western and especially American support, ever since. This civil war and its subsequent political revolution, it must be noted, were both directly motivated by centuries of colonial exploitation of the peoples and resources of the Chinese mainland and its vicinity. The foreign capture of large segments of the Chinese market, ushered in by the Qing dynasty's defeat in the Opium Wars of 1839–1842 and 1856–1860, was perpetrated not only by major European powers such as the United Kingdom and France, but also—and especially during the first half of the twentieth century—by Imperial Japan. Though the new Communist regime (and the one-party-rule system it created) was responsible for millions of deaths and displacements during Mao Zedong's Cultural Revolution (1966–1976), by the early twenty-first century the nation-state that has for millennia referred to itself as the Middle Kingdom (*Zhōng-guó*/中國) once again looms large on the world stage.

With greater exposure and, correspondingly, more tolerant societal attitudes, there have emerged many notable Chinese American and other Asian-American (or Asian-British, etc.) producers, directors, and artists in Hollywood and beyond. Through their works they have helped to bridge what may sometimes appear a yawning chasm between the peoples and cultures of the East and West.

One such author is Laurence Yep (b. 1948). Yep's *Golden Mountain Chronicles*, first published in 1975, portray the Chinese American experience (and especially that of Chinatown, San Francisco, where he was born and raised) between the years 1849 and 1995. The first installment of Yep's historical-fiction series for middle-grade children, *Dragonwings*, begins in the year 1903 as the protagonist, a young boy named Moon Shadow, moves from China to San Francisco to live with his father, a launderer. Moon Shadow experiences many challenges in his new home, not the least of which are racist taunting and bullying from white American children. At one point, Moon Shadow learns about the distinctions between the "Chinese" and the "American" dragon from his father's landlady, Miss Whitlaw, after he has subtly alluded to his sometimes-tempestuous father:

"Perhaps…." Miss Whitlaw tapped a finger against her lips for a moment. "Perhaps the truth of the dragon lies somewhere between [the two] versions. He is neither all-bad nor all-good, neither all-destructive nor all-kind. He is a creature primarily in tune with Nature, and so, like Nature, he can be very, very kind or very, very terrible. If you love him, you will accept what he is. Otherwise he will destroy you."[30]

As an author, Yep is clearly enamored of the dragon, in both its Eastern and Western varieties, as a mythological being representing nature and as a metaphor applicable to many common human experiences. Indeed, he references dragons constantly throughout his oeuvre, to the extent that they are found in several of his books' titles. Yep has also authored several children's books with his wife, Joanne Ryder, which center on friendly, Western-style dragons. In a clever twist, these semi-puerile dragons keep young humans as pets: titles include *A Dragon's Guide to Making Your Human Smarter* and *A Dragon's Guide to the Care and Feeding of Humans*. Whether we consider the Eastern and Western dragons as originally independent phenomena, such cross-cultural or globalized interpretations in the puerile or semi-puerile space of juvenile or young-adult fiction (re)hybridize the two major world-types.

Sadly, discrimination against Chinese and other East Asians in the West does not appear to be a thing of the past. In response to the murders of six women of Asian descent in the Atlanta metropolitan area in March 2021,[31] and in observance of April as National Poetry Month, National Public Radio's poet-in-residence

It is not accurate to ascribe puerility to the Eastern dragon since it has consistently held deep significance as a beneficent creature for millennia in that region of the world. For this reason, children in these cultures have long held an affinity for the figure. Here, Chinese children wave a dragon at the London Chinese New Year celebrations, January 2020, as part of the Medway, UK and Chancheng-foshan Friendship Association (JessicaGirvan/Shutterstock. com).

Kwame Alexander organized and edited a "crowdsourced poem against anti–Asian hate." The piece drew on the contributions of thirty-eight individuals from around the United States. Recited by Alexander and host Rachel Martin on NPR's *Morning Edition* on April 12, 2021, one stanza stands out in particular:

> Today the dragon bends
>> From western winds
>> Blown hot from valleys deep.
>> Scorched skies belie the spring.
>> Heads bowed. All weep.
> Outside my window, the daughter bends to examine the fish in the pond,
>> slowly gliding out of their winter torpor. Her name means
>> celebration in Chinese. It also means blessing.[32]

The figure of an ostensibly Eastern dragon bending "from western winds" speaks to the vicissitudes of globalization as immigrants seek better fortune in faraway lands, and particularly in the United States and other wealthy Western countries. But the costs of this cultural/linguistic assimilation and the prejudice that often accompanies it are often extremely high for such strivers. American capitalism depends upon a strict hierarchy—much like India's traditional society, it has been described as a caste system[33]—that is often hostile to the perceived racial, linguistic, religious, and general cultural otherness of people of Asian origin. Min Jin Lee, Laurence Yep, Kwame Alexander, and others attempt to both express and overcome this dilemma through narratives which focus on shared values of all peoples, regardless of their national or cultural origins. Such values include loyalty to family and community, honesty, diligence, and fortitude.

Another children's book, *The Pet Dragon* by Christoph Niemann, also exemplifies such a yearning for cross-cultural breakthrough. In this juvenile-oriented picture book, the author (who is not himself of Chinese extraction but rather a student of the Mandarin language) tells the story of a young Chinese girl named Lin. Through the book's illustrations, we are introduced to not only the escapades of Lin and her new pet dragon, but also to various common logographs or characters of the Chinese script. The characters for words such as "person," "eye," "father," "speak/words," and several more are depicted as identities, parts, qualities, or movements of the *characters* of the story and their surroundings: Lin ("person"/人), her pet dragon ("small"/小), her father (父), etc.[34] In the form of these clever and lighthearted mnemonic devices, what may otherwise seem an inscrutable system to outsiders begins to be demystified.

The Red Carpet

Though much of the above section concerns Far Eastern or Chinese culture and peoples as they may be viewed through the Western lens, how participants in the domestic Chinese market function and view themselves and the world, whether officially or not, is paramount to this chapter's intended purpose. As the PRC's economic powers and cultural influences—and those of the Chinese cultural sphere at large—continue to expand, it will become ever more important to consider output by Chinese nationals in the areas of cinema, music, cuisine, fashion, technology, and other cultural forms. And as much as possible, it will be necessary to view such content not through the lens of outsiders, but through that of its own context and creators.

With the relative success[35] of Disney's thirty-sixth feature-length animated film, *Mulan*, released in 1998, a considerable segment of the global moviegoing audience was introduced, at least to a certain degree, to Chinese-inspired content. Though the choice by Disney to produce such a film may not seem particularly revolutionary by today's higher demands and standards regarding diversity, equity, and inclusion, even in the late 1990s such an undertaking was a considerable commercial gambit. What's more, some commentators have observed that the film's production was very likely Disney's attempt to appease the Chinese government (and furthermore to court the massive Chinese domestic market) after the PRC's outrage at the 1997 live-action biopic, *Kundun*, about the exiled Tibetan Dalai Lama. The latter was seen as highly politically provocative and furthermore nakedly anti–China.[36]

The plot of Disney's *Mulan* is based on a folktale about a legendary heroine originally named Hua Mulan. Textual evidence of the story can be dated to the 4th to 6th centuries CE. In brief, Mulan, a young woman from the countryside, must pose as a man to serve in the Han army against an onslaught of Hun (Tartar) invaders. She takes this drastic measure to protect her elderly and frail father, the only male in her family, from having to serve. In the animated Disney version, Mulan has a companion named Mushu, a wise-cracking, diminutive red dragon voiced by comedian Eddie Murphy. Several other elements in the film were innovations that departed considerably from the book *Fa Mulan: The Story of a Woman Warrior* (also of 1998) by children's author Robert D. San Souci (1946–2014), on which the Disney version was based.

Though it's unclear where exactly San Souci drew his own inspiration to begin writing an English-language adaptation of this ancient tale, it is likely that he came across a reference to the legendary figure in an influential contemporary book (and also a play) by his fellow northern Californian, the Chinese-American author Maxine Hong Kingston.[37] In her 1977 memoir *The Woman Warrior*, Hong Kingston writes of drawing personal inspiration—along with no small amount of aggravation, given her elders' contradictory messaging on gender roles—from the legend of Hua (or Fa) Mulan:

> At last I saw that I too had been in the presence of great power, my mother talking-story. After I grew up I heard the chant of Fa Mu Lan, the girl who took her father's place in battle. Instantly I remembered that as a child I had followed my mother about the house, the two of us singing about how Fa Mu Lan fought gloriously and returned alive from war to settle in the village. I had forgotten this chant that was once mine, given me by my mother, who may not

have known its power to remind. She said I would grow up a wife and a slave, but she taught me the song of the warrior woman, Fa Mu Lan. I would have to grow up a warrior woman.[38]

Through the nexus of immigration and (often uneasy) biculturalism in the United States of the twentieth century, represented by Chinese American authors like Maxine Hong Kingston and Laurence Yep, this folktale that would otherwise mostly have been confined to the world's Chinese-speaking or -descendent populations thus entered the Euro-American/Western consciousness. But it was the Disney Corporation that made Mulan a rather sanitized global commodity to the extent that, upon the film's international release, many Chinese nationals reported that the cartoon version of their familiar warrior woman was "foreign-looking" and otherwise underwhelming.[39]

By 2000—when foreign movies had only been allowed in China for six years—Hollywood was once again prepared and eager to facilitate the respectful representation of Chinese culture to the world while also attempting to capture the gargantuan Chinese market itself. After *Mulan*, the next major endeavor, adapted from a novel and produced by the Asian subsidiary of Columbia Pictures, was in Mandarin titled *Wò hǔ cáng lóng* (臥虎藏龙 or 臥虎藏龍). It was directly translated into English as *Crouching Tiger, Hidden Dragon*. Perhaps the only Mandarin-language film to become a household name in the West (thus far, at least), the global blockbuster was directed by Ang Lee of Taiwan (Republic of China) and starred Hong Konger Chow Yun-fat, Chinese-Malaysian Michelle Yeoh, mainland–Chinese Zhang Ziyi, and Chang Chen, also of Taiwan.

To date, *Crouching Tiger, Hidden Dragon* has grossed $213.5 million worldwide, making it the first foreign-language movie to break the $100 million mark in the United States. Ironically, and much like the case of *Mulan*, the response to this film in China itself was underwhelming. "There," explains Erich Schwartzel, "moviegoers were watching *True Lies* because it was the kind of action-packed spectacular their own country's filmmakers couldn't produce. *Crouching Tiger, Hidden Dragon*, which had seemed so novel in America, was old hat to Chinese moviegoers reared on kung fu."[40] Such is often the case of cultural breakthroughs or crossovers: something commonplace in one culture may be perceived as not only intriguing but sometimes even spellbinding in another.

Taken from a common Chinese idiomatic expression, the "hidden [or submerged] dragon" of the movie's title is a metaphor for an undisclosed talent or prowess.[41] Therefore, the phrase "crouching tiger, hidden dragon" implies a situation where there are experts posing as ordinary or unskilled people, whatever their reasons. In the context of the film, which is categorized in the *wuxia* martial-arts genre, the "crouching tiger" and "hidden dragon," may also be interpreted as the two lovers (and the junior leads), Lo (Chang Chen) and Jen (Zhang Ziyi), respectively. Jen fits this description because, despite appearing to most as a pampered governor's daughter, she is an advanced practitioner of *Wudang* (or Wu-tang), the fictionalized Chinese martial art depicted in *wuxia* films (and, incidentally, the namesake of American hip-hop collective the Wu-Tang Clan). Also, we learn that despite his reputation, the "crouching tiger," Lo, a nomadic bandit from China's western deserts (i.e., non–Han), is pure of heart.

Since 2000, no film originating in Greater China has surpassed *Crouching Tiger, Hidden Dragon* in terms of worldwide popularity or commercial success. The film opened the gates for Chinese cinema and thus the Chinese cultural milieu at large; many Western viewers otherwise may have remained oblivious or even downright dismissive of this enormous market.

Mulan was remade by Disney as a live-action film (without Mushu the Dragon for comic relief) and debuted in the United States on March 9, 2020. This of course meant that its prospects at the box office were seriously attenuated by the ensuing pandemic. The film was made

The Disney cartoon version of the traditional Chinese hero Mulan. The addition of the small, wise-cracking dragon Mushu (voiced by Eddie Murphy) was pure creative license and omitted from the live-action version of 2020 (Anastasiia Shevchuk/Shutterstock.com).

available the following September by Disney's streaming app Disney+, but its profits were nevertheless underwhelming. And though kung-fu genre films such as 1973's *Enter the Dragon*, starring the widely celebrated and mourned Hong Kong martial-artist Bruce Lee (1940–1973), had proven that there was indeed a considerable worldwide audience for such fare, the market for popular cinema remains culturally asymmetrical, with big-budget Hollywood productions such as those of the Marvel Cinematic Universe (MCU) consistently dominating throughout the world. It is perhaps a sign of things to come, however, that 2021's *Shang-Chi and the Legend of the Ten Rings*, the first MCU feature to star an actor of Chinese descent (Chinese-born Canadian Simu Liu) has set box-office records for the pandemic era.

Dragon Springs

"Dragon sightings have been recorded in Chinese historical annals since ancient times," begins a description of the dragon motif in Chinese culture, part of an explanatory article of the website *shenyun.org*. The article goes on to explain that, in Chinese belief, the dragon "represents the positive energy of *yang*, power and affluence, and is the symbol of the emperor."[42] Such anodyne background material is of course to be expected on the website of an organization dedicated to traditional Chinese cultural expression and performance. However, not all who have seen a live Shen Yun performance—and much less so for those who have merely seen the touring show's widespread marketing materials in the many countries where it operates—may be aware of the troupe's deeper history and associations with the controversial Falun Gong movement.

The new religious movement known as Falun Gong (or Falun Dafa) was founded by Li Hongzhi (b. 1951) in China in the early 1990s. Originally supported by the Chinese government, the sect combines elements of Buddhist and Taoist moral philosophies with *qigong*, the practice of slow-moving energy exercises and meditation (氣, *qi* or *ch'i* = "vital energy" or, more literally, "vapor," "air," or "breath"). While these elements alone may not appear controversial, Falun Gong became a target of the Chinese Communist Party (CCP) not long after its establishment as a political and cultural threat to the CCP's one-party rule. Not only was this due to the movement's spiritual and philosophical tenets[43] but furthermore because it had gained so many adherents in a relatively short amount of time; one expert estimates that there are as many as several hundreds of thousands throughout the world.[44] Faced with political suppression in the PRC, since the late 1990s Falun Gong's leadership, including Li Hongzhi himself, was forced to flee China. The group is now based in an unincorporated community in upstate Orange County, New York, known as Dragon Springs, or simply "The Mountain." Falun Gong is registered as a religious organization known as Dragon Springs Buddhist, thus conferring upon it tax-exempt status.

Shen Yun ("Divine Rhythm," or, according to its website, "the beauty of divine beings dancing"[45]) is the performing-arts branch of Falun Gong. This touring troupe—multiple companies perform simultaneously throughout the world—purports to represent "China before communism" with its classical dance and music show. Such a statement evinces the organization's inherent, if not overt, political stance against the CCP and thus the PRC at large. It could be argued, therefore, that what Shen Yun portrays to audiences outside of mainland China is not only entertainment, but also a form of political propaganda through the arts. Shen Yun disputes this claim, however. As stated on its website, "it is not that Falun Gong itself is political, but rather the communist regime is utilizing political means to persecute Falun Gong and silence anyone who wishes to speak about it."[46] While such an argument is certainly debatable, Falun Gong's news-media arm, The Epoch Media Group, including the newspaper *The Epoch Times*, is much less ambiguous in its political leanings. The overtly right-wing outlet has been a vocal supporter of China-hawk Donald Trump since the presidential election of 2016, and has also lent credence to conspiracy theories related to climate change and the coronavirus pandemic, including ideas and theories which may fall under the QAnon banner.[47]

PART III

Dragons of Today
and Tomorrow

9

Dragons in Global Popular
Media and Culture

For Children (of All Ages)

"My dear little man," said the dragon solemnly, "just understand, once and for all, that I can't fight and I won't fight. I've never fought in my life, and I'm not going to begin now, just to give you a Roman holiday. In old days I always let the other fellows—the earnest *fellows—do all the fighting, and no doubt that's why I have the pleasure of being here now."*[1]

In the summer of 2016 it seemed that all many millions of people wanted to do was to hunt for imaginary creatures. More specifically, these creatures were "pocket monsters," or *Pokémon*, digital cryptids that could, in a considerable proportion of cases, quite reasonably be described as dragons or otherwise dragon-adjacent.[2] The way one hunted them was through an augmented-reality game by Niantic/Nintendo called *Pokémon GO*,[3] played on smartphones. The game was particularly notable for requiring players to go outdoors and search for any nearby cryptids, inspiring many to visit locales that they may have otherwise overlooked. Other physical sites, known as "gyms," were where these "trainers" could deploy their cryptids to fight against those captured by other trainers. Observed one particularly enthusiastic trainer that summer, "Everyone is enjoying the game and they want you to do the same! This game has a crazy way of bringing strangers together!"[4] For a moment, at least, it appeared that a whimsical mobile game could perhaps bridge the gaping political and cultural chasm emerging between Americans on either side of the political spectrum as the 2016 presidential election drew nearer.

Though the *GO* craze died down considerably after that summer, the *Pokémon* franchise's status as a worldwide media phenomenon was nevertheless cemented. Dedicated trainers continued to go outside to play *GO* and collectors continued to trade in the *Pokémon* playing cards that date back to the franchise's beginnings in the late 1990s.

In one recent case, a *Pokémon* card from 1999 was purchased for $57,789 by one Vinath Oudomsine, of Dublin, Georgia (USA). At issue, however, was that Mr. Oudomsine had funded the purchase from the $85,000 he had received in August 2020 as a federal Payroll Protection Program (PPP) loan, intended to be exclusively used for coronavirus relief. As stated in his loan request, these funds were needed to safeguard Oudomsine's ten-person "entertainment services business." However, this business did not actually exist. Of the case, U.S. Attorney David Estes commented, "Like moths to the flame, fraudsters like Oudomsine took advantage of these programs to line their own pockets—and with our law enforcement partners, we are holding him and others accountable for their greed."[5] The cryptid portrayed on this extremely rare (and now-confiscated) card was known as a *Charizard* (#006), a species of dragon evolved from a *Charmander* (#004), via a *Charmeleon* (#005). According to the "Pokédex" of *pokemon.com*, Charizard "spits fire that is hot enough to melt boulders. It may cause forest fires by blowing flames."[6]

Upon his conviction for the crime of wire fraud, the thirty-one-year-old Oudomsine was sentenced to three years in prison. He literally went to prison for a dragon.

A rare Pokémon card, depicting a dragon called Charizard, was at the center of a case of misappropriation of Covid relief funds in 2020 in Georgia, USA (Hethers/Shutterstock.com).

Puffs of Smoke

In the 2000 film *Meet the Parents*, Gaylord "Greg" Focker (Ben Stiller) rides in the passenger seat as his girlfriend's dour father, Jack Byrnes (Robert De Niro), drives. After an awkward silence, Jack turns on the car stereo. It plays the 1963 folk ballad "Puff, the Magic Dragon" by the group Peter, Paul and Mary. For a moment, they listen to the song together. Then, Greg speaks.

GREG: Great song.
JACK: Yeah, one of my favorites.
GREG: Who would've thought it wasn't really about a dragon, huh?
JACK: What do you mean?
GREG: You know, the whole drug thing.
JACK: No, I don't know. Why don't you tell me?
GREG: Some people think that ... to "puff the magic dragon" means to—They're really, uh—to smoke, um, to smoke—a marijuana cigarette.

JACK: Well, Puff's just the name of the boy's magical dragon.
GREG: Right.
JACK: Are you a pothead, Focker?
GREG: No! No.
JACK: What?
GREG: No, no, no, no, Jack. No, I'm—I'm not—I—I pass on grass all the time. I mean, not all the time.
JACK: Yes or no, Greg?
GREG: No. Yes. No.[7]

From there, everything continues to go pretty much downhill between Greg and Jack.

The urban legend that "Puff" was "actually" about "puffing" marijuana smoke by "draggin'" on a joint made by rolling up "the magic dragon" (green like *Cannabis sativa/indica*, it stands to reason), using a leaf of "Little Jackie Paper," doesn't hold up particularly well as mere coincidence, at least at first glance. The song's mythical setting of Honah-Lee (or Honalee, etc.) even bears an uncanny resemblance to Hanalei, Hawaii, on Kauai, a site famous for its marijuana cultivation. Yet the song's writers, Peter Yarrow (music) and Lenny Lipton (lyrics), have for decades consistently and often vociferously asserted that these parallels are sheer happenstance and conjecture. "When 'Puff' was written, I was too innocent to know about drugs," Yarrow stated in 2001. "What kind of a meanspirited SOB would write a children's song with a covert drug message?"[8]

The first mainstream implication of the drug connection is purported to have originated in 1964, about a year after the song's release. Lipton (d. 2022) accused the now long-deceased journalist, gossip columnist, and frequent panelist of the quiz show *What's My Line?* Dorothy Kilgallen (1913–1965) of spearheading the skullduggery. In a personal-blog post of 2009, Lipton wrote, "The first thing I thought when confronted with her newspaper column was disbelief—how could that nice lady say such a thing? The second thing I thought was: What can you expect from a woman without a chin. She had a receding chin. Kind of nonexistent."[9] He reiterated that he held Kilgallen responsible as recently as a 2015 interview.[10] But posthumous, ad hominem potshots and other foggy speculations aside, the bibliographical trail does not bear out this claim, leading to my conclusion that it is very likely apocryphal.

Kilgallen indeed covered Peter, Paul and Mary's meteoric rise to the top of the Billboard charts—"Puff" peaked at number two in the U.S.—in her syndicated column, "Dorothy Kilgallen's Voice of Broadway." But her reporting on the family-friendly, folk-revival act was not nearly so ruthless in tone or nature as Lipton purports. To wit, in August 1963 Kilgallen noted that various parties had made claims to "Puff's" authorship.[11] In December 1964, she revealed that a high-priced contract between the group and a venue had not come to fruition.[12] And, in September 1965, she announced an upcoming performance by the trio at the Cultural Center of the U.S. Embassy in Paris, without any additional commentary.[13] Despite an exhaustive review of the published record, nothing so scurrilous as an intimation of a veiled promotion of drug use turns up. On July 7, 1963, Kilgallen even appeared as a panelist on the same episode of CBS' *What's My Line?* as Peter, Paul and Mary, when the trio were the show's featured mystery guests (Kilgallen correctly identified them). By her familiarity with them as individuals, it seems possible or even likely that they were all already acquaintances, though the look on her face as she questioned them belies a certain subtle disdain, now knowing what she subsequently wrote about them in her nationally syndicated columns. About seven months later Kilgallen established in her column that she wasn't much of a fan of folk music, or at least not a fan of one of the songs Peter, Paul and Mary famously covered. "If I had a hammer," she wrote, "I'd break all recordings of that gruesome song 'If I Had a Hammer,' hit or not...."[14] But since Kilgallen died in late 1965 at the relatively young age of 52,[15] she never had the opportunity to set the record straight about her alleged involvement in starting the Puff rumors, if any. Was she merely the easiest scapegoat? What's more, it appears altogether possible that the rumor began well after Kilgallen's death.

That brings us back to Leonard "Lenny" Lipton (b. 1940). The man now remembered as a prolific filmmaker, producer, and well-respected inventor of revolutionary cinematic 3-D technology was once an undergraduate at Cornell University. In addition to majoring in physics, the young Lipton also had something of a poetic streak. The story goes that he was reading at a campus library in the spring of 1959 when he came across "Custard the Dragon," a 1936 poem by the American poet Ogden Nash (1902–1971). The poem features, as was the major emerging trend in Western dragon narratives of the mid-twentieth century, a beast so meek and mild that a person could keep it as a house pet:

> Belinda lived in a little white house,
> With a little black kitten and a little gray mouse,
> And a little yellow dog and a little red wagon,
> And a realio, trulio, little pet dragon.
>
> Now the name of the little black kitten was Ink,
> And the little gray mouse, she called her Blink,
> And the little yellow dog was sharp as Mustard,
> But the dragon was a coward, and she called him Custard.[16]

Begrudgingly, Custard finds his instinctive courage to repel a pirate attempting to break into Belinda's little white house. But in the end, he returns to his gentle ways: "Belinda is as brave as a barrel full of bears, / And Ink and Blink chase lions down the stairs, / Mustard is as brave as a tiger in a rage, / But Custard keeps crying for a nice safe cage." It's a whimsical piece, and highly representative of the puerility Jorge Borges would lament approximately 25 years later.[17] But the poem, the young Lipton concluded, lacked resonance; he could do much better himself. So later that day, while waiting for a friend to finish preparing dinner for the two of them, he clicked out the first verse of his own dragon poem on a nearby typewriter: "Puff, the magic dragon / Lived by the sea / And frolicked in the autumn mist / In a land called

Honah Lee...." That friend and dinner host, Cornell senior Peter Yarrow, later found the lines on the page, still in his typewriter. He eventually set them to music and fleshed out the rest of the lyrics. About two years later Yarrow brought the song to his folk group, Peter, Paul and Mary, who recorded it in late 1962. The single was the third released early the following year from the group's second LP, *Moving*, released on January 15, 1963.

Up to the end of his life, it appears, Lenny Lipton remained the most vocal proponent of the Kilgallen origin theory for the drugged-out interpretation of "Puff." But other commentators have contributed to the rumor mill by flippantly referencing—but not actually citing—their sources. Even the accomplished musician, composer, and lecturer Robert Greenberg falls prey to this lapse in due diligence. He reported in a *Medium* post in 2020 that "[i]t started with an article in Newsweek magazine, which in 1964 ran a cover story discussing 'hidden drug references' in popular music."[18] Greenberg himself cites Peter Yarrow as the source of the *Newsweek* theory. But like the infamous Kilgallen column referenced by Lipton, neither can this *Newsweek* article be identified; there was neither a cover story nor any other piece in that magazine in 1964 that fits this description. What *does* exist is a letter to the editor in the May 30, 1966, issue of *Newsweek,* responding to its May 9, 1966, cover story on LSD and other psychedelics. "You found an excellent way to get across one of the fastest-growing problems of the youth today," wrote one Denny Kendrick of Largo, Florida. "I would also like to point out that the songs 'Kicks' [by Paul Revere and the Raiders], 'Day Tripper' [by the Beatles] and 'Puff, the Magic Dragon' are all about drug addicts. They are really trying to say something if only people would listen."[19] Could *this* be the source of the Puff-Pot kerfuffle?

The truth seems to be frolicking somewhere in the mists of time and memory, if not exactly a land called Honah-Lee. More likely at play here than intentional subterfuge is rather an organically developed and potent guerrilla-marketing ploy based on the common apocrypha of the urban-legend variety, one edged onwards by a mixture of serendipity, mystique, and plausible deniability. Once the elements had fallen into place, this non-scheme scheme was subtly propagated by the interested parties, namely Yarrow and Lipton. All they had to do was deny it. As a conservative foil to the liberal-leaning Peter, Paul and Mary camp, Dorothy Kilgallen fit nicely into the role of calumniating, youth-hating villain, even in death. Her violent quip about the nakedly pro-labor, Pete Seeger–penned "If I Had a Hammer," even without mentioning by name any of the many 1960s folk artists who covered it, may have provided the spark. But it also may have just been one example of a general, simmering tension between pundits of the left and the right in the culture wars of the period.

Perhaps more ingenuous than their response to the drug link has been Yarrow and Lipton's umbrage at Puff's co-optation as the nickname of a weapon of war. In the mid–1960s, as the communist insurgence force known as the Viet Cong proved surprisingly elusive and the United States military complex began to sink deeper into the quagmire of the conflict in Vietnam, a policy of near-indiscriminate strafing of the local populace began. Towards this end, a series of reconditioned U.S. Air Force C-47 cargo planes (technically the Douglas AC-47 Spooky) were employed. In a spirit of the darkest of gallows humor often found in active theaters of combat, the planes' gunners named their highly destructive charges after the magic dragon of quite-recent popularity. As *Newsweek* reported in 1966,

> Puff owes its name to the fact that its three Gatling-style machine guns lined up on one side of the plane can spit tracer bullets into the night sky at the incredible rate of 450 rounds a second. Firing together, they can put a bullet into every square foot of an area the size of a football field in three seconds.[20]

As vocal opponents of the conflict, and war in general, Peter Yarrow and company were appalled by the military association. Almost twenty years later, in 1984, when news arose that the Reagan administration was considering sending the same model to El Salvador for possible use in the developing conflict there, Yarrow and bandmate Mary Travers again spoke out. "To us and to millions of Americans," Travers wrote in a *New York Times* op-ed, "'Puff' has always been a song for children, not a killer of children." "There's something terribly nihilistic about seeing Santa Claus taking part in a robbery," Yarrow added, "or seeing Puff the Magic Dragon spitting bullets."[21] And in 2009 Lenny Lipton wrote, "There was a point when I ignored *Puff, the Magic Dragon.* That was during the sixties when I distanced myself from the namesake gunship loaded with Gatling guns flown in Vietnam."[22]

On the marijuana front, however, Yarrow and Lipton (and their estates), who have to date collected millions of dollars in royalties and licensing on the popularity of "Puff," continue to have a vested interest in playing it both ways. The song is almost certainly not *intentionally* about marijuana in any way—such pop-cultural saturation of related innuendo, as Lipton and Yarrow have themselves accurately explained at various times, was still several years off. (Indeed, a friendly dragon might quite credibly be named "Puff" because, as we well know by now, many dragons breathe fire. What's more, a reformed, docile dragon of the Land of Honah-Lee, it stands to reason, would be more prone to blowing mere smoke.) But the songwriters lucked out with the historical convergences that allowed the folkniks, the beatniks, the hippies, or whomever to make the connection all on their own. (*Say, man, isn't it far out that this tune makes you think of smoking grass?*) With the intended family-friendly reading of the lyrics (i.e., childhood innocence or whimsy, and the inevitable loss thereof with age), the duo most certainly deemed it unwise to openly concur or otherwise associate with such an illicit or at least family-unfriendly assessment. But it is not as if they could have ever stopped it. The pair have maintained a constant and colossal source of passive income by sticking to their original origin story, snorts and snickers from the cheap seats be damned (and ultimately tolerated). There has been so much revenue generated, in fact, that Lipton's share in the asset greatly assisted in funding his ventures in the motion-picture industry, he openly noted in his later years.[23] His writing of "Puff," however, would be the casual poet's first and last foray into the music industry.

During the Vietnam War, the deadly Douglas AC-47 Spooky gunship was nicknamed "Puff, the Magic Dragon" due to its ultra-high capacity when strafing enemy targets. The original creators of "Puff," all opponents of the war, did not appreciate this coinage (Dan Simonsen/ Shutterstock.com).

When all kinds of people—from tiny tots in daycare, to turtlenecked folkies in the East Village of the '60s, to more contemporary "potheads" like the one portrayed by Ben Stiller as Gaylord "Greg" Focker—can appreciate or even love a song, that is unequivocally what we would call a hit. A well-trod maxim of show business—if not an immutable fact—is that there is no such thing as bad publicity. But when a sweet, melodic reverie on childhood is reinterpreted as an anthem for a new drug-centered counterculture, earning it the opprobrium of square parents all the way up to official prohibitions in Singapore,[24] it has transversed well beyond the hit parade. It has become folklore.

The Many Dragons of Disney

In the 1963 animated film *The Sword in the Stone*, a purple dragon appears at the climax of a wizard's duel. This duel is a fight for magical supremacy between the wizard Merlin (spelled "Merlyn" in the original *Once and Future King* novels by British author T.H. White) and the forest-dwelling witch, Mad Madam Mim. The dragon here is, as in other Disney films such as *Sleeping Beauty*, not an autonomous creature but rather a conjuring by, or magical manifestation of, an otherwise human (or at least humanoid) being.[25] In this case, it's the final form of Mim as she battles Merlyn/Merlin over the right to mentor young (and future king) Arthur, or

"Wart" (originally "the Wart" in White's novels, a nickname that roughly rhymes with "Art," especially in most British dialects). Never mind that Mim herself specifically stipulated beforehand that such mythological creatures were to be prohibited in their duel: "Rule Two: No make-believe things like, uh, oh, pink dragons and stuff." Nor did Mim heed Merlyn when he hastened to add, "Rule Four: No cheating." As a purveyor of dark magic—a classic European witch—to Mim such rules were meant to be broken by technicality. In the movie scene's climax, Merlyn shrewdly overcomes the massive purple (not pink) dragon—"Did I say *purple* dragons?" she taunts—by transforming himself into a microscopic virus (not technically invisible, he contends) and infecting her, though not mortally. Victorious, Merlyn leaves Mim pouting and screeching, laid up sick in her bed with a hole punched in her thatch roof so she might get "lots and lots of sunshine," according to Merlyn. Of course, the patently dreadful Mim hates such a "horrible, wholesome" cure.

Interestingly, the later American edition of T.H. White's novel *The Sword in the Stone*, the first in the tetralogy later titled *The Once and Future King* and fully published by 1958, omits this wizard's duel episode entirely. However, it was White's original (British edition) text of 1938 that the 1963 Disney film was based on. In that edition, as opposed to the final round of the duel in the film, the dragon transformation occurs right away: "At the first going Madame Mim immediately turned herself into a dragon. It was the accepted opening move and Merlyn ought to have replied by being a thunderstorm or something like that. Instead, he caused a great deal of preliminary confusion by becoming a field mouse...."[26] This latter action was also shuffled in the film version: Merlyn instead becomes a mouse to scare off Mim's elephant, echoing a classic, if hackneyed, trope in both folklore and pop culture alike, despite its scientific inaccuracy. Regardless of the sequencing, it seems apt that Disney reclaimed the dragon from the first-edition text: How strange would it be to make a children's animated feature set in medieval times without at least one?

Though the first dragon to appear in a Disney film is technically the nameless, puerile star of *The Reluctant Dragon* (1941), much more vivid in the popular memory and consciousness of today is that of 1959's *Sleeping Beauty*. The ancient European folktale on which the latter Disney film was based was most popularly recorded in literary form by French author Charles Perrault (1628–1703). In 1697, Perrault published *Histoires ou contes du temps passé, avec des moralités*, which included the tale *La Belle au bois dormant* (literally, "The Beauty of the Sleeping Forest"), more commonly known in English as "Sleeping Beauty." However, no traditional telling of the story includes a dragon; it would take Walt Disney and his team of screenwriters for that embellishment, a power of transformation bestowed upon the evil fairy or sorceress, Maleficent.

The ATU Index categorization of the "Sleeping Beauty" tale is Type 410. Of its essential premise, American folklorist Stith Thompson wrote rather sparingly: "A fairy who has not been invited to the princess's christening celebration makes a wish that the princess will die from a spindle wound. Another fairy changes the curse

The draconic manifestation of the sorceress Maleficent in Disney's *Sleeping Beauty* is here depicted using only LEGO bricks at the LEGO Store, Anaheim, California, USA (Rosamar/ Shutterstock.com).

from death into a hundred-year sleep."[27] He adds that "it has never become a real part of oral folklore."[28] Indeed, if Perrault had not preserved and popularized the tale-type in his seventeenth-century book, the rather convoluted original story most likely would never have become the household name that it has been ever since. But with the Disney treatment, its fate was secured as one of the most recognizable and iconic fairy tales in the Western canon.

The contrast between the ferocious, neon-green-plasma-breathing Maleficent of 1959's *Sleeping Beauty* and the kind-hearted, foppish turquoise dragon of 1941's *The Reluctant Dragon* exemplifies the new extreme in the broadening of the dragon's range in the West, and especially in the United States. Such a drastic departure from the creature's once exclusively sinister profile accelerated as the pop-cultural/media engines of the era achieved greater and greater saturation, leading to an unprecedented demand for novelty. Such a process had begun in earnest by the 1930s and was still ongoing by the late 1950s, as we saw above, respectively, with Ogden Nash's "Custard the Dragon" and Peter, Paul and Mary's "Puff, the Magic Dragon." Yet the classic, nefarious manifestation of the Western dragon was still clearly at writers' disposal.

In *Reluctant*, released between the latter two works, in 1941, the irony is firmly set in the conceit of a dragon who refuses to fight a brave knight to the death: everyone knows that a dragon is supposed to be a ruthless and bloodthirsty monster and not a zoftig, tea- and poetry-loving pacifist. In the short film, both the humorist Robert Benchley (playing himself) and his wife (played by Nana Bryant) agree that a certain children's book, the eponymous short story by Kenneth Grahame (1898), is charming enough to bring to the attention of Mr. Walt Disney himself for consideration of animated adaptation. Lucky for them, the couple lives not far from Mr. Disney and his Burbank, California, studio—they can just drive on over. But they are in fact too late (not to mention that the Benchleys were not nor ever have been the story's rights holders). Mr. Disney, Benchley discovers after an all-access adventure through the company's back lots and studios, has already adapted it. We are made privy to the final version of *The Reluctant Dragon* in its entirety as an even shorter film within the short film itself.

Of note, the dragonslayer-for-hire of the original story is none other than St. George himself; in the short film, his name is Sir Giles, and he is an elderly knight with a fine Received Pronunciation. The name change is curious, though it is likely that the intention was to avoid any religious references in such a vehicle intended for secular mass consumption. (In a 1987 British stop-motion version of the tale, however, the knight is once again named St. George.) At any rate, the Disney film was intended to be a profit engine for other, more sophisticated projects in production, namely *Dumbo* (1941) and *Bambi* (1942). "[Walt Disney] also regarded it as a kind of advertisement for the Disney studio," writes Disney historian Neal Gabler, "and recommended including references to *Bambi* and *Dumbo* as 'teasers.'"[29] These references, however, were not ultimately included. Due to its combination of live action and animation, Disney referred to *The Reluctant Dragon* as a "bastard picture,"[30] portending other misfortunes. Namely, a labor strike interfered with the film's commercial potential: About twelve hundred lower-ranking staff, such as assistant animators, walked off the job to call for better compensation and conditions. In June of 1941, when *The Reluctant Dragon* debuted in Los Angeles, the strikers used a dragon cut-out to picket the theater. Its head was a caricature of Walt Disney himself, its body labeled with the word "UNFAIR."[31]

Video Games

For those of us who weren't yet old enough to have seen it in its original form during the arcade era (1978–85), the look of the game *Dragon's Lair* is almost unfathomable as having been released when it was: 1983. A glimpse at one of its stills suffices to elicit a virtually universal response: How in the world did the designers achieve such rich and high-resolution graphics and gameplay in the era of the otherwise exclusively 8-bit graphics, as in *Donkey Kong* or *Space Invaders*? "Everybody remembers the first time they saw *Dragon's Lair*," writes Simon Parkin in his

Illustrated History of 151 Video Games. "In the near-instantaneous shift from *Space Invaders'* jagged blobs to the curvaceous, cel-animated style of *Dragon's Lair* it was as if video games had skipped five stages of visual evolution and, in this one game, arrived at their final, mesmerizing form."[32] Graphically, the game indeed looks like an animated feature film, every bit as dynamic as the groundbreaking animated film *The Secret of NIMH*, released the year before. What's more, astoundingly, a player can control the action of the "film" of *Dragon's Lair* with a joystick and "sword" button. So why, if this feat was possible at such an early date, didn't all (or at least more) contemporary games endeavor to look this stunning?

The reason *Dragon's Lair* was so uncannily different from its contemporaries is that, at its core, it was. Unlike other video games of the era, which were powered by RAM (random access memory) chips, *Lair* depended on the new technology of the quasi-digital LaserDisc video format. This allowed for the game's "cutscenes" to be recorded for playback at a high resolution, similar to how they would appear on television or film.[33] Furthermore, this was a "film" unlike any other: it could be navigated by a player. In the same manner a compact disc or DVD might skip forward, either internally within a track or to the next one, the action of *Lair* operated upon the method known as "quick time event" (QTE). If a player correctly and immediately followed each lighted prompt (for either direction of movement or sword use against a foe), the avatar, a young and slightly clumsy knight named Dirk the Daring, advanced to the next cutscene. But autonomy in such a game was highly restricted; it operated "on the rails," whereby one could only follow the predetermined plot of the action already burned onto the LaserDisc—or not. If commanded incorrectly, instead of advancing Dirk would perish in a variety of scene-specific fashions (e.g., strangled by a snake or burnt to a skeleton by the dragon's flame), also known as "death sequences." Over fifty of these were programmed. The game's creators intended them to be almost as entertaining as *not* dying: "Because I thought that would be the humor of the thing," one designer commented, "you know, how to do it so that it wasn't just gruesome or cruel or anything like that."[34] The only way to get good, and finish the game, was by spending mounds of quarters. But, as Tim Skelly puts it, "After a while, even the show-offs stopped playing."[35]

In the second season of the 80s-set Netflix series *Stranger Things* (2018), Dustin (Gaten Matarazzo) gets all the way to the eponymous dragon's lair at his local arcade in fictional Hawkins, Indiana. However, as Dustin begins to fight the green, purple-fringed, and yellow-bellied dragon, Singe, with Princess Daphne looking on and gasping, he dies suddenly. Dirk surreptitiously dissolves into a pile of bones for the death sequence. "I hate this overpriced bullshit!" Dustin shouts, banging on the cabinet in a rage. (In the game's defense, its technical components were much more expensive than the average arcade game, necessitating the higher price.)[36] Despite these common complaints, Bluth and Dyer's creation was a massive and immediate financial success, reportedly netting the creators $45 million in 1983.[37] And though critiques of the clunky and monotonous gameplay itself were not far behind its high

Highly innovative for its LaserDisc technology, *Dragon's Lair* has been ported to various gaming systems, such as the Super Nintendo (SNES), since its original release on arcade cabinets in 1983 (seeshooteatrepeat/Shutterstock.com).

cost, *Dragon's Lair* was revolutionary in that it gave millions of arcade gamers a glimpse into the future: it wouldn't be until the mid–1990s, or over ten years later, with Nintendo 64 and other higher-bit consoles that video-game graphics would even begin to be comparable. As a result, *Dragon's Lair*—doubly read aloud as "dragon slayer," it stands to note—has its place firmly secured in the halls of video game history; it has never gone out of publication in its more than 40 years of existence on countless platforms. It seems not at all surprising that such a historic feat of gaming technology would comprise, narratively speaking, an archetypal hero's quest to rescue a beautiful maiden from a loathsome and mighty dragon. The trope would continue in earnest with a then still up-and-coming franchise, *Super Mario Brothers.*

The dragon-as-final-boss trope continued apace as video games shifted venues from the arcade to the home. Considering the now near-ubiquity of characters such as Mario, Luigi, Princess Peach, Toadstool, King Koopa (also known as Bowser), and others, it's easy to forget how revolutionary the *Mario* franchise was when the Nintendo Entertainment System (NES) debuted internationally, in 1985. Originally called Famicon in Japan, Nintendo mastermind Shigeru Miyamoto shrewdly surmised that if his company's new console for the home was to succeed, he would need a highly inventive (and furthermore seriously popular) flagship game to accompany it. With the massive arcade-format hit of Nintendo's *Donkey Kong* (1981), Miyamoto had cut his teeth on game and character design, proving that he understood the demand for dynamic yet learnable gameplay. (The latter element, of course, is the secret to any video-game hit, especially in the arcade: hook players with a chance to play, lose, learn, and then keep p[l]aying over and over.)

Miyamoto plucked the protagonist or "sprite" of the NES megahit *Super Mario Bros.* from *Donkey Kong.* At that earlier stage, the bouncing, mustachioed workman was the boyfriend of the game's damsel, Pauline, herself kidnapped by the eponymous villain, the workman's own pet gorilla gone rogue.[38] Based on his principal mode of movement, Miyamoto naturally dubbed the little sprite "Jumpman." It wasn't until after *Donkey Kong* was a hit under the Nintendo of America subsidiary that the little fellow changed names and, ostensibly, gained an ethnic identity. Miyamoto honored the company's Italian-American warehouse landlord in Seattle, a man named Mario Segale, with such a distinction due to the latter's flexibility with their rent ... as well as the perceived similarity of appearance between Segale and the 8-bit sprite.[39] Also in *Donkey Kong,* interestingly, Jumpman is portrayed as a carpenter rather than a plumber; his profession would not be permanently solidified as the latter until the pipe-and-tunnel-heavy *Super Mario Bros.* of 1985.[40]

Donkey Kong was indeed a bona-fide arcade sensation in its own right: Nintendo of America sold 67,000 cabinets of the game over its production run.[41] After almost 100 years of existence in Japan as an otherwise domestic-focused company that manufactured traditional Japanese playing cards (*hanafuda*) and children's toys, Nintendo had now made serious inroads into the American market. But the narrative as we now know it hadn't quite arrived. "As little Mario gallantly battles his way up the barriers," one early ad for *Donkey Kong* tantalizes, "he is taunted and teased by Donkey Kong, who brazenly struts back and forth, beating his chest in joyful exuberance at the prospect of having the beautiful girl all to himself."[42] Despite such classically monstrous vices as wrath and—not so subtly, according to the aforementioned ad copy—*lust* for human females, a dragon Donkey Kong is not. The now-iconic pixelated gorilla (who later went on to be a protagonist in other Nintendo games such as *Donkey Kong Country* for Super Nintendo [SNES] in 1994) is rather more emblematic of the killer-ape trope in the mold of *King Kong* (various versions since 1933), *The Planet of the Apes* (multiple sequels [and a reboot franchise] since 1968), and even the opening sequence of Stanley Kubrick's monumental *2001: A Space Odyssey* (also 1968). It would take the erstwhile "Jumpman's" journey from the arcade to the home console for the next archvillain to take on a form more resembling this book's quarry.

So how did Nintendo make the leap from a gorilla-fighting carpenter to a turtle-toppling plumber? And what ever happened to Jumpman's girlfriend? Under the direction of a less inventive game designer, the nemesis of *Super Mario Bros.* may very well have remained Donkey Kong and the "princess," Pauline. *Donkey Kong*'s financial success as an arcade game would have reasonably justified a rehash for Nintendo's slated home console. But Shigeru Miyamoto was neither an average designer nor one to rest on his creative laurels. "In his games," writes journalist

Mario may have originated as a gorilla-fighting sprite in Jumpman in *Donkey Kong* (1981), but he and his brother Luigi are best known today for their pursuit of Princess Peach, captive of the evil Bowser (also known as King Koopa), a creature best described as a dragon-turtle (Ken Weaver/Shutterstock.com).

Nick Paumgarten, "Miyamoto has always tried to re-create his childhood wonderment, if not always the actual experiences that gave rise to it, since the experiences themselves may be harder to come by in a paved and partitioned world."[43] For his next trick, his intention was to create even more elaborate levels and, essentially, a degree of worldbuilding that would feel much more narratively rich and therefore more cognitively intriguing than the "platform" (one screen per level) design of *Donkey Kong*. This transition included a switch from the latter model to the more dynamic, left-to-right "side-scrolling" mechanism of *Super Mario Bros.* on the NES home console.

To rescue the princess, Mario or Luigi must pass through eight worlds with four levels each. The rank and file of the Brothers' foes are Koopa Troopas (ostensibly turtles) and Goombas (angry, semi-anthropomorphic mushrooms). But the archvillain is seemingly unique, and of a different species altogether: Bowser, King of the Koopas, the Big Boss. The mythozoology of Miyamoto's Mushroom Kingdom is fascinatingly whimsical unto itself, but not unprecedented whatsoever given the designer's cultural background. As we saw in Chapter 3, due to the physical proximity of Japan to China, and the latter's early rise as a cultural and commercial juggernaut, the influences of Chinese culture upon that of Japan are myriad and diffuse.

The dragon-turtle of Chinese geomancy (*feng shui*) is a hybrid of two of the four magical creatures in that tradition. Despite Bowser's malevolence, the dragon-turtle is traditionally viewed as an auspicious creature, one associated with wealth and good fortune (ST239/Shutterstock.com).

Though the principal languages of the two countries are not considered genetically related, the modern Japanese written language, especially in its main form, *kanji*, is infused with assimilated Chinese characters and their concomitant folklore, logic, and accrued wisdom. Thus, similar mythological creatures are present in both countries and have been for many centuries, if not millennia. Such is true of the dragon-turtle (龍龜/*lónggui*, literally "dragon-turtle"), a hybrid of two of Eastern folklore's most significant motifs.

In Chinese mythology, as we saw in Chapter 8, the turtle is also one of the four celestial animals, otherwise known as "The Four Gods," "The Four Guardians," or "The Four Auspicious Beasts." Each is the guardian of one of the cardinal directions—the Turtle (or Black Tortoise) of the North; the Azure Dragon of the East; the Phoenix (or Vermillion Bird) of the South; and the White Tiger of the West. It is worth noting that of the four, two are fictitious (dragon, phoenix) and two are real creatures (turtle, tiger). When the dragon and the turtle combine, they form the *lónggui* and this is precisely what King Bowser Koopa of the Mushroom Kingdom—with his dragon's head and turtle's body—is probably meant to be.[44] Then again, Bowser is also a case of creative license: in traditional Far-Eastern folklore the

The Four Gods of *feng shui*: dragon, phoenix, turtle, tiger. Notably, two of these creatures are mythical and two are real (insima/Shutterstock.com).

lóngguī is auspicious, whereas in *Super Mario Bros.* he is clearly *inauspicious* as the violent kidnapper of Princess Peach. In this regard, Miyamoto was probably influenced by the Western/malevolent interpretation of the dragon, a phenomenon discussed in Chapter 3, as has occurred in many other cases of globalized Japanese pop culture since the mid-twentieth century. With Nintendo's conquest of the American market and beyond, the now-common trend of cross-pollinating elements of the two major dragon world-types was already in full effect.

10

Dragons in Global Popular Media and Culture

Just for Grown-Ups

For that summer, from the outskirts
of some far off even whimsical place
came the low resolute moo of a dragon[1]

Not long ago, in June of 2021, my father, John, happened to meet George R.R. Martin, creator of the *A Song of Ice and Fire* (*ASOIAF*) series, including the novels *A Game of Thrones* and *A Dance with Dragons*.

John was on the downtown–Chicago campus of Northwestern University, where he works as a pediatric orthopedic surgeon, and by chance he recognized Martin standing on the sidewalk. After a brief greeting, John then asked for a photograph with Martin, who was himself at Northwestern (of which he was already an alumnus) to claim an honorary doctorate from the university's Medill School of Journalism.[2] Martin's personal assistant quickly interceded and declined the photo op on her client's behalf, understandably concerned that it might draw a crowd that could then potentially become unwieldy. Instead, the assistant graciously offered my father two coins. Both depicted on the obverse (front) the figures of *ASOIAF*'s Queen Daenerys Targaryen and her three dragons, Drogon, Rhaegal, and Viserion; on the reverse was a pyramid behind manacled hands breaking free. (Given that my father is an amateur numismatist, such an offering was particularly auspicious. More on dragons in coinage will be covered in Chapter 12.) According to the website of the coins' manufacturer and retailer, Arkansas-based Shire Post Mint, "[Daenerys] had this coin minted to replace the concept of slaves as currency on the city. The golden Mark is worth about half as much as a Westerosi Dragon, or the equivalent of 105 silver Stags."[3] Along with these mementos, my father was of course gifted with the marvelous anecdote of having met and chatted with one of the most notable authors of original high-fantasy fiction in modern history, if not the most notable *living* author in that category. John gave one of the coins to me and it now sits next to my ever-growing personal research library on the topic of the dragon.

After massive successes with both the books and television adaptations of his *A Song of Ice and Fire* series, George R.R. Martin (b. 1948) has established himself as the early twenty-first century doyen of the high-fantasy genre, established in the mid twentieth century by J.R.R. Tolkien (d. 1973). The author (left) here joins actors Lily Collins (center) and Nicholas Hoult (right) for the Hollywood premiere of the *Tolkien* biopic on May 8, 2019 (Kathy Hutchins/ Shutterstock.com).

A Little More Bite

"One of the writing decisions I wrestled with was whether or not to include actual dragons," George R.R. Martin is quoted as saying. "I always knew, for some reason, the Targaryens would have dragons on their banners, but were they real or was it just a symbol? I finally decided they would be real ... and I'm glad I did."[4] To wit, in the teaser to the HBO prequel series *House of the Dragon* (2022), the latest installment of the *Song of Ice and Fire* franchise (based on Martin's novel *Fire and Blood*, published in 2018), actor Matt Smith as Prince Daemon Targaryen speaks ominously in voiceover. "Dreams didn't make us kings," he intones. "Dragons did." Though of course dragons are introduced as essential figures in the six published novels (to date) and seven television seasons of the *A Song of Ice and Fire* franchise, *Fire and Blood*, whose second season is scheduled to be released in summer of 2024, offers a particularly rich trove of dragon lore and background detail to Martin's principal storyworld of Westeros.

Most immediately in the novel *Fire and Blood*, the dragon Balerion or "The Black Dread," is described. Balerion is an individual dragon also referenced starting as early as *A Game of Thrones* (the first novel, published in 1996)/*Game of Thrones* (season one of the HBO series), so the reference has been established now for some time. In an April 2014 article for *The Daily Dot*, published amid the immensely popular HBO series, writer Rob Price mused on some of the finer details of Balerion's anatomy to establish the growth potential for Daenerys Targaryen's dragon triplets, Drogon, Rhaegal, and Viserion. "If we assume a steady rate of growth," Price wrote, "this means by the time of Balerion's death [at the age of about 200] ... he may have been in excess of 150 meters [almost 500 feet] in length. That's five times as long as a blue whale, or one and a half times the length of a football field." Balerion, Price hastened to mention, "is supposed to be able to swallow a mammoth whole."[5] Lots of room for growth for the young triplets, it seemed.

The backstory of Balerion in *Fire and Blood* offers what fans of the earlier novels and/or the TV series have likely wondered for years: How, specifically, did the Targaryens conquer Westeros? Geographically and genealogically speaking, Aenar, the grandfather of Aegon the Conqueror, and his sister-wives Rhaenys and Visenya, had first captured the small but strategic island of Dragonstone, off the southeastern coast of Westeros. Aenar had made this move in large part due to his homeland of Valyria being destroyed by the "Doom"—ostensibly a massive and land-sinking series of earthquakes that left the ancient and influential city-state uninhabitable (think Ancient Greece if it had been somehow physically destroyed). After a time, when the conditions were right, Aegon and his sisters advanced with their dragons on the much larger landmass of Westeros, taking most of its dragonless kingdoms by surprise. "Of the five dragons who had flown with Aenar the Exile from Valyria," Martin writes, "only one remained to Aegon's day: the great beast called Balerion, the Black Dread. The dragons Vhagar and Meraxes [corresponding to Aegon's

The worldwide success of the *A Song of Ice and Fire* franchise continued in 2022 with the debut of the HBO series *House of the Dragon*, a dragon-heavy prequel to *Game of Thrones*. A billboard in Madrid, Spain promotes the series in October of 2022 with the tagline "The heart of *Game of Thrones* keeps strongly beating" (Julian Prizont-Cado/Shutterstock.com).

sister-wives] were younger, hatched on Dragonstone itself."[6] Without these dragons, and especially Balerion, the Targaryen dynasty would have never been established in Westeros. This family's ouster from the throne by Robert Baratheon and the Lannisters, and the resulting power vacuum, is the predicate of the entire *Game of Thrones* saga.

In Martin's conception, dragons are domesticable, as opposed to, for example, J.R.R. Tolkien's or Gary Gygax's wild and untamable (yet also often sentient) dragons and other dragonesque creatures (see Chapters 7 and 11, respectively). Thus do the Targaryens possess the ability to not only mount and drive the mighty forces of dragons, but also to form strong, quasi-maternal or -paternal bonds with them. This is most deeply exhibited in the relationship between Daenerys Targaryen and her three dragons, whom she constantly refers to as her "children." Indeed, the implication throughout the franchise is that the Targaryens were not only bonded to their dragons (a trope also employed in the case of the Na'vi and their mountain banshees, or *ikran*, among other creatures, in the *Avatar* franchise), but furthermore were, somehow, genetically related to them. "[T]he strictures of the Faith [of the Seven, the principal religion of Westeros] might rule other men," Martin expounds in *Fire and Blood*, "but not the blood of the dragon."[7] Lacking this inheritance precludes a person entirely from even approaching a dragon safely, much less riding and commanding one to spew fire with a shout *Dracarys!*[8] Furthermore, this is also given as the principal rationale for the practice, otherwise seen as wholly taboo among the Westerosi, of Targaryen siblings marrying one another.

The Elephant and the Dragon

The mythological peridexion (or perindeus) tree was first attested in the didactic Christian text known as *Physiologus* (Greek, third century CE) and appears later in several medieval European bestiaries. As the legend goes, in India, where the peridexion is supposedly endemic, it is a common sanctuary for doves as they flee their natural predator, the dragon. The doves hide in the tree's branches and are further protected by its shade, which the dragon abhors as if it were poison. The peridexion, we are meant to understand, represents Christ's grace and furthermore the eternal salvation of souls from the clutches of evil and perdition. So long as we meek doves remain among the branches, the dragon will never corrupt or devour us.[9]

While doves must be a mere snack to the likes of a dragon, they are not the only creatures at odds with the evil monster. One of the most prominent specimens from the bestiary lore of both late antiquity and the Middle Ages is the elephant, sometimes presented as a well-matched nemesis to the dragon, but often as another of its victims.

As for the elephant's characterization as a worthy foe, one sly and much-debated reference has appeared quite recently, in the seventh and eighth seasons of *Game of Thrones* (2018–19). Preparing to do battle against Khaleesi Daenerys Targaryen (Emilia Clarke) and her massive dragons for control of the Seven Kingdoms of Westeros, Queen Cersei Lannister-Baratheon (Lena Headey) purchases the allegiance of the Golden Company, an army of mercenaries from Essos across the Narrow Sea. Cersei had previously sent a message through her agents that she specifically also wanted the notorious sellswords to bring war elephants, which in the show's universe are native to the continent of Essos. However, when the Company's general reports for duty, he solemnly informs Cersei that "They are excellent beasts, your grace, but not well suited to long sea voyages." Later, after a tryst with her deranged lover and new military ally, Prince Euron Greyjoy of the Iron Islands, Cersei distractedly mutters to herself, "I *wanted* those elephants." In addition to the use of elephants (and dragons) as pieces in the original *ASOIAF* novels' chess-like board game, *cyvasse*, the TV series is also well supported by accurately historical, and specifically medieval, modes of thinking about the enormous beasts and their attributes. As the most important consultant to the series, George R.R. Martin, deeply versed in such arcane knowledge of topics classical and medieval, certainly must have signed off on the rationale that, in pitched battle, if one cannot have dragons, elephants are the next best thing. What's more, as attested by both historical events and common sense,

Dragon statue, Parco dei Monstri ("Park of the Monsters"), Sacro Bosco, Bomarzo, Lazio, Italy. In the background is seen an elephant, long considered the natural foe to the dragon in traditional European folklore. However, here the dragon fends off a trio of lions or possibly dogs (Sergei Afanasev/Shutterstock.com).

horses (and, of course, people) are naturally terrified by charging adult elephants on the battlefield or, frankly, in any context.

Several other variables play into the antipathy between elephants and dragons in ancient folklore and literature. One is the seemingly backwards notion, according to modern science, that dragons are warm-blooded, and elephants cold-blooded creatures.[10] It is both stated and implied in the *ASOIAF* universe that dragons are fire incarnate, and this notion is congruent with the medieval lore made most explicit in bestiaries and earlier classical sources, such as Pliny the Elder's *Natural History* (Latin, first century CE). This is also true of what is considered the earliest recorded bestiary, the anonymously written Greek text known as *Physiologus*.[11] Elephants, perhaps because they are largely hairless and spend ample time in watering holes—but also very likely because Europeans simply did not know much, if anything, about them or their physiology—were deemed by ancient scholars to be cold-blooded. And for the purposes of spinning a yarn, the maxim of "opposites attract" seems germane, especially in the context of predation and/or mortal combat within literature and/or folklore. "For (say they)," wrote Pliny, "the elephant's blood is exceeding cold, and therefore the dragons be wonderful desirous thereof to refresh and cool themselves therewith, during the parching and hot season of the year."[12] However, as Pliny claimed later in his work, elephants are often so heavy and cumbersome that it is common for them to fall and crush blood-sucking dragons as they feast, causing both creatures to die. As they lie in a heap, he continues, their oozing blood mixes and reacts to create the mineral cinnabar (mercury sulfide), often used as a pigment to represent blood in painting. Pliny referred to this toxic substance as "dragon's blood."[13,14]

But the lore continues. Pliny the Elder, or Gaius Plinius Secundus (23–79 CE), was a well-connected patrician from an old and prestigious Roman family. Naturally, given his time and place, he was also a pagan. The author had no connection to the then brand-new cult of Christianity, which had only just emerged when he was an adolescent. Though beginning to wane, the classical Greco-Roman world and worldview—including its popular religions and mythologies—were still very much in their prime during his lifetime. Pliny's *Natural History* is more of a catalog of his acquired personal knowledge and should not be categorized as a bestiary; as mentioned, the *Physiologus* of about two centuries later is considered the first of this genre. It is with this latter text, purportedly written by a Greek Christian monk in Alexandria, Egypt that explicit Christian allegory is first applied to a survey of the world's known creatures, the pattern of which would then be followed throughout the medieval era, as seen in Chapter 5.

"Actual" Dragons

At the core of the human inclination towards religion and religious modes of thinking is a natural response to forces over which we have little to no control, and particularly to that most universal of preoccupations: our own mortality. When we sense that death is imminent, many pray to be (or to have others) spared. This urge is even seen in such cases as the "Hail Mary" pass by a quarterback in American football: He only employs this tactic when his team is down by at least six and at most seven points—he and his team are about to "die" (lose the game), and the "Hail Mary" is the final chance to "stay alive" (tie or win). Or observe the rigor of a whispered prayer to God or any other deity to survive an encroaching tornado or wildfire or hurricane or bombing while trapped in a basement or car or closet. Even in the form of a simple votive candle, lit in a chapel on behalf of a critically ill loved one, is this inclination abundantly clear. In all these fraught moments and countless others can the religious urge provide great comfort, or at least constitute an appeal of last resort. When ritualized by a particular society, this instinct becomes normalized, structured, and elaborated upon. Its doctrines become ensconced in the local or chosen liturgical language, whether oral or written. Paired with political or military might, the resulting organized religion may become the sharpened speartip of the society and culture which wields it. Mitigating or neutralizing any external threats or obstacles to the maintenance of this force thus become religious as well as political concerns.[15]

In the case of evangelical American Christianity, in current times predominantly practiced by those identifying with the political right, the perceived loss of previously held political or cultural privilege may be overestimated but it is nonetheless viewed as personally and even existentially threatening. To many who equate American exceptionalism with Christianity, any diminution of the status of the latter inherently implies an attack on the former. What's more, and especially in the United States, the correlation between this significant voting bloc's values and the material advantages of its inherent identifications with (or otherwise alliances with) the socio-political or caste construct of whiteness is inextricable. Such anxiety and outrage in the face of an ever-secularizing (and generally diversifying) society is an extension of the historically entrenched systems of privilege and supremacy that compose the most fundamental power dynamic of the United States and other post-colonial societies (besides capitalism itself), particularly in the Americas. Though advancements have been made through federal legislation in the United States, such as the Civil Rights Act of 1964, many attempts at establishing a fully representative system of democracy have been met with fierce opposition from the predominant caste. "When you're accustomed to privilege," maintains one commonly cited maxim, particularly popular among contemporary activists, "equality feels like oppression."[16]

After Donald Trump lost his bid for reelection in November 2020, the culture wars that he had fomented during both of his presidential campaigns and throughout his one-term administration did not suddenly disappear. Many of the grievances Trump had espoused took on a markedly revanchist dimension in the wake of his defeat, reaching a historic fever-pitch as thousands of his supporters protested, mostly peacefully, to "Stop the Steal." Meanwhile, a more radicalized subset, composed of several hundred of the President's most ardent acolytes, violently stormed and breached the United States Capitol on January 6, 2021, in an attempt to disrupt or reverse the Constitutionally mandated transfer of power. Though the 2020 presidential election was nevertheless certified, and Trump accordingly left office—as of this writing he still publicly claims that the election was stolen from him—the conspiracy theories circulated among his supporters have continued, seemingly unabated. The rampant misinformation and propaganda then pivoted from alleged election fraud (though this, too, persists) to fearmongering centered around three particular hot-button issues: the recently developed and now widely available Covid-19 vaccine (and the various federal, state, and local policies therein appertaining); the related (and highly variable, by jurisdiction) public mask mandates associated with attempting to hinder the coronavirus' spread; and the tenets of an ill-defined representation of "critical race theory" (CRT), and their purportedly divisive effects on society at large, as well as on the politics of gender and sexuality. How children and their mental and physical wellbeing should (or should not) play a part in all these novel wedge issues has been the unequivocal nexus of them all. Much of this discourse has first materialized on social media platforms such as Facebook and

Twitter before entering more traditional forums such as parent-teacher and school board meetings.

One internet meme, posted to a Facebook group page on March 1, 2022, was illustrative of the rhetoric emerging from this novel crucible of predominantly right-wing outrage. The background graphic of the meme depicts the head and neck of what appears to be a mechanical dragon with steam billowing from its mouth. The text in the left corner reads,

> HUSBAND: "I'm sorry we have to raise our children in times when our world is in such turmoil."

And along the bottom:

> WIFE: "Never feel sorry for raising dragon slayers in a time where there are actual dragons."—unknown

At the time of this writing, only one week after it was posted, the meme has received 194 "likes" or "loves" and has been shared fifty-six times. Among the post's thirty comments, one user wrote, "Are there currently any classes on dragon slaying? I feel in need of one." Another user responded with information on an upcoming, weekend-long conference on "Personal Tactics in Kingdom Warfare" to be held in Indianapolis just a few weeks later.

The venue for this meme was, more specifically, the public page for "Purple for Parents Indiana," a special-interest group representing conservative parents concerned about what kinds of rhetoric or indoctrination their children may be exposed to at public schools.[17] But the reference to "actual dragons" is intriguing, if not patently histrionic. (What's more, the author of the quotation is most likely "unknown" because that individual and the meme's creator are one and the same.) Did the meme's anonymous author not understand the meaning of "actual"? Or do they believe that dragons are real? Regardless, the distinction between the figurative and the literal in the language of evangelical Anglo-American Christianity is one that is often so fine as to be nonexistent. The reason for this, as it is in other fundamentalist religious traditions, is to immerse the beholder in a realm where dogma and orthodoxy must be upheld by any means, including magical modes of perceiving reality, often despite all evidence to the contrary. Herein lies the essence of the religious-political "speartip" mentioned above, the necessary ideology for maintaining established hierarchies of power and privilege. Linguists and other social scientists refer to this common phenomenon as "word magic," though the same may also be applied to less drastic contexts such as conferring of an academic degree at a graduation ceremony, or the binding of two individuals together, "forever," in matrimony. Present-day instances of word magic such as this case of "actual dragons" thus fit into the same propagandistic imaginary from which the St. George the Dragonslayer legend itself was embedded centuries ago, as detailed in Chapter 5. In a non-religious context we might refer to such rhetoric as "make believe," but it is also the preacher's or the propagandist's prime directive to do just that for a given congregation or other audience: make *them* believe.

Political Monsters

In a recent opinion piece in the *Washington Post*, the political theorist Danielle Allen laments that "two dragons" menace American democracy: "an out-of-balance electoral college and gerrymandering. How can we slay them?"[18] The use of the dragon as political metaphor is not new, but what continues to be striking is its lasting efficacy; immediately, the author claims the reader's attention to introduce policy suggestions that are not only complex, but also controversial given the current American political climate. (Allen's solution—"Two dragons, one stone. How can we just leave it lying on the ground?"—is to expand the number of seats in the U.S. House of Representatives.)

The very origin of the term "gerrymandering," that particularly fraught American method of engineering political influence through the reshaping of congressional districts, is germane to this discussion as well. The portmanteau ([Massachusetts Governor Eldridge] *Gerry* + *salamander*) first appeared in print over two-hundred years ago in the *Boston Gazette*, on March 26, 1812, along with a now-famous woodblock image. In the graphic, the newly redrawn Essex South District of the Massachusetts state senate (done so at the behest of then-governor Gerry to benefit the Jefferson Republican Party) is indeed conspicuously serpentine in its contours. On the suggestion of the *Gazette*'s editors (who had contributed to the term's coinage), the painter, designer, and engraver Elkanah Tisdale (1771–1835) cleverly stylized the salamander-shaped district into a winged, arrow-tongued dragon (specifically a wyvern, given its two clawed feet).[19] "The Gerry-mander," the article's title reads: "A new species of monster, which appeared in Essex South District in January last." Broadside posters were also produced using Tisdale's illustrations and distributed throughout Massachusetts during the 1810s.[20] The original gerrymander woodcut blocks (four pieces in total) were purchased by the Library of Congress in Washington, D.C., in 2002 and since then are available for viewing in the Geography and Maps Division.[21] The practice of gerrymandering[22] itself of course continues to enjoy wide currency in American electoral geography.

The dragon as political symbol is also frequently deployed on the international stage. Not surprisingly, this manifests overwhelmingly in the form of the Chinese dragon, as mentioned in Chapter 8. To wit, the influential British weekly *The Economist* regularly employs "the dragon" as a stand-in for the People's Republic of China, whether in its reporting or in articles' accompanying graphics. A cursory search shows that, in 2022 alone, the term in this context appears in the publication at least eight times. The evocative titles of these articles include "Fatter elephant [i.e., India], leaner dragon" (18 November 2022), "Democracies and the dragon" (21 April 2022), and "Chasing the dragon" (19 February 2022).

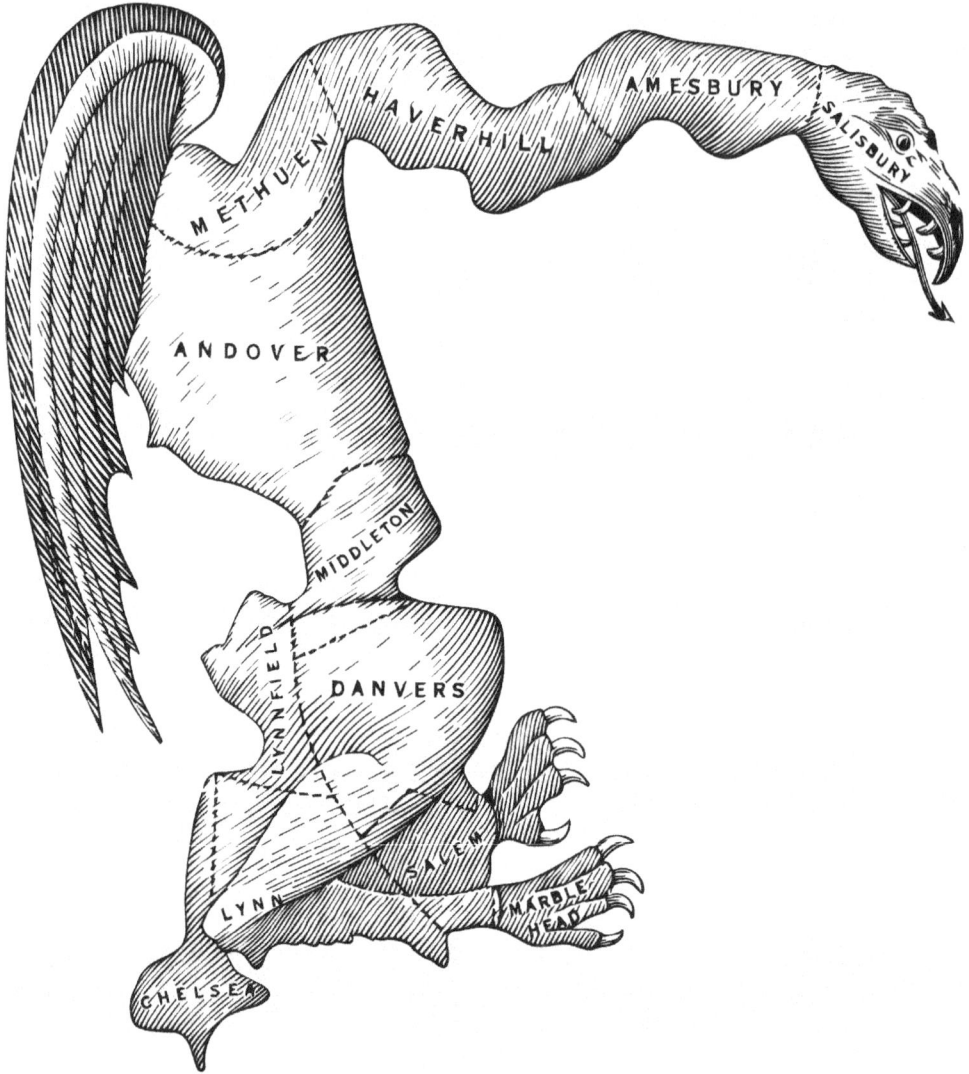

The original graphic depicting the concept of gerrymandering, by engraver Elkanah Tisdale, debuted in the *Boston Gazette* on March 26, 1812. The paper's conflation of the novel and questionable practice with the sinister nature of the Western dragon is unmistakable (Morphart Creation/Shutterstock.com).

One final use of the dragon in the political milieu is worthy of mention. This comes in the form of a high-ranking office of the American racist-terrorist group the Ku Klux Klan: "Grand Dragon." The term refers to the second tier of rank under the Imperial Wizard, thus making it akin to a governor (this is particularly apt given that the "Realms" of the Klan are coterminous with the states in which the organization is active). From its beginnings in 1867, and despite the group's national dismantling in both 1870 and 1944, each Grand Dragon has under him eight "Hydras."[23] The implication is crystal clear in that the dragon should be repurposed from a negative to a positive—or otherwise positively threatening—connotation among Klansmen.

Especially in the aftermath of the slavocratic Confederacy's defeat and dismantling, the precept of Christian lore that all dragons are unholy and evil was thus superseded by an unequivocal desire among many erstwhile Confederates and other Americans to uphold white supremacy. The dragon can just as soon be used as a vector of terror as it is of other, less immediately threatening forms of awe.

11

Dungeons & Dragons
A Realm unto Itself

The disco hot spots hold no charm for you
You can concern yourself with bigger things
You catch a pearl and ride the dragon's wings[1]

In "Discos and Dragons," the eighteenth and final episode of the short-lived teen comedy-drama *Freaks and Geeks* (1999–2000), the five members of the William McKinley High School Audio/Visual Club plan for their next campaign (gaming session) of the role-playing game (RPG) *Dungeons & Dragons*.

Meanwhile, an outsider is among them in the cramped A/V storeroom. He sits broodily in a chair against the wall, listening as he fumbles with a film reel. This is Daniel Desario (James Franco), one of the series' eponymous "freaks."

Daniel is a gritty cool guy in a leather jacket with, according to his math teacher and nemesis Mr. Kowchevski, "bedroom eyes and … stringy hair," as well as a strong anti-authoritarian bent. "He's a loser," the disgruntled educator sneers to junior Lindsay Weir, one of the show's two protagonists (the other being Lindsay's brother Sam, a freshman who is also a member of the A/V Club).

Daniel has been ordered to assist the group in providing A/V services and equipment to classrooms as punishment for his attempt to pull a school fire alarm. (He had tried to avoid a test he expected to fail … until Kowchevski caught him in the act.) Daniel, otherwise sullen during his confinement among the "geeks," pipes up to ask about their animated discussion of something called a "dancing sword." One of the geeks, seizing on Daniel's piqued interest, invites him to play. After some discussion, including pushback from Neal, a precociously cynical freshman geek, Daniel—himself a fifth-year (or possibly more) senior—accepts the invitation. "I'll play," Daniel, still surly, agrees. "Just don't expect me to be good at it or anything."

The scene depicting the geeks' campaign serves less as a primer to the rules of the tabletop, pen-and-paper RPG *Dungeons & Dragons* than as a monument to its cultural significance and appeal. At the time of the show's setting, in the fictional Detroit, Michigan, suburb of Chippewa during the 1980–81 school year, the game was already a seven-year-old phenomenon—an underground hit, if not yet the household name that it is today.

The geeks' de facto leader, sophomore Harris Trinsky (played by Stephen Lea Sheppard, himself the real-life author of several modules for the role-playing game *Exalted*) begins by explaining to Daniel that Harris is the Dungeon Master, or DM, who will administer and guide the campaign. Harris and the others also clarify to Daniel that, though Daniel has, disappointingly to him at first, rolled the dice for a dwarf player-character (PC), dwarves are strong fighters and "good at finding jewels." Daniel accedes and names his PC "Carlos."

Amazingly, the campaign goes off with gusto, as we see in montage, with all six teens, including Daniel, drinking cans of Faygo, eating junk food, and otherwise having a fun time. After the campaign's successful conclusion, a smiling Daniel asks if the group would want to play again the next night. They would, of course. He then walks off to get another drink. In hushed, conspiratorial tones, Bill Haverchuck (Martin Starr) leans in and asks his four fellow geeks: "Does him wanting to play with us again mean that he's turning into a geek? Or we're turning into cool guys?" After a beat, the others agree: "Definitely cool guys," says Sam Weir (John Daley), the group's kindly, pre-pubescent everyman (and kid brother to the show's everywoman, Lindsay, played by Linda Cardellini).

There's a certain very specific pathos, and nostalgia, that this scene conjures. For one, what plucks the heartstrings is the longing, particularly among Gen-X viewers, for the wood-paneled, shag-carpeted era before both the internet and widespread, at-home video gaming divided and conquered our attention spans. It's a simpler, quainter time. Second is the sheer sweetness of the geeks' innocence and naiveté, especially as juxtaposed against Daniel's world-weary delinquency; it seems the geeks' quirky wholesomeness might have, at least momentarily, chipped away at this freak's cynicism. The five friends may certainly be geeky in the eyes of their peers, but they are nevertheless highly sociable and collaborative—no matter what, they have each other. As actor, model, *and* avid *D&D* player Joe Manganiello explains, "People want to get together on Friday night or Saturday night with their friends around a table, and be social and play a social game, rather than staring at their phone and netting zero for the next five hours."[2] Back in 1981, the particular subculture of these fictional geeks—as well as that of the show's creator Paul Feig and his friends, upon which said geeks were closely based—was emerging throughout the United States and beyond. It had and continues to have a distinct set of rituals, a dialect (or at least a jargon), referential touchstones, and values that all members have shared, developed, and propagated together since their coalescence. The newcomer Daniel may or may not actually show up the following night to play *D&D* and continue his initiation into geekdom, and the five geeky underclassmen face slim odds of ever being considered "cool guys" at their high school. But they'll always have this one particularly glorious adventure in a realm where, as fellow-geek Gordon Crisp had quipped earlier, "[T]he best part is, you get to pretend to be somebody you can't be in real life!"

The fact that this scene serves as one of the final vignettes of the series—along with the A-plot of Lindsay ditching a summer enrichment program to instead follow the Grateful Dead—is apt. These two underground youth subcultures, by 1981, had finally reached critical mass among teenage American suburbia; they even had significant overlap in their ranks. From their origins in the heady, revolutionary social movements of the 1960s and '70s, each of these scenes presented—and, to an extent, they continue to present—not only alternative lifestyle choices but furthermore alternate worlds of imagination for freaks and geeks alike. Further, both the Grateful Dead and *Dungeons & Dragons* conjured and wove medieval, fantastical, and even semi-occult mythology and lore into their aesthetic storyworlds, very much in opposition to the mainstream sociopolitical and technological trends of the middle of the twentieth century.

There's No Such Thing as a Neutral Dragon

Fantastical beasts such as dragons, through their constantly evolving interpretations and representations, allow for extended flights of fancy in the literary sphere. But how did such things ever become an interactive game? The difference between a medieval bestiary such as the one translated by T.H. White as *The Book of Beasts* (see Chapter 5) and the various editions of the *Monster Manual* first developed by *Dungeons & Dragons'* creator Gary Gygax lies in the latter's capitalizing on such literary and mythological potential for the purposes of gameplay. We see in countless works throughout history and world cultures that such magical monsters are liberated in their fictive potential precisely *because* they are not beholden to the rules and restrictions of anatomy, biology, or reality whatsoever. To echo the fanciful, pseudo-early-modern style commonly found in the early writings of Mr. Gygax and company: dragons dwell betwixt planes. In *Dungeons & Dragons*, as lore becomes play, this in turn propagates a variety of escapism that is socially and intellectually stimulating as well as simply fun, as its many adherents have attested since 1974.

Of course, there would be no *Dungeons & Dragons* without specimens of the latter marauding in the former. According to several first-person accounts, the game's famous name itself was decided after Gygax presented several options to his young children, who had been helping him beta-test before going to market. One of Gygax's daughters was drawn to both the name's rhythmic alliteration as well as the perfect distillation of the role-playing game's fantastical aesthetic, and, according to Gygax, it is thanks to her positive reaction that such an appropriately marketable name was bestowed.[3]

In the game's roughly edited, forty-page first-edition "Monsters & Treasure" booklet, dragons are given four pages.[4] Wyverns, the smaller, two-legged "relatives of Dragons," are listed separately from, and just before, the section on "true dragons": "A Wyvern hasn't the fearsome breath as a true Dragon, but they are equipped with a poisonous sting in their tail and poison enough to use it repeatedly."[5] Due to its shading, the anatomy of the creature featured on the booklet's cover is some-what ambiguous but arguably that of a wyvern. All six of the "true Dragon" varieties described are assumed to be quadrupedal with separate wings, following the common but anatomically dubious representation of the Western dragon. Listed by color and in order of hit-point strength, they are as follows: white, black, green, blue, red, and golden.

"Breath weapons" are important attributes of *D&D* dragons. Though the common trope of fire is represented as the weapon of the Red Dragon, Gygax and company diversified the range to include, in order of each dragon's hit-point strength: "cold" (white), acid (black), chlorine gas (green), lightning (blue), and gas (golden, along with fire). "The Dragon is able to use its breath but three times per day, so sometimes it will bite instead," the authors warn.[6] Players may attempt to kill *or* to subdue a dragon, though either intention "must be announced before melee begins."[7] As for the latter option, a detailed example scenario is given, which also demonstrates the essential element of statistical probability—determined by both character attributes and rolling various types of die—to the rules of the game.

> A "Very Old," 11[-]Hit[-]Dice Red Dragon is encountered asleep in its cavernous lair. Three fighters creep in a strike to subdue. All three hit scoring respectively 2, 3, and 6 points total. 11 [2 + 3 + 6] ratioed over 66 (the number of hit points the Dragon can absorb before being killed or in this case subdued) is ⅛th or 17%. The referee [Dungeon Master] checks to determine if the Dragon is subdued and rolls over 17 on the percentile [two 10-sided (10–00 and 1–10)] dice. The Dragon is not subdued, and a check is then made to see whether he will bite or use his breath weapon during the second melee round. The result indicates he will breathe. The attackers strike again and once more all hit for a total of 12 points. The Dragon breathes and as none make their saving throws the attackers are all killed for they take 66 points of damage from the Dragon fire. Subsequently, the referee rolls 01 on the percentile dice (any roll up to 34 would have indicated success) indicating that [if] the attackers survived they would have subdued the Red Dragon that turn.[8]

(This is not a game for the mathematically faint of heart.) Furthermore, a subdued dragon can theoretically be sold for 500–1,000 Gold Pieces per hit-point potential, e.g., 33,000–66,000 for the Red Dragon mentioned above. However, this mercantile option was not continued in later versions of the game.

Three years and surely many thousands of *D&D* campaigns later, the number of the game's dragon species was doubled. In TSR's *Monster Manual,* a "special reference work" on the creatures of *Advanced Dungeons & Dragons* (*AD&D*; first published in 1977), twelve different dragon species or types are described, all by color and, as an additional innovation from the first edition, each with its own pseudo–Latin nomenclature. Alphabetically by color, they are black (*Draco Causticus Sputem*), blue (*Draco Electricus*), brass (*Draco Impudentus Gallus*), bronze (*Draco Gerus Bronzo*), chromatic (*Tiamat*), copper (*Draco Comes Stabuli*), gold (*Draco Orientalus Sino Dux*), green (*Draco Chlorinus nauseous Respiratorus*), platinum (*Bahamut*), red (*Draco Conflagratio Horriblis*), silver (*Draco Nobilis Argentum*), and white (*Draco Rigidus Frigidus*). Six types are morally aligned as evil and six as good; ethically, five are chaotic and seven are lawful; zero are neutral (see *Table 2* below).[9]

As the medieval scholar Jonathan D. Evans observes, this diverse range of draconic alignments comes in opposition to the starkly static counterparts of Tolkien's storyworld, for "None of the dragons of Middle-earth appear as powers of Good...."[10] Two of the dragon species in the *Manual* are represented by single individuals: Tiamat (chromatic) and Bahamut (platinum). The introduction to the dragon section also details such generalities as: "Dragons pass through eight ages in their lives," from very young (1–5 years) to ancient (401+ years); "All dragons see equally well in daylight or darkness," astutely referencing the original Greek meaning of *drakōn* or, "the sharp-sighted one"; and "A considerable percentage of dragons have the ability to speak one or more human languages in addition to the language of their species."[11] In addition to the twelve types, there are four dragon-like creatures: Dragonne (a lion/dragon hybrid), Dragon Turtle, Fire Lizard, and Pseudo Dragon.[12]

In *D&D*, all player-characters and non-player-characters are "aligned" in terms of their moral and ethical predispositions. Alignment is represented by a matrix and set and interpreted using a combination of a reference book (i.e., the *Monster Manual*), the rolling of dice (for player-characters), and, to a certain degree, the discretion and imagination of the Dungeon Master. With its two axes: moral (good/evil) and ethical (lawful/chaotic), the three-by-three matrix yields the following grid of nine distinct character alignments (*Table 1*):

Table 1.
Character Alignment in *Dungeons & Dragons*

Lawful Good (LG)	Neutral Good (NG)	Chaotic Good (CG)
Lawful Neutral (LN)	True Neutral (N)	Chaotic Neutral (CN)
Lawful Evil (LE)	Neutral Evil (NE)	Chaotic Evil (CE)

In the early 2010s, a popular internet meme emerged as a play on this concept, whereby nine characters or things (e.g., food, cities, etc.) are plotted—according to the judgment of the creator—onto the grid. In a March 2020 *Atlantic* article, Kaitlyn Tiffany attests that the meme was first popularized in 2012 on the now-defunct Polyvore forum, a progenitor of Pinterest, and then quickly disassociated from its origins in *D&D*. "Today," she writes, "sharing an alignment meme has much less to do with nerdy hobbies than it does with the internet's favorite petty debates, such as 'Are you supposed to wash your legs?' and 'How would dogs wear pants?' (Don't even get me started on whether cheesecake is pie.)"[13] In a game of strategy and creativity such as *Dungeons & Dragons*, this device is an important engine for character diversity and consistency. (Among other implications, the Dungeon Master may inflict penalties for straying from one's established alignment.) And while it provides part of the scaffolding on which player-characters may determine their pathways through dungeons and fight against dragons (et al.), it is not surprising that alignment has spun off from the tabletops of RPGs and into the realm of social media and the internet at large, where it has gained a wholly autonomous second life.

"If we could decide, once and for all, what is the exact best way to live," muses Kaitlyn Tiffany, "maybe everything would fall into place."[14] The desire for such control is a major appeal to role-playing games on the whole: they offer a chance to experience a series of events—the "campaign"—through an invented proxy that may serve as an alternate version of oneself and/or a distinct persona altogether, depending on individual preference as well as how the campaign's storyline progresses. The overlay of character alignment allows for a further suspension of disbelief within a surrealistic or fantastical storyworld by providing such rational parameters to player-characters and non-player-characters (e.g., monsters) alike.

Table 2.
Alignment of All Dragons Described
in *Advanced Dungeons & Dragons Monster Manual*
(First Edition, 1979 printing)

Bronze, Gold, Platinum (aka Bahamut), Silver (Lawful Good)	N/A (Neutral Good)	**Brass, Copper** (Chaotic Good)
N/A (Lawful Neutral)	N/A (True Neutral)	N/A (Chaotic Neutral)
Blue, Chromatic (aka Tiamat), Green (Lawful Evil)	N/A (Neutral Evil)	**Black, Red, White** (Chaotic Evil)

In the first episode of the *Dungeons & Dragons* Saturday-morning cartoon series (1983–85), the main characters—a band of contemporary youngsters transported to the *D&D* storyworld by an enchanted roller-coaster—first encounter an adversary in the form Tiamat the Chromatic Dragon. As in the *Monster Manual*, this version of Tiamat has five heads, each of a different color and nature: white, black, green, blue, and red, with breath weapons corresponding to the color of each head.[15] And as is Tiamat's namesake in Babylonian mythology, this dragon is female.[16] According to her entry in the *Manual,* "Tiamat rules the first plane of the Nine Hells where she spawns all of evil dragonkind. She hates all good as fiercely as she loves cruelty and hoards wealth."[17] Also according to the *Manual,* Tiamat's alignment is lawful evil. Conversely, the other singular dragon, Bahamut the Platinum, is male, lawful good, and "the King of Good dragons." He "dwells in a great fortified palace behind the east wind," his entry floridly explains. Tantalizingly, the entry continues, "(No one knows for certain if this place is on the elemental plane of air or some plane betwixt it and the Seven Heavens or Tri-Paradises, save Bahamut and his court.)"[18] Like Tiamat, Bahamut's namesake is drawn from ancient Semitic sources. A *bahamut*[19] in Arabic lore is a sea-monster, more akin to the whale-like leviathan of several books of the Hebrew Bible. In older Hebrew sources, however, the cognate *behemo(th)* ("beast[s]") is more akin to a dragon—the terrestrial counterpart to the marine leviathan. At any rate, Gygax et al. were nothing if not consistent in evenly calibrating the game's "thunder" of dragons[20] along the lines of both alignment and world mythology: the parallels of Tiamat to the Western (malevolent) and Bahamut to the Eastern (benevolent) dragons, respectively, are unmistakable, if not exactly faithful to traditional Semitic lore.

In the most recent edition of the *Monster Manual*, published in 2014, dragons remain as prominent as ever. They are first described as "large reptilian creatures of ancient origin and tremendous power." Also remaining are the alignments of the ten listed species or types of dragons (whimsical, pseudo–Latin names have been jettisoned), including the beneficence of metallic dragons and the malevolence of the chromatics.[21] Clearly, there is a consistently stark dichotomy between good and evil classes; there is no such thing as neutrality among "true" dragons in the world of *D&D*. However, the categories have been revised somewhat. Whereas "chromatic" and "platinum" once referred to two individual dragons (Tiamat and Bahamut, respectively), the former is now a general category that includes blue, green, black, red, with Tiamat as their evil queen.[22] As follows, Bahamut remains King of Good (Metallic) Dragons.[23]

As in the original 1974 "Monsters and Treasure" booklet and the *Manual*'s first edition (1977–79), in this most recent edition wyverns and pseudodragons are also relegated to "less powerful, less intelligent, and less magical" status.[24] Other draconic creatures of the 2014 edition include *dracoliches* ("dragons ... which allow themselves to be transformed by necromantic energy and ancient rituals...."[25]), as well as *shadow dragons* ("true dragons that were either born in the Shadowfell or transformed by years spent in its dismal confines"[26]) and dragon turtles, which resemble gigantic (perhaps around 75-foot-long) snapping turtles. Wyverns, as mentioned, are not lent equal status with the prestigious chromatic or metallic "true" dragons listed above. They are unaligned and considered cousins of true dragons, and they "hunt the same tangled forests and caverns as their kin."[27] Wyverns of *D&D* appear less sentient than the "true" (though, again, anatomically questionable) quadrupedal dragons, and function more as wild predators than mystical beasts. "A wyvern can be tamed for use as a mount, but doing so presents a difficult and deadly challenge," the *Manual* advises. "Raising one as a hatchling offers the best results. However, a wyvern's violent temperament has cost the life of many a would-be master."[28] No explanation is given for how or when true dragons evolved their four limbs and separate, scapular wings, but the implication is that they represent a more advanced variety than the wyverns, whose wings are formed by webbing between their fingers, much as a bat's, a physiognomy similar to that of all the dragons depicted in the *Game of Thrones* television series, as we have seen.

The *Manual*, in its several editions, functions as a latter-day bestiary, in many ways still akin to the one translated and interpreted by T.H. White as *The Book of Beasts* (1954). The distinction lies in the literary intention of each. Whereas White's source material, a Latin bestiary of the twelfth century likely transcribed at Revesby, Lincolnshire, England,[29] was an earnest attempt to catalog known Western zoological science, the *Manual* of 1977 and its successors allow Dungeon Masters to more systematically create and portray the foes he or she will unleash against player-characters as they advance through a campaign. What links both texts is the mystique and imaginative stimuli of exotic creatures. Some beasts featured in both texts are more prosaic, like dogs, categorized as "war" (uncommon) or "wild" (common) in *Advanced D&D*[30]; in White's *Book*, the description of dogs is allotted seven pages of facts, lore, and multiple illustrations,[31] while most other creatures' entries have one or two pages maximum, including dragons.

Straight Out of the Dungeon

In the 1982 made-for-TV movie *Mazes and Monsters*, based on the 1981 novel by Rona Jaffe, a college student named Robbie—incidentally, played by a young Tom Hanks in his first feature-length role—disassociates from reality and becomes psychologically trapped in the storyworld of the eponymous fantasy role-playing game. After various shifts in his personality, he eventually flees from his campus in Pennsylvania and makes his way to New York City. There, he encounters large, thunderous dragons (subway trains) and smaller, anthropomorphic ones, called "gorvils" in the fictional game's nomenclature (merely regular people whom he encounters on the street). Robbie never escapes from this delusion, though he is saved from jumping to his death from the World Trade Center by his loyal friends, also fellow gamers.

Clearly, the fictionalized game of *Mazes and Monsters* is a facile representation of *Dungeons & Dragons* and, if one had followed the national news of the previous few years, a manifestation of a contemporary moral panic. The plot is loosely based on the highly publicized real-life case of teenager James "Dallas" Egbert, who himself had had a mental breakdown and then fled from Michigan State University, his college campus. Before he was found, however, and thanks to an overly imaginative and press-loving private detective who took the case, Egbert's interest in *Dungeons & Dragons* was catapulted to the status of primary motive of the young man's troubles and disappearance, solidifying the game as suspect (or culprit) in the minds of hysterical parents throughout the United States. The incident caused no shortage of woes for the game's creators, though the heightened publicity had one major positive effect: sales of the game skyrocketed. "In the year or so following the Egbert case," writes Gygax biographer Michael Witwer, "*D&D*'s sales had jumped from $2 million to over $8 million, more than double the company's projections."[32]

When *Dungeons & Dragons* was first published in early 1974 by Tactical Studies Rules, Inc. (TSR) in small-town Lake Geneva, Wisconsin, the American pop-cultural brew of the fantastical, the subversive, and the tech-geeky had already been at a slow, rolling boil for about a decade. The game's principal creators, E. Gary Gygax (1938–2008) and Dave Arneson (1947–2009), had themselves emerged from the Upper Midwest's small but vibrant miniature-tabletop wargames scene. Such games combined historical military battles with rules that allowed for alternate outcomes, often using small figurines to represent battalions or other infantry or cavalry units. A large component of Gygax and Arneson's innovation lay in the reimagining of the figurine (or, even better, the player her/himself) as, instead of a *group* of individuals, a *singular* individual: the "player-character." Once the pair ascended from Gygax's basement after years of tinkering and toying with the concept, the word-of-mouth-fueled demand was almost immediate.[33]

The new myth, magic, and folklore-rich RPG found its audience among, at first, a set of college students highly correlated with enrollment in computer science programs. The game then very quickly attained broader cult status, spreading within only a few years to middle- and high-schoolers not unlike, respectively, the main characters of Netflix's 1980s-set *Stranger Things* (2017-present) and Dungeon Master Harris Trinsky and company on *Freaks and Geeks*. The cultural impact was targeted but widespread, as a certain subset of esoteric-minded youths finally had an outlet that was both entertaining and stimulating of creative inclinations that they otherwise may have pursued in isolation through reading, writing, or drawing. Most parents or other elders during this early stage were largely oblivious to the finer details of the game. However, by the very end of the 1970s and into the early 1980s, the phenomenon interacted with several emergent societal factors at once. Despite most of its players reporting almost nothing but positive experiences, as in the case of Dallas Egbert, *D&D* would be implicated in a years-long, nationwide moral panic over what some purported as the game's corrupting influence on particularly intellectual, sensitive youths. Included in these claims were supposed ties to not only antisocial behaviors generally but furthermore Satanism/the occult, suicide, and murder.[34]

Ultimately, any supposed causation of tragic events would be understood as what they were all along: correlations. The novelty and particular appeal of the new genre of fantasy role-playing games was what drew the attention of scandalized parents, law enforcement, and psychologists away from nuanced mental-health and societal ills; *Dungeons & Dragons* was offered up as a convenient scapegoat. But where would these authority figures have gotten this idea of the game's supposedly occult leanings? While deeply ensconced in the popular culture of today, by the early 1970s the popularization of works based in historical or revisionist medievalism (and otherwise in pre- or non–Christian cultures of the world) had yet to fully take root in the West. The original literary influences on *Dungeons & Dragons'* storyworld may at first appear to be a foregone conclusion, namely those originating in J.R.R. Tolkien's Middle-earth magisterium. But this is not without a set of caveats.

Gary Gygax, as the game's principal creator and original-rules copywriter, did acknowledge his desire to forge an immediate link with distinctly Tolkienesque humanoid races and other creatures such as hobbits, balrogs, and ents due to their inherent popularity and subcultural relevance. "The seeming parallels and inspirations are actually the results of a studied effort to capitalize on the current 'craze' for Tolkien's literature," Gygax admitted in a 1985 column. "To attract those readers…. I used certain names and attributes in a superficial manner, merely to get their attention."[35] However, he was not personally a fan of *The Lord of the Rings*

(LOTR) trilogy: "It was so dull. I mean, there was no action in it. I'd like to throttle Frodo," he clarified years later.[36] But with Tolkien references already bolstered and well-ensconced in pop culture—for example, see the LOTR- and *Hobbit*-inspired lyrics to chart-topping songs by British rock group Led Zeppelin such as "Ramble On" (1969); 1971's "The Battle of Evermore" and "Misty Mountain Hop" (if only in the title for the latter); and "Over the Hills and Far Away" (1973)—one might forgive Gygax for this somewhat disingenuous gambit. Tolkien himself had been abstractly if not presciently reticent of his work being interpreted in such an immersive way, though not necessarily from an intellectual-property standpoint. As he commented in a letter to a friend in 1955 (as the three books of *The Lord of the Rings* were still in the process of being published), "I am not at all sure that the tendency to treat this whole thing as a kind of vast game is really good—certainly not for me, who find that kind of thing only too fatally attractive."[37] Others, clearly, tended to disagree.

The matter of Gygax's sleight of hand indeed did come to a litigious head by 1977, when TSR, Inc. had grown prominent enough to be noticed and sued by a particularly aggressive representative of Tolkien's estate named Saul Zaentz, for copyright infringement. The suit was settled out of court, leading Gygax and company to instead opt for "halflings," "balor demons," and "treants" as adequate replacements for the proprietary "hobbits," "balrogs," and "ents," respectively, in the game's upcoming second edition. Despite his efforts, however, Zaentz's attempt to claim infringement over the term "dragon," was a bridge too far and ultimately deemed frivolous.[38] With or without the uniquely Tolkienesque nomenclature, Gygax had shrewdly and symbiotically fused the two franchises in the minds of serious gamers. Those who found a particularly striking appeal in fantastical, personalized quests were also statistically likely to be well acquainted with Bilbo Baggins' and his nephew Frodo's narrow escapes, respectively, in the halls and tunnels of the dragon-plagued Lonely Mountain of Erebor or the orc-haunted Mines of Moria. Thus, *Dungeons & Dragons*, officially the world's first fantasy role-playing game, steeped in sundry global motifs and creatures, especially from the pre–Christian European traditions, could not escape association with the novels that had done so much to introduce the fantasy literary genre to a mass audience earlier in the twentieth century.

Gygax's close reading of mythologist Joseph Campbell's *The Hero with a Thousand Faces* (1949) set the stage for *Dungeons & Dragons* to appeal to worldwide audiences on both an anthropological as well as on a ludological level, whereby games take on broader human concerns and meanings. By marriage, Gygax, the original Dungeon Master, was a practicing Jehovah's Witness.[39] Philosophically, however, he tended to view the world, its history, and peoples through a lens of allegory not unlike that of an animist shaman. As religious studies scholar Joseph P. Laycock writes, "The origins of *D&D* lie in fantasy, and the origins of fantasy lie in historiography[,] the product of modern man's nostalgia for sacred time."[40] It is constructive, Laycock argues, to understand gaming—and especially fantasy role-playing

Members of the Japanese organized crime syndicate known as *Yakuza* are notorious for their many tattoos. Here, gang members proudly display their ink during the 2014 Sanja Matsuri Festival, one of the three great Shinto festivals in Tokyo (M. Toth/Shutterstock.com).

games—as highly interconnected with this universal human impulse. And though derogatory claims of heathenism, Satanism, and occultism dogged Gygax and TSR while *Dungeons & Dragons* began to skyrocket in both its "cult" popularity and mainstream notoriety, he was vocal until his final days that he had never ceased believing in a higher power and strong polarities of good and evil, if not an exclusively Christian conception of God. "There's got to be a hand behind everything," he remarked in the summer of 2007, not long before his death the following spring. He was then reported as quoting the thirteenth-century Catholic theologian Thomas Aquinas: "Out of nothing, nothing comes."[41] This sense of deistic, cosmic morality is exemplified in not only his game's general rules, but also in its system of character alignment, first introduced in the rules to the game's 1974 first edition, and developed further in the 1977 *Advanced Dungeons & Dragons Players Handbook*.[42]

Out of the dungeons of his imagination had come dragons, and much more: a worldwide horde of loyal gamers that has enjoyed, celebrated, sustained, and built upon his strategic, fantastical vision for what is now almost half a century.

As for the "puerilization" of dragons so lamented by Jorge Borges in the 1960s, with the contributions of innovators like Gygax the creature experienced a further boost to its reversal as the twentieth century progressed into its final quarter.

Authority figures and "moral entrepreneurs"[43] had so relegated and discounted such mythological beasts to the realm of children's entertainment that they were wholly unprepared for their emergence in this new light. Fearmongers wrongly blamed the novel *D&D* subculture for its correlation with shocks related to the restructuring of the American family. These changes included rapidly rising rates of households with two working parents—or perhaps a single parent working two jobs—the resulting phenomenon of "latchkey kids," and the growing social acceptance of divorce and remarriage. Ironically, what may very likely have been an oasis for troubled youths was, at least for a few years, portrayed in mainstream media as a potential or actual catalyst for their insanity. (Dallas Egbert was eventually found about three weeks after his disappearance from East Lansing, Michigan, though he committed suicide the following year. The cause was clearly attributable to severe mental illness, including depression; in hindsight, playing *Dungeons & Dragons* was a respite to the troubled young man, and not the cause of his troubles.)

What *Dungeons & Dragons* has most successfully leveraged, including in its recent film adaptation, *Honor Among Thieves* (2023), is the primordial and universal human fascination with rendering the fantastical into allegory. Translator Seamus Heaney, in his analysis of the dragon in *Beowulf*, claims that the dragon possesses "real oneiric power, one that can easily survive the prejudice which arises at the very mention of the word 'dragon.'"[44] This "oneiric" or dreamlike power is perhaps linked to Jungian notions of the collective unconscious, but more practically is a reconciliation of our own dreams or nightmares against our perceptions and navigation of the regular world of our waking hours. The most inventive among us have devised the storyworlds and other structures into which this longing for the fantastical may be readily inserted. And while manifestations of the beast have nevertheless remained declawed in the now highly lucrative juvenile entertainment market up to the present day, in its fiercer forms Gygax had returned it to the focused, awed gaze of young adults through the creation and establishment of the fantasy role-playing game as a genre. As seen in the dragons of massively popular early twenty-first-century franchises such as George R.R. Martin's *A Song of Ice and Fire*, the erstwhile awesome, fearsome Western dragon has returned in even greater force after a century or so of dormancy. And is seemingly here to stay.

12

Dragons in Historical
and Contemporary Popular Visual
and Material Cultures

The beast and dragon, adored
You been gone so long
Where you been for so long[1]

The clothes and accessories we wear. The color(s) we paint our house. The type of car we drive. Our haircut. These are all representations of who we are, but also *what* we are—members of the society, country, culture, and/or time in which we are born or otherwise find ourselves. And when there exists a wide range of choices for our visual or material representations, such as in industrialized, capitalistic societies like those of the United States, much of western Europe, or Japan, the deeper meanings of these choices become even more nuanced.

Though many of the dragons discussed thus far have been literary, artists throughout the ages have sought to visually represent these monsters in media as varied as rock art (petroglyphs), tapestries, flags, coins, paintings, cartoons, comics, toys, computer-generated images, tattoos, and others. In these forms, the dragon is brought into the world in a dimension evocatively parallel with its narrative or textual counterpart, further solidifying it as the psychic presence that it has maintained since time immemorial.

Tattoos

The practice of tattooing (and scarification, as well as other forms of ritual mutilation or body modification) is ancient, originating in prehistoric times in cultures throughout the world. In English, "tattoo" itself comes to us from the common word—*tatu*, *tatau*, or something similar—a cognate found in most of the Polynesian languages (e.g., Marquesan, Samoan, Tahitian) of the south Pacific. The word was first attested in the writings of the first major British explorer of the region, Captain James Cook (1728–1779). Though common among many societies, in European or Western societies the practice has been seen as taboo (incidentally, another

Polynesian borrowing) and thus was relatively rare, at least until the last thirty to forty years. Especially among younger Americans the practice of tattooing has become not only accepted, but downright popular. According to an Ipsos poll conducted in 2019, 30 percent of Americans now have at least one tattoo, and those under fifty-five years old are twice as likely to have a tattoo as their older counterparts.[23] Not surprisingly, dragons have been and remain popular as a principal motif within this unique medium.

Recently, an acquaintance from my youth, Danny, documented his large tattoo's progress via the photo-sharing app Instagram. Danny was born in the early 1980s and has had multiple tattoos since he was in his late teens, starting in the late 1990s. His latest tattoo covers his entire back. He reported that it took approximately twenty-five hours to complete over the course of a year and a half. The artist, Gyungwook "Zen" Kim, originally of South Korea, based the design on Danny's novel concept, which comprises two main elements. The first element is the robot Evangelion Unit-01 from the Japanese anime series *Neon Genesis Evangelion* (1995–6). The second is an Eastern dragon in the style of the traditional tattoos of the infamous Yakuza organized crime syndicate, also of Japan. Though Danny is neither a Japanese national nor of Japanese descent, the iconography of that culture resonates with him, and especially so in the form of a particular trope: that of a samurai fighting a dragon. "It represents humanity in conflict with god/nature/any other higher powers," he explained. "[S]o I told the artist that I wanted a samurai versus [a] dragon [as a] back tattoo, but replace the samurai with this giant fighting robot...."[4] Danny thus combined a traditional and ancient icon (the dragon) with a figure from a much more contemporary graphical idiom (anime) to commission a piece of body art both resonant with and representative of himself as an individual and as a cultural actor. "Not only is a samurai fighting a dragon just plain cool," Danny continued, "but it also represents humanity in conflict with god/nature/any other higher powers. That concept fits with the theme of the anime as well, and once I made that connection, all the pieces for the tattoo started falling into place."

The Japanese themselves have a long tradition of dragon-themed tattooing, though its associations nowadays also include organized crime. More than their own elaborate full-body tattoos, often of dragons, which of course are often concealed by clothing, some members of the Japanese crime syndicate known as *Yakuza* are easily identified by another body modification: a mostly amputated pinky finger on the left hand. The practice, known as *yubitsume* (指詰め, literally, "finger shortening"), is a form of atonement for an offense committed, so does not apply to all members. But what is clear is that the criminal element of Yakuza and their notoriously extensive tattooing on the back and other prominent areas of the body, often including depictions of large Eastern-style dragons, are correlated, especially in the view of the Japanese public. In other words, in socially conservative Japan there is still very much a tattoo taboo. Because of tattoos' association with organized criminality, "most bathhouses will absolutely not let anyone in with tattoos," another informant (an American who is expert in Japanese language and culture) wrote to me from his home in Tokyo. "[There are] some exceptions for foreign tourists," he continued, "but in the country [i.e., rural areas] even this is not allowed. I remember once we had an orientation for foreign teachers [and] there was a [...] dude from LA with a tattoo of *kanji* [script] for 'death' on his neck. We were like, 'Buddy, you are gonna have to cover that up.'"[5]

Mascots

The NCAA Men's Basketball Tournament, popularly known as "March Madness," took place while I was writing this chapter. After a one-year hiatus due to the coronavirus pandemic, the 68-team tournament returned in 2021 as usu-

Danny Frank, a resident of Chicago, Illinois, opted for this intricate tattoo by artist Gyungkwook "Zen" Kim to combine two main elements which resonate with him: the traditional/naturalistic and the modern/technological worlds (© Gyungkwook "Zen" Kim).

ally scheduled, from late March to early April. Extra precautions were taken to avoid the spread of Covid-19, including holding most of the games in one location, in Indianapolis, to limit players' travel and thus their exposure. As in most cases of American popular culture, the dragon was not far from March Madness, either. This came in the form of that much-beloved phenomenon of (North) American popular culture, the sports-team mascot. The mascot is a subject that could potentially warrant an entire academic treatise unto itself, but a brief overview will suffice here.

Compared to other countries that may either casually employ the practice or not at all, the United States is awash with thousands of discrete and often intensely revered team mascots. The practice itself dates to at least the 1880s and arose with the popularity of baseball after the Civil War. In the 1889 book *Athletic Sports in America, England, and Australia*, which includes an account of one American baseball team's wide-ranging tour to introduce and promote the sport to other countries, the concept of the mascot is described in plain and introductory terms, ostensibly for the non-initiated reader outside of the United States. "He may be a boy possessed

of some special attainment or physical peculiarity," wrote Harry Clay Palmer, the *New York Herald* reporter who accompanied the American baseball delegation and edited the book, "or he may be a bull-pup with a prominent patch over his left eye. It matters not whether a mascot be brute or human, so long as his presence upon the players' bench insures a victory...."[6]

Sadly, the inextricable link between American mascotry and racist minstrelsy is also on full, unapologetic display in Palmer's account of "Spalding's Australian Baseball Tour." The delegation, he details, was accompanied by a young Black man named Clarence Duval who served as their mascot. Duval had "a remarkable talent for plantation dancing, 'hoe-downs' and 'walkarounds,' and the gift of baton twirling to a degree well calculated to make the average drum-major wild with envy." Lamentably to the oblivious Palmer—but most certainly not to the plainly habitually mistreated, insulted, and abused mascot—Duval "proved a deserter."[7]

Many of the modern cultural hallmarks of American athletic spectacle began to coalesce after the American Civil War with the rise of semi-professional baseball and the beginnings of the professional game. Other popular sports, such as American football, were soon to follow. Though they began as either non-human or human animals, mascots as we know them today are often a synthesis of the two: a person dressed in a costume which somehow emulates a revered or otherwise totemic creature of some kind, whether real or fictional. The "special attainments" noted by Palmer still come in the form of physical prowess or comedic skill, including but not limited to acrobatics, mime-like pratfalls, or other sight gags. In the (diminishing but still extant) cases of mascots and/or team logos that continue to portray Native American peoples, the overtly racist stain of minstrelsy remains to this day as well.

But as for dragons: One outstanding example is the mascot of one 2021 March Madness team, Drexel University of Philadelphia, Pennsylvania: a navy-blue dragon named Mario the Magnificent. According to the Drexel Athletic Department's website, the mascot was named after an alumnus named Mario V. Mascioli, "who didn't miss a Drexel game for more than 20 years." As is common to most college and professional mascots, "[Mario the Magnificent] can be seen rooting on teams from the sidelines, dancing on the court during timeouts, and causing general lighthearted mayhem...."[8] According to another, more recent Drexel alumnus, Mario is indeed generally beloved on Drexel's campus. "But the funny part about it was having a mascot that wasn't an actual, real animal," my informant told me.[9]

As it happened, Drexel University played the University of Illinois Urbana-Champaign in the first round of 2021 March Madness tournament play.[10] Mario's lighthearted mayhem was, sadly, nowhere to be found: Due to Covid-19 social-distancing and other restrictions, all team mascots were excluded from participating in the 2021 tournament.[11]

Several collegiate and professional teams are called "The Dragons" (or something similar/reminiscent thereof), in addition to those of countless elementary and high schools throughout the United States and the world. At the collegiate level,

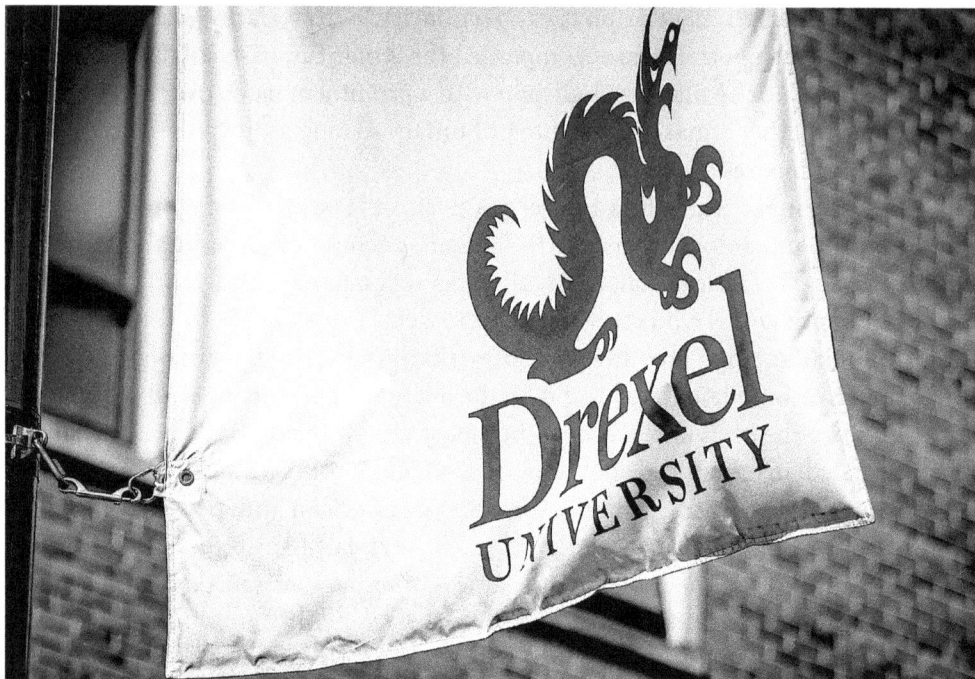

The Drexel Dragons are perhaps the best-known of collegiate teams bearing the name (Benjamin Clapp/Shutterstock.com).

Statue in honor of Drexel's Mario the Magnificent, Philadelphia, Pennsylvania, USA (quiggyt4/Shutterstock.com).

besides Drexel, examples include the University of Alabama–Birmingham—technically the Blazers, though the mascot/logo is clearly a dragon; Minnesota State University Moorhead; the State University of New York at Cortland ("Red Dragons"); Tiffin University (Ohio); and Lane College (a historically Black college in Tennessee). A total of forty-nine schools with a dragon as a mascot, at all levels and throughout the world, are listed on the website Ranker.com, not counting variations of the term such as "Blazers" or "Red Dragons."[12]

The Dragons of Drexel appear to be the most likely candidate as the first of these dragon mascots, as student-newspaper documentation shows. The previous team nickname had been, simply, "The Engineers," though this proved inadequate as the school's academic offerings diversified. A brief article of April 16, 1928, in *The Drexel Triangle* rather unceremoniously revealed the origin of the rebranding. "Due to the fact that both the Engineering and Business Administration Schools are being represented on the various athletic teams of Drexel," it read, "it has been decided to call or nickname, as the case may be, these teams, 'The Dragons.'"[13] No additional rationale for the new name was given, though it is probable that the alliteration between "Drexel" and "dragon" was a deciding factor. The following year, 1929, saw the debut of a large, multi-person dragon apparatus, one not unlike a traditional Chinese "lantern dance" dragon costume. One year later, further improvements were made to the mechanical monster, including a steel frame and new paint. In addition, as documented in a *Triangle* article of November 1930, "A small jar of titanium tetrachloride has been placed in the head with tubes leading to the nostrils. When the liquid comes in contact with the air a dense smoke is formed, resembling the traditional fiery breath of the historic [*sic*] monsters."[14] One would guess that only a team of student-engineers could be behind such a boldly scientific operation.

Flags

Dragons are quite well represented in flags from around the world, especially if we expand our scope to the historical record. On the national level, as detailed in Chapter 1, dragons serve as the central devices of the current flags (and coats of arms and emblems) of both Bhutan and Wales. And, although minuscule, there is also a dragon in the national flag (and arms) of the Republic of Malta. From the late nineteenth to the early twentieth century, an Eastern-style dragon also appeared as the central device of the flag of the Chinese Empire under the Qing dynasty. Dragons feature in the flags of one English county, as well as that of the former Anglo-Saxon kingdom it was once a part of. And the modern dragon flags of several municipalities located throughout Eurasia (whether in their flags' current or historical manifestations) are no less noteworthy. Two formerly colonial–European flags of what is now the People's Republic of China will also be considered below. In all, there are at least thirty official, current flags that feature dragons in some way, representing various levels of government throughout the world.[15] When we add verifiably historical flags, this figure leaps to something closer to fifty.

Despite the importance of dragons to the mythology of the country, China does not boast of any dragon flags. But it once did. The "Middle Kingdom" was ruled during its last imperial period by the Qing, a dynasty founded by northern Manchu (non–Han) people whose reign lasted from 1644 until 1912 (and then again briefly in 1917). At various points during this 268-year span, the domestic integrity, if not the sovereignty, of the Empire of China was severely undermined by external forces, and especially by the emerging and ever-encroaching Western colonial powers—especially Portugal, France, and Britain. These three seaborne empires maintained their military and commercial strongholds in mainland China, respectively, in the colonies or concessions of Macau; Tianjin and Kwangchow Wan (or Guangzhouwan); and Hong Kong. In 1860, at the conclusion of the Second Opium War, the power of "The Great Qing" was again undermined as it conceded trading and diplomatic rights to Britain, France, Russia, and the United States. This meant that China was forced, through treaty, to open itself to the rest of the world in a way that had hitherto been forbidden, and particularly to the highly extractive trade practices of its European and American foes as the global demand for opium and other commodities soared. Signaling this rather coerced pivot to the world stage, in 1862 the Empire of China began to represent itself with a standard national flag.

Historical accounts indicate that this initiative was motivated, at least in part, by British requests for a means to distinguish Chinese naval vessels from their civilian counterparts.[16] However, since standardized and officialized vexillography (ultimately derived from Western heraldic tradition) was a relatively novel and still semi-foreign concept in China, the "Yellow Dragon Flag" was meant to accommodate this more pragmatic, commercial need and not necessarily any other purpose.[17] Naturally, given the powerful symbolism of the dragon in *feng shui* (Chinese geomancy) and Chinese culture in general (combined with the flag's field of yellow, the color traditionally representing the Manchu people), the Qing leadership chose an azure *lóng* pursuing an auspicious flaming pearl as the nation's sigil.[18] In 1889, the flag was altered from a triangular banner to a rectangle to better assimilate to the emerging worldwide standards for national flags.[19] This latter iteration would remain in use until 1912, when the Qing monarchy was overthrown, the imperial era ended, and the Republic of China (now coterminous with the island of Taiwan only) was established.[20]

The dragon of the Republic of Malta's national flag (and coat of arms) is so relatively small that it is almost imperceptible at first glance. But embedded in the emblem at the top left corner ("upper-hoist canton" in the jargon of vexillology) is an even-limbed and red-fimbriated (outlined) cross containing the popular image of St. George on horseback as he dominates the dragon with his lance. This decoration is known as the "George Cross" and is not to be mistaken with St. George's Cross, the simple red device seen in the flags of England and the Republic of Georgia. Rather,

The first standardized international flag of the Chinese Empire, under the Qing dynasty, 1862–1889 (imperial standard) (Anupong Boonma/Shutterstock.com).

The second flag of the Chinese Empire, 1889–1912 (dancsomarci/Shutterstock.com).

the "George" in the case of Malta's cross refers not to the famous saint but to one of the saint's many namesakes, the historical King George VI of the United Kingdom and the Dominions of the Commonwealth (1895–1952; r. 1936–1952).[21] King

Detail of the George Cross bestowed by King George VI of England, the emblem found in the canton of Malta's national flag, as well as its coat of arms. The British monarch's ultimate namesake, St. George, is centrally featured (Save nature and wildlife/Shutterstock.com).

George awarded his cross to Malta—a British crown colony from 1813 to 1964—on April 15, 1942, to "bear witness to the heroism and devotion of its people" while the tiny island was besieged by the Italians and Germans in the early years of the Second World War. Echoing England's devotion to the legendary saint, within a silver medallion over the cross is a depiction of St. George and the dragon. Surrounding this is a ring which reads, "FOR GALLANTRY." Each corner of the cross is adorned with a "VI" cipher representing the now-independent nation's erstwhile British sovereign and patron, George VI.[22]

"The Saxons of Wessex," wrote the vexillologist (flag scholar) W.G. Perrin, "adopted as their principal war standard the dragon, which in various forms was destined to appear at many crucial moments in English history."[23] From 519–927 CE, Wessex was not a mere shire (county) but rather an independent kingdom in southern Britain under Anglo-Saxon (as opposed to Celtic) rule. The territory's name essentially means "[the Kingdom of the] West Saxons."[24,25] As the King of the

West Saxons (871–886 CE) and later of all the Anglo-Saxons (886–899), Alfred the Great and his countrymen had staved off the Vikings of the Danelaw (what is now northern and eastern England) with a primordial version of the Wessex flag in hand. Almost two-hundred years later, Harold Godwinson, the Earl of Wessex and the last Anglo-Saxon king of England, also supposedly had by his side the dragon standard of Wessex—more specifically a golden (or sometimes red) wyvern—when he was killed in battle on October 14, 1066, by knights under the command of Duke William of Normandy. The victorious duke would forever be known to history as King William I or simply "William the Conqueror," the first Norman king of England. This dramatic battle scene—including the dragon standard of Wessex— is depicted in embroidery on the sequentially narrative Bayeux Tapestry, itself created not long after the fateful Battle of Hastings in the late eleventh century.[26] The elaborate, 230-foot (70 m) by 20-inch (50 cm) piece was lost for several centuries but rediscovered in 1729; it is presently housed and exhibited at Musée de la Tapisserie de Bayeux in the arrondissement of Bayeux in Normandy, France. Inspired by its renowned emblem of yore, the current regional or community flag for Wessex—a golden wyvern on a field of red—was designed by William Crampton and registered with the UK's Flag Institute in 1974.

The English traditional and ceremonial county of Somerset lies in the western reaches of what was once the Kingdom of Wessex. Like Wessex, Somerset too boasts of a dragon flag, clearly indicating an affinity between its red dragon on a field of

Detail view of the Bayeux Tapestry, Bayeux, France, wherein King Harold Godwinson's shield bears the golden-dragon emblem of the Kingdom of Wessex (jorisvo/Shutterstock.com).

The flag of the Anglo-Saxon Kingdom of Wessex (519–927 AD) was recreated by vexillographer William Crampton in 1974 (Momcilica/Shutterstock.com).

The modern flag of the County of Somerset, UK (twenty1studio/Shutterstock.com).

yellow, and Wessex's (usually) golden wyvern on red. Though influence from the flag of Wessex is also likely, according to the Association of British Counties (ABC), both cases suggest an older Roman via Celtic origin. (Somerset lies just across the Bristol Channel from Wales and, furthermore, all of Britain was predominantly Celtic before the Anglo-Saxon migrations of the early Middle Ages.) This theory would imply that the Welsh *Ddraig Goch* itself possibly also drew inspiration from the *vexilla draconis* of the occupying Roman legions. "In essence therefore," states the ABC, "the flag is a traditional design with a pedigree of over a thousand years." A contest was held in 2013 to determine the County of Somerset's official flag and, naturally, this ancient motif was chosen as the winner.[27]

The *zilant* is a variety of dragomorph particular to the Russian Federation, but it is not Slavic or even Indo-European in origin. Rather, it originates from the Tatars, the Turkic people of Tatarstan, in the southwest of the Russian Federation. Kazan, the capital of this republic, bears the wyvern-like zilant on its flag in a context that potentially interacts with that of the greater national capital. According to a synopsis of the city's legendary origin published by the Museum of the Kazan National Research University (KAI),

> Kazan was built on a place where there was a multitude of snakes. A Tatar sorcerer lit bonfires and spoke magic words. The snakes perished, but the snake-king Zilant escaped to a neighboring mountain, called *Dzhilantai* (Snake Mountain). On the site thus liberated people built a city. However, they were unable to live in peace, as the snake-king who had settled nearby brought misery on them. Fortunately, in the city there appeared a mighty magician, Hakim, who was able, by mighty conjurations, to kill the snake-king. In memory of this occurrence a representation of Zilant is still a civic emblem among the Tatars.[28]

According to some scholars, the familiar image of the dragon being speared by St. George—the central device of Moscow's municipal flag—may be interpreted as a thinly veiled reference to Russian colonialism and domination over the federation's Turkic (and predominantly Muslim) minorities.[29] This is but one interpretation, of course, as symbolic modes or systems such as vexillology and heraldry may be interpreted in myriad ways based on their specific uses and contexts. But the case bears contrasting the roles of dragons as potent metaphors among these two distinct ethno-linguistic groups: for the Tatars, their "snake-king" has been repurposed as protector and champion, a great friend of the people to be honored and revered; and for the ethnic Russians (as it is for many other, but not all, Christo-European groups), the dragon is a vile foe to be destroyed in the name of all that is holy. At any rate, the word *zilant* comes to Russian from the Tatar language, wherein *yılan* (or *елан* in Cyrillic script) is the common word for snake. When Tatar speakers specify a large, dragon-like serpent in their own language, however, they more commonly use *Ajdaha-yılan*, "dragon-snake," borrowing the Persian word for the mythological creature as a modifier.[30]

Like Tatarstan's Kazan, Ljubljana, the capital of the Republic of Slovenia, is a city protected by a dragon. Its municipal flag (and coat of arms) shows a green quadrupedal dragon atop a white castle, the claws of its front and back feet balanced on the tower's crenellations.[31] The iconic creature is also found in local statuary, most famously on the city's *Zmajski Most* or Dragon Bridge. Like the Welsh and the Tartars, in their iconography the Slovenians have maintained a less purely antagonistic

The principal device of the flag of the city of Kazan, Tatarstan is the *zilant*, a benevolent draconic creature of Turkic legend (Baka Sobaka/Shutterstock.com).

The flag of the City of Moscow, Russian Federation displays the familiar St. George the Dragonslayer motif, perhaps as a point of Euro-Christian hegemony (grebeshkovmaxim/Shutterstock.com).

relationship with the dragon and instead view it as a potential—if not fully domesticated—ally; it serves as a brute guardian against outside threats and foes. However, Ljubljana's municipal website explains that such a symbiotic arrangement was not achieved without a "fight":

> Between the present-day Vrhnika [another city in Slovenia] and Ljubljana the Argonauts [of ancient Greek legend] found a big lake surrounded by a marsh. It was here that Jason came across a terrible marsh monster, which he fought and eventually slew. This monster was the Ljubljana dragon, which today has its permanent abode on top of the castle tower in the Ljubljana coat of arms.[32]

As also seen in the case of Kazan, before Ljubljana's dragon could be reborn as a symbolic protector, it first had to be "slain." It also displays a close affinity with the Byzantine (and likely older) tale of St. George, detailed in Chapter 5. This same lore is also the source of the dragon-flag of another Slovenian city: that of Kozje, on the border with Croatia.[33]

Five thousand, five hundred fifty miles (8,931 km) away from Ljubljana, and 6,825 miles (10,984 km) from Lisbon, Portuguese merchant-adventurers had established Macau as their colonial outpost in China when they first leased the coastal area from the then-ruling Ming dynasty in 1557. The small concession would remain under Portuguese rule until 1999, when, as Hong Kong had been two years prior (from the British), it was handed over to the People's Republic of China as a special administrative region (SAR). Throughout this almost half millennium, a distinct culture arose in Macau fusing primarily Portuguese with Chinese (Cantonese) elements. Despite such extended contact, however, today only a small minority—less

The flag of the city of Ljubljana, Slovenia (Illustration Contributor/Shutterstock.com).

than 3 percent—of the Macanese population (about 700,000) reportedly speaks Portuguese fluently.[34] Mandarin, as the undisputed majority language of China, is on the rise in Macau and even English appears to have surpassed the territory's former colonial language in common usage. As for its other cultural touchstones, a 2018 *Reuters* article reported, "These days, the only real remaining elements of Portuguese influence are colonial architecture and its distinctive cuisine."[35] It comes as no surprise, then, that Macau's heyday as a uniquely Sino-European hybrid came and went before the waning Portuguese Empire's last-ditch attempts at maintaining a "pluricontinental nation" in the twentieth century, an era in which its colonies were half-heartedly granted the status of "overseas provinces." As such, a series of insignias for all the colonies-cum-provinces was proposed whereby each was integrated into a shield in the lower-fly canton (bottom right corner) of Portugal's still-current national flag (standard), popularly known as the *Bandeira das Quinas* (literally, "Flag of the Sets of Five"). Prior to this proposal, all eight of the remaining Portuguese-controlled territories—Angola, Cabo Verde, Goa, Portuguese Guinea (Bissau), Macau, Mozambique, São Tomé and Príncipe, and Timor—would have simply flown the Portuguese standard.

The proposed shield/coat of arms for the *Província Ultramarina de Macau*, described in a 1935 decree by the Portuguese Colonial Ministry, is as follows: "In a field of blue, a golden dragon with a red tongue and claws, and outlined in black, holds in its claws one of the *quinas* of Portugal."[36] This unique device occupied the right-hand third of the shield; the other two thirds, which were standard for all eight overseas colonies/provinces, were, at left, a set of five *quinas* (described below) and, at bottom, white and green waves indicating the sea. A *quina* ("set of five [things]"), of which the standard Portuguese flag already has five within its principal coat of arms, is a smaller blue shield (*escutcheon*) with five silver dots (plates or *bezants*) in a saltire or *quincunx* pattern (much like the "five" side of a die). Macau's overseas-provincial flag, therefore, would have included a total of eleven *quinas* and thus fifty-five bezants. But of most interest is the phenomenon of Macanese cultural fusion, herein exemplified by a classic, four-fingered Eastern golden dragon proudly bearing a quintessentially Portuguese *quina*. Later in the twentieth century, and until the power transfer of 1999, this golden dragon/*quinas* insignia was reset over a five-castled armillary sphere to become Portuguese Macau's *de facto* flag. Since 1999, an entirely different design—featuring a lotus flower on a field of green and otherwise reflecting exclusively Chinese rather than predominantly Portuguese motifs—has been hoisted as the official flag of the newly incorporated SAR Macau.

It is easy to observe the parallels between the political history of Macau and that of Hong Kong. Both concessions were the result of European military and colonial opportunism during an era of sovereign vulnerability in China, before its massive and often tumultuous projects of political and ideological consolidation in the aftermath of the Communist Revolution of 1949. Unlike Portugal's sixteenth-century acquisition of Macau, Great Britain had captured and established

The coat of arms featured on the flag of the former Portuguese Overseas Territory of Macau (1976–1999) combines both Portuguese and Chinese symbolism (Mauro Rodrigues/Shutterstock.com).

its Chinese merchant-colony relatively late; it was awarded by the Treaty of Nanking of 1842, which had ended the First Opium War in Great Britain's favor. The new crown colony of Hong Kong quickly overtook Macau in strategic and commercial importance. As mentioned, Hong Kong transitioned to Chinese rule only two years before Macau, in 1997, though Hong Kong's relationship with the People's Republic of China since then has been undoubtedly more fraught, and especially in the several years leading up to and including 2020. These factors have resulted in a marked topicality regarding the old colonial Hong Kong flag of 1959–1997 that does not find a direct analog in the case of Macau.

Wrote one observer of Hong Kong's transfer of power from Great Britain to the People's Republic of China on July 1, 1997,

> For flag fans, the handover ceremony was a real bonanza thanks to the British for putting on a real pomp and circumstance show. For vexillologists, we were given a real treat as we watch [*sic*] all the various proceedings from the British Governor leaving his Residence and watching the Union Jack defaced with the Governor's badge being lowered for the last time to the cutover to Beijing where thousands were gathered holding both the China and the Hong Kong Special Administrative Region flags to the final hour when everyone was gathered for the formal flag ceremony.[37]

Like SAR Macau's current official flag, SAR Hong Kong's has little to nothing to do with its former colonial counterpart. Yet such a distinction has only heightened

As in Macau, the coat of arms featured on the flag of the former British Overseas Territory of Hong Kong (1959–1997) presents a fusion of European and Chinese symbolism (Illustration Contributor/Shutterstock.com).

the latter's semiotic resonance among Hong Kong's pro-democracy activists as they have protested Beijing's encroaching control over the territory, which was intended to exist under a "one country, two systems [of government]" policy after 1997. Since July 2020 and the passage of the "Law of the People's Republic of China on Safeguarding National Security in the Hong Kong Special Administrative Region (HKSAR)," such a special arrangement is effectively no longer the case. But leading up to such autocratic legislation, massive and often violent street protests against the forces of Beijing erupted throughout Hong Kong. Especially before the coronavirus pandemic overtook the global narrative in early 2020, this political movement caught the world's attention. Often seen among the throngs of predominantly young dissident Hong Kongers was their old colonial flag, established on July 27, 1959: a blue Union Jack ensign defaced[38] by a badge or coat of arms featuring two golden lions rampant (one facing right, the other left), two square-rigged sailing ships, and, much akin to Macau's own erstwhile emblem, a golden, red-clawed, red-tongued, and four-fingered Eastern dragon. The messaging of the bearers of this flag, given the context, was abundantly clear: Hong Kong's tradition of and preference for British- (or Western-) style, parliamentary democracy is embedded in the territory's hybrid culture, and it would not be replaced without a fight.

Coins and Stamps

Like vexillology (the study of flags), the practices of numismatics and philately (the study or collection of coins and stamps, respectively) might be dismissed by the incurious as esoteric or even trivial hobbies.[39] And while "coin collecting"

The former flag of Hong Kong, along with those of the United States and others, *in situ* during protests against Beijing on September 29, 2019 (Amar Aziz/Shutterstock.com).

and "stamp collecting" may be more so household terms than "the study of flags" (much less the mouthful of "vexillology"), all three pursuits are significant subfields of semiotics. All are also made particularly relevant by the habitual and perpetual usage of flags, coins, and postage stamps throughout most modern human societies. All three are furthermore representative of material forms imbued with a wide range of symbolic meanings relevant to both the political, historical, and economic spheres (often all three), hence their high collectability. It is also no coincidence that the dragon figure is well represented in coins and stamps, both (usually) state-issued artifacts that, like flags, serve to efficiently represent the values and interests of the governments and/or societies which produce them.

Most experts estimate that metal coins have been in use since about 900 BCE, originating among the Lydians of what is now Turkey. The first postage stamps have a much more recent vintage, however, having emerged as a standard practice only since about 1840, when the British "Penny Black" stamp was first issued. Of course, another distinction between the two forms is that the former is almost always metallic and thus highly durable, often lasting many centuries or more in recognizable form; the latter is almost always made of paper and thus quite fragile, necessitating more meticulous care for proper preservation.

Many of the oldest coins which feature dragons were minted and circulated in imperial China and Japan. As in these nations' flags and other iconography, the dragons on these coins were invariably all beneficent representations.[40] Interestingly,

This British two-pound golden coin of 1893 displays Queen Victoria (d. 1901) on the obverse and St. George the Dragonslayer on the reverse (Yaroslaff/Shutterstock.com).

This Japanese silver one-yen coin of 1885 features a dragon guarding a pearl, a common motif in Far Eastern folklore (Yaroslaff/Shutterstock.com).

with the advent of the People's Republic of China in 1949, creatures more commonly struck onto coinage than dragons include unicorns and pandas.[41] As in its national flag, several series of Bhutanese coinage feature their interpretation of the Eastern dragons as well.[42] Representative of the commonly malevolent dragon depicted in most Western nations, that which appears on the coins of Great Britain, for example, is either the familiar image of St. George's quarry as it is trampled by his horse or, in the case of coins referring to Wales, the equally familiar *Ddraig Goch* of that principality.[43] Though even more difficult to discern than the image on Malta's state flag due to its tiny scale, St. George's dragon-slaying scene within the George Cross is

The Aztec god Quetzalcoatl was featured on the obverse of this Mexican five-peso coin of 1980 (Yaroslaff/Shutterstock.com).

found on a fiftieth-anniversary commemorative coin the tiny island nation issued in 1992, among others.[44] We predictably also find St. George and his dragon on coinage from Ethiopia minted in the early 1930s, immediately prior to the Italian invasion and short-lived conquest.[45] And a five-peso piece minted by Mexico in 1980 depicts that country's dragonesque pre–Columbian (Aztec) god, Quetzalcóatl.[46]

Relative to flags and especially coins, the ephemeral nature of postage stamps is due in large part to the enormous volume of physical mail sent every day throughout the world, especially before the advent of the internet and email. A high degree of design variation and stylistic turnover are thus commonplace. But, more practically speaking, national postal services are incentivized to regularly produce new designs not only because of the frequent changes in postage pricing, but also because a considerable market exists among philatelists (the collectors of postage stamps) for commemorative, historically notable, or otherwise rare specimens. These products thus generate considerable sums for their respective services' own operations. And to keep production costs low, the images depicted on postage stamps may sometimes be drawn, seemingly at random, from the public domain. This practice is seen, for instance, in a 1983 Laotian stamp featuring a segment of Italian Renaissance painter Raphael's *c.* 1505 painting of St. George slaying the dragon, a masterpiece currently housed at the Louvre. But what does the Southeast-Asian nation of Laos have to do with Raphael? Practically nothing. Using such well-known works that are not under copyright and thus free to reproduce is simply preferable to procuring original designs by professional artists, whose labor is invariably much more expensive and time-consuming. Another interesting "fair use" of the St. George-versus-the-dragon image is seen in a Greek stamp from 1960: to commemorate fifty years of the Scouting Movement in the country, a Greek Boy Scout in full dress takes the place of the famous holy warrior, his spear about to plunge into the gaping maw of the hideous

This Laotian stamp of *c.* 1983 bears the public-domain image of Raphael's *St. George and the Dragon* (*c.* 1505) (YANGCHAO/Shutterstock.com).

beast. The Christian symbolism remains potent, however, as the silhouette of the scout is clearly that of St. George himself—shield, halo, and all. National and societal virtues are thus efficiently signaled, all within the minute confines of a common postage stamp.

A stamp commemorates the 50th anniversary of the Boy Scout Movement in Greece (1960) via the familiar imagery of the St. George the Dragonslayer legend (Lefteris Papaulakis/Shutterstock.com).

Whither the Dragon?

The Twenty-First Century and Beyond/Conclusions

Imagine Dragons? No thanks; I'll have nightmares![1]

My working title for this book, *Big Dragon Energy*, was tongue in cheek. This will be self-evident to even casual sojourners to the realms of popular/youth culture embedded in today's internet-based and Americanized English-speaking (or, at least, -reading) world of mass media. But to be perfectly transparent, it is a fusion of two separate coinages from internet culture/slang: "Dragon energy," as we saw in Chapter 1, is a novel though not entirely original phrase popularized via Twitter by the now-disgraced rapper and artist Kanye West in 2018. It was likely drawn from or at least influenced by an early exposure to concepts common to Chinese Taoism, though the particulars remain unclear. The other element—the expression "big dick energy"—also emerged and gained traction around 2018.

According to the crowdsourced UrbanDictionary.com, the top-rated definition of "big dick energy" is as follows:

> The loud and boisterous energy emitted by someone who has a colossal phallus and doesn't have to tell anyone about it. The energy speaks for itself. The Big Dick tells it's [*sic*] own story. Everyone strives for big dick energy. Only few possess such a gift. People with big dick energy possess qualities such as leadership, kindness, positivity towards others, great humor, and a "dont [*sic*] fuck with me" aura. Great hair too.[2]

For reasons that I hope are obvious given the above, a combination of the two phrases made perfect sense as the title for a book with a focus on both the distant past and immediate present of dragon lore. Even though this book's present, more anodyne title eventually won out, this "Big Dragon Energy" powered me through its writing.

Given the timeliness of so much of the dragon-related popular culture considered in this book, the broader historical moment that coincided with its writing should also be further addressed.

The period 2020–22 (and arguably beyond) has been defined by not only a pandemic of the body, but also by one of the mind. Many scholars and journalists now refer to this latter condition as an *infodemic*. Admittedly, infodemic is not quite a household term yet—it is not even recognized as a word by the version of Microsoft

Word that I am currently using to write this text. Though it has recently been critiqued by some as a facile summation of a highly complex set of phenomena,[3] it is nevertheless worthy of mention here.

The online, crowd-sourced dictionary Wiktionary.org defines "infodemic" as

1. (*informal*) An excessive amount of information concerning a problem such that the solution is made more difficult
2. (*informal*) A wide and rapid spread of misinformation[4]

And, as to not rely exclusively on an online dictionary sometimes critiqued for its open-access model (itself a critique that we may place firmly within the infodemic hypothesis), the following is the *Oxford English Dictionary*'s definition: "A proliferation of diverse, often unsubstantiated information relating to a crisis, controversy, or event, which disseminates rapidly and uncontrollably through news, online, and social media, and is regarded as intensifying public speculation or anxiety."[5] The latter further attributes the word's coinage to the *Washington Post*'s David J. Rothkopf in an article of May 2003 about the SARS outbreak. It had virtually disappeared in both news media and academic literature until Covid-19 and its worldwide impacts brought it roaring back.

The year 2020, even before the worldwide ravages of Covid-19 fully set in, one could argue, was one already infected by unhinged conspiracy theories, toxic political discourse, and outright lies at multiple levels of power throughout the world. Add to this quagmire of nightmarishly magical thinking and autocratic motives a novel virus that cared neither for international borders nor political affiliations; the tragic result was an explosion of mis- and disinformation, confusion, despair, and rage alongside equally shocking levels of sickness, violence, and death. And though, primarily thanks to an unprecedentedly rapid development of vaccines, this two-headed dragon of a plague has subsided somewhat—at least as of the time of this writing, in 2023—it continues to threaten both human life and the very systems of liberal democracy that the world has come to know since the end of the Second World War.

What particularly stands out to me about this moment, and more specifically in my home country of the United States, has been the markedly extreme adoption of, or perhaps reversion to, powerful symbols and tokens—totems, we may call them—as subjective guiding principles against the objective systems that underlie them. An immediately glaring example of this has been the often-obstreperous controversy over simply wearing a mask to help prevent the spread of an uncontrolled (and, before vaccines were introduced, mostly uncontrollable) virus. To a not insignificant segment of the population, the totem of *not* wearing a mask as an assertion of political affiliation or ideology outweighed any risks of contracting a potentially deadly virus.

Such paroxysms of unreason are anything but new—the span of human of history is riddled with them. But why and how do they keep happening? One way to view these issues is through the lens of semiotics, the study of signs, symbols, and meaning.

In the late nineteenth century, the Swiss linguist Ferdinand de Saussure (1857–1913)—considered the founder of the field of semiotics—developed what he dubbed the "model of the sign." This theory established the relationship between *signifiers* (such as the words in a language) and the *signified* (those words' empirical meanings). Signifiers are (mostly) arbitrary sounds or their corresponding written symbols,[6] whereas the signified are linked more firmly to phenomena governed by the natural laws of physics. For example, the sign "water" in the English language is a two-syllable utterance (/ˈwɔːtə/ or /ˈwɔtəɹ/,[7] in the standard British and American dialects, respectively), or otherwise a set of five written characters of the Latin alphabet: *water*. Empirically, what we're referring to is the liquid form of H_2O (or "dihydrogen oxide" in the slightly more universal, though still ultimately arbitrary, Greek-derived jargon of physical science). Most importantly, what we're referring to here is that clear, wet stuff that we feel compelled to drink when we're thirsty and is also abundant on Earth in oceans, lakes, rivers, etc. In the Tagalog (*Filipino*) language, however, "water" is not *water*; it's *tubig*. Though these two ultimately arbitrary signs may differ, the substance signified is nevertheless one and the same.

In times of confusion or turmoil this already tenuous relationship between signifier and signified may be in effect reversed: abstract, figurative representation—the signifiers or symbols that overlay ideology and, especially the ideologies of fundamentalist religion and authoritarian politics—often violently overtake the signified substance. The result is a re-appropriation or even negation of those observable objects and phenomena that form the basis of our shared, observable reality. To continue with our analogy from above, this would be as if those who use *tubig* declared war against those of us who call it "water." *How can it be both? It must be only one!*

The signifier, in the most recent infodemic, *became* the signified. What was once the deeper, signified meaning (the *signification* in Saussure's model) was either marginalized or discarded outright. Thus, statements such as "I am covered in the blood of Jesus" became a relatively common retort of some who were asked why they were unfazed by the threat of contracting the fast-spreading coronavirus, or otherwise were opposed to receiving a free and abundantly available vaccine against it. We can more accurately label this semiotically reversed or scrambled mode of perceiving reality as magical thinking, or even word-magic—the act of willing something to be (or not) through linguistic formulae, spells, or incantations.

The relation between these more topical or political matters to a book that is ostensibly about dragons of all things may seem, at first glance, tenuous, I'll readily admit. Yet the link is inherent to the reversion to magical thinking that has not only taken place but spread in tandem with the novel coronavirus itself. Such a shift is still the result of a consensus, albeit a stochastic one—in this case the "spray" of human psychology through our newfangled and imperfectly regulated (yet highly effective) prisms or filters of information-technology, telecommunications, and social-media platforms. Mythological or totemic stories, figures, or systems constitute symbolic, metaphoric, or literary manifestations of real human concerns, and thus also present a kind of prism, albeit one much more ancient than our modern technologies. In the case of the dragon, and especially in the West, the fears which such figures represent often include that most basic dread of physical predation; of the more abstract but still potentially urgent spiritual damnation, if not more precisely a kind of societal and/or genetic annihilation; or otherwise of individual or collective futility amid some brute or otherwise irresistible force. Though unequivocally disturbing, it is thus not an entirely random tragedy that a man from Santa Barbara, California, in August of 2021, murdered his own small son and daughter because he believed that their mother, his wife, "possessed serpent DNA and had passed it on to [them]." Influenced by the unhinged conspiracy theories of "QAnon," an amorphous, internet-centric ideology which in part purports a covert reptilian-alien invasion of Earth, this now-convicted murderer appears to have truly believed that he was "saving the world from monsters."[8]

On the contrary, in other cultural contexts—namely, as we have seen, the East-Asian sphere, with China at its gravitational center—the dragon as it emerges from the mythological/allegorical prism is instead one of beneficence: sentiments of luck, fertility, abundance, auspiciousness, or prosperity dominate to a charismatic degree. For many centuries, and still in many societies today, such monsters were not only believed to be real, but furthermore played and may still play outsized roles in daily modes of life, from common medicinal remedies to foundational oral folklore and societal moral structures; to the interpretation of natural cycles, such as the seasons and annual harvests; and to traditional cosmogonies and cosmologies on their broadest terms.

Based on general trends, it appears that these disparate interpretations across human cultures may be correlated directly with a given society's relationship with nature, a postulate that has been explored elsewhere in this book. Suffice it to say, some scholars argue that what we call "dragon" in the West is a mythological creature altogether unrelated to that which the Chinese call *lóng* (龍).[9] Others, such as the American linguist Robert Blust, firmly (though controversially) contend that the dragon, in all its possible manifestations, "stands as one of the supremely instructive examples of convergent evolution in the symbolic life of the mind."[10]

Whatever the cultural context, it is important to establish that, despite humans' advances in technology or systems of social and/or legal justice, magical thinking, for better or for worse, is nevertheless inherent to our species. But magical thinking plus the world-beating technology of modernity strikes a distinctly novel chord. As the late American biologist E.O. Wilson wrote,

> Humanity today is like a waking dreamer, caught between the fantasies of sleep and the chaos of the real world. The mind seeks but cannot find the precise place and hour. We have created a Star Wars civilization, with Stone Age emotions, medieval institutions, and godlike technology.[11]

These "Stone Age emotions," so often leading to the very magical thinking in question, present the most consistent foils to our faculties of reason. Our inability to reconcile the two presents an inherent liability on a societal or even a species-wide basis. Yet this conflict or dissonance is also the source of much of our finest works of literature and other narrative arts: the questions and hypotheticals that emerge from this crucible can deeply enthrall and enchant us, as both creator and beholder. And though they may often be in conflict, magical thinking and reason are perhaps even better described as being in a state of symbiosis. This duality is why the dragon has never gone extinct ... even though it never existed. Spanish master-painter Francisco Goya framed this dynamic most aptly when he captioned his eponymous aquatint of about 1799. In his

This haunting late-eighteenth century aquatint by Spanish painter Francisco Goya (d. 1828) bears the caption "The sleep of reason produces monsters" (Everett Collection (1868 reproduction)/Shutterstock.com).

phrasing, "The sleep[12] of reason produces monsters (*El sueño de la razón produce monstruos*)." Put another way: When we set aside our waking reason, monsters (not to mention angels) often begin to appear. For most of us, reason sleeps just as we do, every night or (usually) at least once every day or so. But when we wake, our dreams and nightmares do not always disappear into oblivion. Rather, some of them hide in the shadows, waiting.

Cyber Dragons

Among the lobster, tortoise, cat, dog, whale, and many other creatures available as emoji, the logographic characters now ubiquitous in digital text messaging systems, the dragon stands alone as the only mythological one. This is telling. Without fanfare, the ancient monster has followed humanity straight into the throes of the digital era in this and myriad other ways. It is not surprising that the dragon should be represented as a creature both endemic to the internet, but also one where its many pre-internet manifestations are thoroughly documented.

One relatively early denizen of cyberspace has been documenting dragons for over twenty years now. "One of my favorite toys was a big green dragon that I stole—I mean *borrowed*—from my sister," reports Kylie McCormick, by way of introduction. "I've always been very interested in dragons." By vocation, McCormick, a native of Connecticut, is a software engineer living in North Carolina. But her longer-term avocation is as a webmaster, and more specifically as a digital dragonmaster. Since 2000, McCormick, who also goes by the pseudonym "drago," has built and maintained the online dragon encyclopedia and forum *The Circle of the Dragon* (*blackdrago.com*). I wanted to know more about the nexus of dragons and the internet, so naturally I turned to McCormick, whose site appears at the top of Google search results on the topic.

McCormick first created the basic components of her dragon site when she was still in high school, and just as a hobby, she admits. It didn't have its own domain until about 2002 and for quite a while the project "started out as an excuse for finding more information," she explained. "This was around the time when websites started to be about information."[13] Before that, in the dragon realm at least, the trend towards puerility was still in full effect. But McCormick strove to capture the full range of dragonology in the then still-novel medium of the website, which held an advantage over all others in its potential for constant revisions, additions, and reinventions, not to mention accessibility to a wide and indeed global readership.

But that global access was also revealing. As McCormick began to receive feedback on her site, she came to realize the need for greater cultural sensitivity. She also noticed the seemingly inevitable tendency of a certain subset of netizens towards the occult and conspiracy theories. As such, she decided that an "About" page would be helpful to preempt frequently asked questions and concerns. She thus offers the following set of rather stern caveats to all readers:

1. This site doesn't provide information on contacting dragons, serpents, or other religious spirits, past or present, through any form of magic, medium, or supernatural means.
2. This site doesn't provide information on religious or spiritual practice of any variety, pertaining to dragons or otherwise.
3. This site doesn't provide information of any kind that suggests, insinuates, or implies any methods of summoning, conjuring, or otherwise contacting a dragon in anyway [*sic*], shape or form.[14]

McCormick explained to me that such fine print became necessary over the years, as she saw an increase in the volume of email inquiries as the site rose in exposure. After filtering out questions that are already answered by the "About" section, she fields questions as broad as students looking for general help with dragon-related research papers and as specific as why Catholics have two more chapters in their Book of Daniel than Protestants do.[15] But most importantly, what McCormick's and others' expansive, web-based reference projects reveal is the massive shift of literary sources from a predominantly print-based medium to a digital/electronic-focused context. This shift has proceeded in earnest since around 1995, and the implications of it on the content of narrative storytelling and cultural imaginaries themselves have been profound.

To maintain scholarliness on her website, McCormick has incorporated a thorough bibliography, even though, as she told me, "I started this [website] before I even knew what a bibliography was or why you should have one."[16] She confirmed that, as interest in her site and its contents continues to grow, such epistemological diligence is even more crucial. And considering some visitors may sincerely wish to attribute magical significance to their reading and interpretation of her website's contents, as belied by its three notices above, the more citations the better.

Then again, if one truly believes in the existence of dragons, perhaps no number of caveats or citations on a website (or elsewhere) will change one's mind.

Dragons in Space/of Dystopia

There are stylistic and thematic through-lines connecting Stanley Kubrick's *2001: A Space Odyssey* (1968) to Ridley Scott's *Alien* (1979) that are unmistakable. But it is in each film's dramatic approach that we find interesting distinctions. While *2001* takes a macro view of human evolution as our species begins to explore, inhabit, and fathom the greater cosmos, *Alien* deals with the immediate concerns of individual humans attempting to survive not only in the far reaches of that greater cosmos, but furthermore in close quarters with an imminent and hitherto unknown threat. ("In space, no one can hear you scream," ran the latter's infamous tagline.) Taken together, the pair presents a complement of groundbreaking science-fiction storytelling, rich in complex philosophical and practical questions made ever more relevant by human societies' continuing reliance on new technologies, especially as means of transcending our very mortality.

In *Alien*, the fierce and resourceful heroine Warrant Officer Ellen Ripley (Sigourney Weaver) proves to be a well-matched opponent to the eponymous and bloodthirsty extraterrestrial creature with which she is trapped. In the sequel, *Aliens*, the monster is first referred to as a *xenomorph* (from the Greek for "foreign [or 'alien'] shape" or "form"), a term which has stuck with fans and commentators alike, despite it technically referring to any alien lifeform in the context of the film. Regardless, the Alien's species is variously known as Xenomorph XX121, *Internecivus raptus*, and *Linguafoeda acheronsis* in the franchise's canon.[17]

Though clearly inspired by the "biomechanical" imagery of Swiss artist H.R.

Giger (1940–2014), the xenomorphs of *Aliens* are, in essence,
extraterrestrial dragons. "Actress
Sigourney Weaver [is] a classic dragonslayer," the anthropologist David E. Jones contends,
"pure of heart and defender of
the weak[.]"[18] In the character's
own words, quoted in a companion book to the entire franchise,
Ripley describes her bane—or
is she *its* bane?—as "giant, over
two meters tall, humanoid in
form but with a long, segmented
tail. There were these skele-
tal ridges extending off its back,
like spines, or maybe pipes. Its
skin was hard, black, and shiny,
like a beetle's shell, and it looked
organic … but mechanical, too."[19]
Though as a species these creatures are formidable predators in
their final "drone" stage, perhaps
equally frightening is Xenomorph XX121's means of reproduction: An egg, laid by a queen,
launches a parasitic "facehugger,"
which attaches to a host's face
and then inserts an embryo into
the chest cavity.[20] The embryo
then transforms into a "chest-
burster" which is subsequently

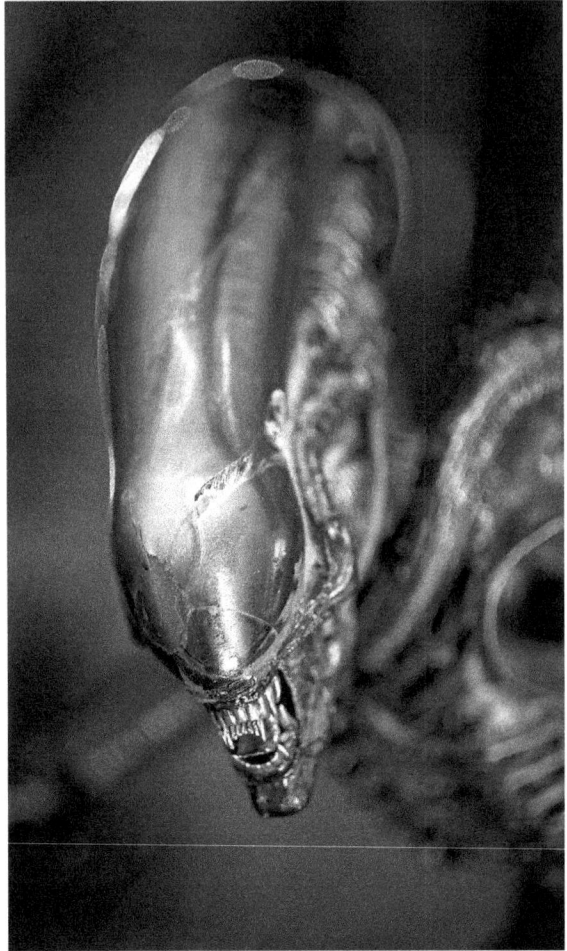

A dragon for the Space Age, the xenomorph of the
Aliens franchise was deeply inspired by the "biomechanical" paintings of Swiss artist H.R. Giger
(d. 2014). This replica is housed at the H.R. Giger
Museum in Gruyères, Switzerland (Wirestock Cre-
ators/Shutterstock.com).

"born" as it emerges violently from the chest of its host. The larva then very rapidly
molts and metamorphoses into a full-grown drone whose prime directive, ostensibly, is to build hives—along with the collection of new hosts—and furthermore
to propagate the species. More unsettling still: while inside its host, the parasitic
embryo implanted by a facehugger "mates" with the host via horizontal (as opposed
to vertical, i.e., parent-to-offspring) gene transfer, essentially absorbing a considerable amount of its host's DNA to be better adapted to the ecosystem into which it
will soon emerge. Scientists in the *Aliens* franchise, understandably, speak in awed
terms of the Xenomorph as a an eminently well-evolved (and evolving) organism,
despite its predilection for killing practically all humans it encounters. "You still

don't understand what you're dealing with, do you?" utters the mangled form of the android Ash (Ian Holm) in *Alien*, just before going permanently offline. "Perfect organism. Its structural perfection is matched only by its hostility."[21] Another interpretation of the horrifying species might be by analog with viruses; like the latter, xenomorphs replicate by co-opting the genetic material of their hosts on a cellular or molecular level.

Another species of dystopian space dragon appears in the 2021 disaster comedy *Don't Look Up*, directed by master satirist Adam McKay. Midway through the film, tech-billionaire-with-a-God-complex Sir Peter Isherwell (Mark Rylance) chats with U.S. President Janie Orlean (Meryl Streep) as they attempt to resolve the film's principal conflict: a massive comet hurtling towards Earth. Knowing that Isherwell has the power to accurately predict an individual's cause of death using his company's massive (and unethically sourced) archive of personal data, Orlean playfully asks him how *she* will die. Isherwell abides: Orlean will be eaten by something called a "brontoroc." "We don't even know what that means!" he chuckles as she looks on, also amused. In the film's epilogue, we finally learn that Isherwell and Orlean have escaped Earth on a spaceship just before (practically) all life on it was destroyed by the comet. Over 20,000 years later, the cosmic ark's population of less than 2,000 ultra-rich and/or well-connected people has arrived at a distant planet suitable for human habitation. The good fortune is short-lived, however, as the party quickly encounters a flock of large, vibrantly colored bird-like creatures. The intrepid yet foolhardy President Orlean approaches them, curious about their beautiful plumage … and is immediately devoured alive. *These* are the brontorocs, Isherwell promptly realizes and announces to the others before the epilogue cuts back to the credits. What's clear after this reveal is that *brontoroc* is a composite of the familiar prefix from the ancient Greek word for thunder, plus the giant bird of Arabian and Persian folklore.

On September 18, 2008, SpaceX CEO Elon Musk specifically stated in an interview that his company's Dragon spacecraft was named after "Puff, the Magic Dragon." Moreover, he referred to the persistent urban legend that the song is about marijuana: "So many people thought I must've been smoking weed to do this venture," he told his hosts.[22] But as we saw in Chapter 9 with the complicated backstory of "Puff" itself, and just as SpaceX has performed as a company since 2008 (most recently, in April 2023, its Starship rocket exploded on launch), the situation isn't nearly as simple as puffing smoke.

Back on Earth, dragons have lately been employed in much more banal professions than spacecraft, but perhaps ones that are just as topical. Reflecting the precarity of the modern state of employment, a fictional job listing by Maeve Dunigan on the site *McSweeney's Internet Tendency* offers a play on the fire-breathing dragon motif. The piece concludes, "Interested applicants should send a résumé, cover letter, and a 500-word essay on their favorite shiny object to dragon@kingarthursux.net. Dragon is an equal-opportunity exploiter."[23] Not surprisingly, and though it offers

The SpaceX Dragon spacecraft was named, rather ironically, after "Puff, the Magic Dragon" (Evgeniyqw/Shutterstock.com [elements of this image furnished by NASA]).

potential college credit and "free pizza lunch on Tuesdays," this opportunity to serve as an intern to an actual dragon is unpaid.

All Tomorrow's Dragons

What is to become of the dragon? As I have demonstrated, though the figure has passed through approximately one century of marked puerility in the West, its psychological presence has been restored to its original awe over the last twenty-five years or so. Now with proven marketability among children and adults alike, there appears to be very little stopping media creators and producers from including dragons in their content. The newfound interconnectedness between the cultures and media of the East and the West only facilitates this expanded dynamism. Thanks to the advent of at-home streaming media and a pivot away from movie theaters or other more communal spaces (most acutely due to the Covid-19 pandemic), the most essential criteria in this brave new world of virtually unlimited bandwidth are whether the storytelling is compelling, and the visual style and effects are convincing. This is clearly the case, as discussed throughout, of the wildly popular franchise, *A Song of Ice and Fire* (*Game of Thrones*, *House of the Dragon*).

Yet, despite the malleability of this classic motif, old perceptions of the dragon may still die hard depending on one's media habits and specific cultural background.

When I mention this project to particularly erudite friends, otherwise vocal supporters of my research interests, their facial expressions may range from engaged to glazed to seemingly bemused, if not slightly befuddled. "My (grand)children [or nieces, nephews, etc.] really like a certain show about dragons," or something along those lines, is the usual desultory remark. A somewhat awkward silence may follow. Other friends have just as readily referenced their or their (very young) loved ones' favorite dragon toys, whether plush or plastic, animated or CGI. The default cultural response to "a book about dragons" in my usual social circles has seemed to be almost exclusively oriented to the creature's puerile manifestations. And though I readily admit that such responses do indeed mirror a large component of my own interpretation of the phenomenon, taken alone they also leave much by the wayside. Based on these interactions, I soon found myself altering my elevator pitch in casual conversation. "It's a book about the intersection of folklore/mythology and modern pop culture," I've found myself saying instead. And if I can tell that at least some interest is piqued: "…through the lens of the dragon." The responses to this re-phrasing have been markedly more enthusiastic and less patronizing. (Though I suspect that some might have nevertheless found the idea of the project a bit too whimsical, if not wholly bizarre. I accept this as an honest reaction, but I also hope that this book itself presents a convincing counterargument.)

Conversely, young children, I am happy to report, have been almost unequivocally excited to discuss dragons with me. They have not only permitted but also actively encouraged me, in their wonderfully unselfconscious way, to talk with me about dragons in a spirit of sheer fun and wonder. Sometimes this is in the contexts of the storyworlds where dragons "naturally" exist, but just as often it is in the realm of pure imagination. Jorge Borges' observation of the ascendent puerility of the dragon in the West, as he recorded it in the mid-twentieth century,[24] was indeed astute for the time. But it need not have been a definitive, universal lamentation. What the last century's revolution in popular culture has unleashed represents a democratization of popular folklore and its remarketing through mass media, moreover as an approach keenly refocused on the child. The Disney Corporation, through its films, amusement parks, publishing, and myriad other ventures, has led this vanguard with great aplomb, if not near-military rigor, as shown in Chapter 9. But the response from other authors and producers, and especially those targeting more "mature audiences," as a certain television rating indicates, has been more than robust too, as we have seen. The result today is that dragons are neither exclusively puerile nor exclusively for adults. Rather, their semiotic bandwidth has been greatly expanded, revised, and diversified for a much wider range of audiences.

Inevitably, there will be dragons or dragon-related stories that I will have omitted, whether intentionally or not, from this book. There are so many instances of fantastical, reptilian monsters throughout the world that it would be impossible to capture so much content in one place. (Recall that scholar Michael Carr identified more than one hundred names for dragons [*draconyms*] in classical Chinese literature alone.[25]) And so I'll end here with an observation. It would be wonderful for our world's monsters to be primarily of the safe, fictive kind. But of course the world has never been anything close to perfect, much less entirely safe, even for the most sheltered and privileged among us. Since time immemorial we as a species have eked out our individual and communal existences in a reality that can instantly prove fatal, tragic, or exhaustingly difficult. Much is at stake, now as ever before, with factors such as epidemic disease, political strife, and economic tumult dominating the headlines. And more recently, nuclear proliferation and climate change have presented acutely existential threats not only to humans, but also to the Earth's entire biosphere. It behooves us to remember, whether through our individual or collective storytelling and mythologizing, that we are all fragile and we are all mortal. However we choose to present or interpret it, the dragon reminds us that we are not only human, but also ourselves animals and living things generally. We as the human species are distinguished from all others by our strong predilection for storytelling. We keep the dragon alive and well within our stories because we have never ceased having poignant, and widely varied, cultural and symbolic uses for it. Whether in our literary or metaphorical or other creative visions of a fantastical past, the tumultuous present, or a dys- or utopian future, the dragon is time and again the storyteller's choice as an essential vector of power, wonder, terror, and awe.

Chapter Notes

Preface

1. Watkins, Calvert, *How to Kill a Dragon: Aspects of Indo-European Poetics*. Oxford University Press, 1995, p. 447. A related word is δέρκεσθαι (*derkestai*), "to look, see."
2. Huxley, Francis, *The Dragon: Nature of Spirit, Spirit of Nature*. New York: Collier Books, 1979, p. 6.

Introduction

1. d'Huy, Julien, "The Evolution of Myths." *Scientific American*, Vol. 13, No. 6, December 2016, p. 69.
2. Porada, Edith, *Monsters and demons in the ancient and medieval worlds: papers presented in honor of Edith Porada*. Mainz on Rhine: P. von Zabern, 1987, p. 2.
3. This first human's name per biblical tradition is a generic term for "man" in Hebrew, itself ultimately deriving from the word *adamah* (אֲדָמָה), "ground," in reference to his essential nature, *cf.* English "earthling."
4. Genesis 2:16–17 (King James Version).
5. *Idem*, 3:4–5.
6. Miller, Robert D. II, *The Dragon, the Mountain, and the Nations: An Old Testament Myth, Its Origins, and Its Afterlives*. Eisenbrauns/The Pennsylvania State University, 2018, p. 204.

Chapter 1

1. Bear, Elizabeth, "She Still Loves the Dragon." *Uncanny*, Issue 20, January/February 2018. Online: https://uncannymagazine.com/article/still-loves-dragon/.
2. West, Kanye, Tweet sent 25 April 2018. Online: https://twitter.com/kanyewest/status/989179757651574784.
3. Anonymous, "Kanye West: Politics." *Wikipedia*. Accessed 12 December 2021. Online: https://en.wikipedia.org/wiki/Kanye_West#Politics.
4. "Dragon Energy." *Urban Dictionary*. Accessed 19 June 2020. Online: https://www.urbandictionary.com/define.php?term=Dragon%20Energy.

5. West, Donda, *Raising Kanye*. New York: Pocket Books, 2007, pp. 85–93.
6. See Hartz, Paula, *Taoism*. New York: Facts On File, 2004.
7. Lebowitz, Shana, "Kanye West says he loves Trump because they're both 'dragon energy'—here's what that means," *Business Insider*, 15 April 2018. Online: https://www.businessinsider.com/kanye-west-trump-dragon-energy-2018-4?r=UK.
8. Jin, Tee, "Dragon Energy Magic Power." *Tin Yat Dragon Blog*, 22 January 2022. Online: https://www.tinyatdragon.com/blogs/spiritual/dragon-energy-magic-power.
9. In his public behavior, as well as in media interviews and other statements on his religious beliefs, Kanye West has vociferously and almost exclusively self-identified as a Christian. This is to such an extent that we may accurately call him an evangelical. In late 2022, he effectively ended his career as a legitimate artist when he allied himself with right-wing conspiracy theorists like Alex Jones and the openly white-supremacist internet personality Nick Fuentes.
10. West, Kanye, Tweet sent 24 April 2018. Online: https://twitter.com/kanyewest/status/988795997869391873.
11. West, Kanye, "Monster." *Next Level*, Roc-A-Fella/Def Jam, 2015.
12. Smith, Gregory A., et al., "In U.S., Decline of Christianity Continues at Rapid Pace: An Update on America's Changing Religious Landscape." Washington, D.C.: Pew Research Center, 2019. Online: https://www.pewforum.org/wp-content/uploads/sites/7/2019/10/Trends-in-Religious-Identity-and-Attendance-FOR-WEB-1.pdf.
13. See: https://www.bbc.com/news/newsbeat-63833338; West, now widely known as "Ye," was reinstated by owner Elon Musk on July 29, 2023 as Twitter was rebranded as X.
14. Borges, Jorge Luis (Trans. Andrew Hurley), *The Book of Imaginary Beings*. New York: Penguin, 2005 [1967], p. 71.
15. *Ibid.*
16. Senter, Phil, Uta Mattox, and Eid E. Haddad, "Snake to Monster: Conrad Gessner's *Schlangenbuch* and the Evolution of the Dragon in the Literature of Natural History." In *Journal of Folklore Research*, Vol. 53, No. 1 (January/April 2016).

Bloomington: Indiana University Press, pp. 67–124.

17. Smith, G(rafton) Elliot, *The Evolution of the Dragon*. Manchester, UK: The University Press, 1919, p. 76.

18. *Idem*, p. 82.

19. More flags featuring or evoking dragons are considered in Chapter 12.

20. From Norman French (the source of most heraldic terminology), meaning "striding."

21. For more on the significance of red in Welsh folklore, see Chapter 6.

22. This configuration, one more evolutionarily and anatomically plausible—*cf.*, birds and bats—than that of four independent limbs plus scapular wings, is often called a *wyvern*. More on this in later chapters.

23. Penjore, Dorji and Sonam Kinga, *The Origin and Description of the National Flag and National Anthem of the Kingdom of Bhutan*. Thimphu, Bhutan: The Centre for Bhutan Studies, 2002, p. 4.

24. Jones, David E., *An Instinct for Dragons*. New York: Routledge, 2002, p. 8.

25. *Idem*, p. 4.

26. "Dragon." *Britannica*. Accessed 30 March 2022. Online: https://www.britannica.com/topic/dragon-mythological-creature.

27. For a brief recounting of the initial comedy of errors surrounding the scientific discovery of dinosaurs, see Lauren Davis' "The first scientific name ever given to a dinosaur? *Scrotum humanum*." *Gizmodo*, 28 October 2012. Online: https://io9.gizmodo.com/the-first-scientific-name-ever-given-to-a-dinosaur-foss-5955550.

28. Jung, C.G. and Violet Staub de Laszlo (Ed.), *The Basic Writings of C.G. Jung*. New York: Random House/The Modern Library, 1993 [1959], p. 150.

29. Jones, *Op. cit.*, p. 17.

30. Ogden, Daniel, *Drakōn: Dragon Myth and Serpent Cult in the Greek and Roman Worlds*. Oxford University Press, 2013, p. 25.

31. Mayor, Adrienne, *The First Fossil Hunters: Dinosaurs, Mammoths, and Myth in Greek and Roman Times*. Princeton: Princeton University Press, 2011, p. 225.

32. Huxley, Thomas Henry, *Evidence as to Man's Place in Nature*. Project Gutenberg, 2013 [1863], p. 8. Also quoted in epigraph in White, T.H., *The Book of Beasts: Being a Translation from a Latin Bestiary of the Twelfth Century*. New York: Dover Publications, 1984 [1954], p. 3.

33. See Chapter 2.

34. Jones, *Op. cit.*, p. 4.

35. Isbell, Lynne A. *The Fruit, the Tree, and the Serpent: Why We See So Well*. Harvard University Press, 2009, pp. 3–6.

36. *Idem*, p. 78.

37. *Idem*, p. 4.

38. *Idem*, p. 55.

39. Ogden, *Op. cit.*, *Ibid*.

40. *Idem.*, p. 2.

41. Mayor, *Op. cit.*, pp. 15–53.

Chapter 2

1. Hislop, Susanna, *Stories in the Stars: An Atlas of Constellations*. New York: Penguin Books, 2015, p. 76.

2. Campbell, Joseph, *The Hero with a Thousand Faces*, 2nd Ed. Princeton, NJ: Princeton University Press, 1968 [1949], p. 3.

3. Ford, Clyde W., *The Hero with an African Face: Mythic Wisdom of Traditional Africa*. New York: Bantam Books, 2000, p. 12.

4. *Idem*, p. 13.

5. This group includes Arabic, in the Semitic sub-group, which comprises several distinct spoken dialects. These "dialects," however, may more accurately be deemed separate languages united by a common standard written form, preserved most actively via the Muslim religion. Also included among Afro-Asiatic languages are Berber and Tuareg of the Sahara/North Africa region; and Coptic, the direct descendent of the language of the ancient (i.e., non–/pre–Arab) Egyptians.

6. The Guinean and Bantu families are sometimes grouped together into one Niger-Congo superfamily.

7. Luo also happens to be the native language of both actress Lupita Nyong'o and Barack Obama, Sr., the late father of the former U.S. President.

8. See Chapter 5 for an extensive analysis of the St. George the Dragonslayer cultus throughout the world.

9. See Chojnacki, S., "The Iconography of Saint George in Ethiopia: Parts I & II." *Journal of Ethiopian Studies*, January 1973, Vol. 11, Part 1, pp. 57–73; July 1973, Vol. 11, Part 2, pp. 51–92.

10. *Idem*, Part 1, p. 57.

11. See Chapter 5.

12. Chojnacki, *Op. cit.*, Part 2, pp. 56–59.

13. *Idem*, p. 74.

14. "St. George and Ethiopia's dragon," *The Guardian*, 12 September 1974. Online: https://www.theguardian.com/theguardian/1974/sep/12/fromthearchive.

15. The mysterious Sumerians were not ethno-linguistically Semitic nor Afro-Asiatic whatsoever; their language was an isolate. They are credited with inventing the cuneiform ("wedge-shaped") writing system later adopted by their Semitic successors the Babylonians and Assyrians.

16. See Chapter 11.

17. Miller, *Op. cit.*, p. 126.

18. Jacobsen, Thorkild, "The Battle between Marduk and Tiamat." *Journal of the American Oriental Society*, vol. 88, no. 1, American Oriental Society, 1968, p. 105.

19. Miller, *Op. cit.*, p. 203.

20. To wit, the star Betelgeuse of the Orion constellation (or Alpha Orionis), which was popularized as the eponymous ghoul of the 1988 film (spelled *Beetlejuice* in the title but *Betelgeuse* within the film itself). The creepy-sounding name—to English speakers—is a linguistic coinci-

dence due to corruption (via Latin) of the Arabic for "the hand of Orion," or *Yad al-Jauza*.

21. Kerrod, Robin, *The Book of Constellations: Discover the Secrets in the Stars*. London: Quarto, 2002, pp. 56–7.

22. Al-Jazari, Ismail (Trans. Donald R. Hill), *The Book of Knowledge of Ingenious Mechanical Devices [Kitāb fī ma 'rifat al-ḥiyal al-handasiyya]*. Dordrecht and Boston: D. Reidel, 1974, p. 279.

23. *Idem*, p. 59.

24. The Kurds, like the Persians, are also ethno-linguistically categorized in the Iranian subgroup of the Indo-European family.

25. See the discussion of *zilant* in Chapter 12.

26. The toponym of the multinational isthmus in question, the Caucasus, is also the source of the now mostly antiquated racial category "Caucasian," commonly referring to white people or otherwise those of European (or sometimes North African) ancestry. The highly imprecise term was coined and popularized by German anthropologists in the late eighteenth century based on both biblical and classical sources. The term's link with the purported *Urheimat* or ancestral homeland of the Proto-Indo-Europeans is convenient, but incidental.

27. See Damgaard, Peter de Barros et al., "The first horse herders and the impact of early Bronze Age steppe expansions into Asia," *Science*, 29 June 2018: Vol. 360, Issue 6396.

28. Olalde, Iñigo et al., "The genomic history of the Iberian Peninsula over the past 8000 years." *Science*, 15 Mar 2019: Vol. 363, Issue 6432, pp. 1230–1234.

29. Zubiri, Nancy, "Mr. Basque: A Look Back at William Douglass' Years Studying the Culture." *Euskal Kazeta (Basque News)*, 2 October 2020. Online: https://euskalkazeta.com/william-a-douglass-is-mr-basque/.

30. Interview via email with Iñaki Arrieta Baro, 18 January 2022.

31. Thompson, Stith, *The Folktale*. Berkeley: University of California Press, 1977 [1946], p. 243.

32. This system, the Aarne-Thompson-Uther Index, will be further described in later chapters.

33. Webster, Wentworth, *Basque Legends*. London: Griffith and Farran, 1879, xiv–xv.

34. *Idem*, p. 22.

35. *Idem*, p. 87.

36. *Idem*, p. 28.

37. See Chapter 7.

38. Watkins, Calvert, *How to Kill a Dragon: Aspects of Indo-European Poetics*. Oxford University Press, 1995, p. 7.

39. Webster, *Op. cit.*, pp. 88–94.

40. *Idem*, p. 88.

41. *Ibid*.

42. Thompson, *Op. cit.*, p. 26.

43. *Ibid*.

44. See Ingersoll, Ernest, and Tarl Warwick (Ed.), *Dragons and Dragon Lore: Cryptozoology and Mythology*. Public domain reprint, 2017 [1928], p. 10.

45. See Gidwitz, Adam, *The Unicorn Rescue Society: The Basque Dragon*. New York: Dutton Children's Books, 2018.

Chapter 3

1. *Ajagar* (अजगर) is also the Hindi word for "python." It derives from the Sanskrit word *ajagara* (अजगर), literally "goat swallower."

2. Dobson, Kenneth and Arthur Saniotis, "Dragons: Myth and the Cosmic Powers." *Prajñā Vihāra: Journal of Philosophy and Religion*, Vol. 15, No. 1, January–June 2014, pp. 89–90.

3. Williams, George, *A Handbook of Hindu Mythology*. Oxford University Press, 2008, pp. 90, 112.

4. Ingersoll, Ernest, *Dragons and Dragon Lore. Cryptozoology and Mythology*. Public domain reprint, 2017 [1928], p. 34.

5. *Idem*, p. 35.

6. Tawada, Yoko (trans. Susan Bernofsky; Yumi Selden), *Where Europe Begins*. New York: New Directions, 2002, p. 127.

7. Other examples include *biru* (building), *terebi* (television), *aisukurīmu* (ice cream), and *sutairu* (style). For a more extensive list, see Abe, Namiko, "Common Loan Words in Japanese." *ThoughtCo.*, 26 June 2019. Online: https://www.thoughtco.com/most-common-loan-words-in-japanese-2027852.

8. Immerwahr, Daniel, *How to Hide an Empire: A History of the Greater United States*. New York: Farrar, Straus and Giroux, 2019, pp. 365–8.

9. *Godzilla [Gojira]*, Toho Co., Ltd., 1954. Online (English-language script): https://subslikescript.com/movie/Godzilla-47034.

10. This explosive reputation is also the reason why French designer Louis Réard chose *bikini* as the name of the now-ubiquitous women's bathing suit, which he debuted in 1946.

11. Immerwahr, *Op. cit.*, pp. 351–2.

12. Blair, Gavin J., "Japan Box Office: Toho's 'Godzilla Resurgence' Opens With $6.1 Million." *The Hollywood Reporter*, 1 August 2016. Online: https://www.hollywoodreporter.com/news/general-news/japan-box-office-tohos-godzilla-916071/.

13. Lai, Stephanie, "Americans Learn Cartoon Japanese—Anime fans sprinkle Nihongo into their speech; how kawaii!" *The Wall Street Journal*, 23 March 2022, p. A1.

14. Blust, Robert, "The Origin of Dragons." In *Anthropos*, Vol. 95, No. 2, 2000, p. 524.

15. *Ibid*.

16. Mercatante, Anthony, *The Facts on File Encyclopedia of World Mythology and Legend*. New York: Facts on File, 1988, p. 546.

17. Blust, *Op. cit.*, p. 520.

18. *Idem* (Table 1).

19. See Chapter 1.

20. Blust, *Op. cit.*, p. 525.

21. *Idem*, p. 528.

22. Leeming, David Adams and Margaret Adams Leeming. "Australian Aborigine Creation."

Oxford Reference. Oxford University Press, 2009 [1994], n.p.

23. Mol, Hans, *The Firm and the Formless: Religion and Identity in Aboriginal Australia.* Waterloo (Ontario): Wilfrid Laurier University Press, 2006, p. 10.

24. Clarke, Philip A. *Discovering Aboriginal Plant Use: The Journeys of an Australian Anthropologist.* Rosenberg Publishing, 2014, p. 147.

Chapter 4

1. Online: https://www.merriam-webster.com/dictionary/indigenous.

2. According to census data, the segment of the U.S. population identifying as "American Indian" or "Alaska Native" (and no other race) grew by nearly 27 percent between 2010 and 2020—from 2,952,087 to 3,745,005 (see http://census.gov).

3. In both the Shawnee and Fox languages, the cognates of *manitou* mean "snake" (See Costa, David J., "Culture Hero and Trickster Stories." *Algonquian Spirit: Contemporary Translations of the Algonquian Literatures of North America*, edited by Brian Swann. University of Nebraska Press, 2004, p. 300).

4. *Idem*, p. 297.

5. The original pictographs (there were at least two and likely many more) have since been eroded or destroyed. The longest-surviving original was located a short distance away from the modern reconstruction.

6. Marquette, Jacques, *The Mississippi Voyage of Jolliet and Marquette, 1673.* New York: Charles Scribner's Sons, 1917, pp. 248–9.

7. Lewis, Meriwether, William Clark, and Reuben Gold Thwaites (Ed.), *Original Journals of the Lewis And Clark Expedition, 1804-1806: Printed from the Original Manuscripts in the Library of the American Philosophical Society and by Direction of Its Committee on Historical Documents, Together with Manuscript Material of Lewis and Clark from Other Sources, Including Note-books, Letters, Maps, Etc., and the Journals of Charles Floyd and Joseph Whitehouse, Now for the First Time Published in Full And Exactly As Written.* New York: Antiquarian Press, 1959, p. 40.

8. Armstrong, Perry A., *The Piasa, or, the Devil Among the Indians.* Morris, IL: E.B. Fletcher, 1887, p. 12.

9. Credit is due to Duane Esaray for his excellent talk on this subject on behalf of the Illinois State Archaeological Survey, available on YouTube at https://youtu.be/gP2nR_PqIMk.

10. Costa, *Op. cit.*, pp. 304.

11. *Idem*, p. 305.

12. For more on the dragon as a sports-team mascot, see Chapter 12.

13. Interview with David McPike, 15 November 2021: "Alton in general is very weird when it comes to spirits and lore and ghosts and myths. There are so many haunted tours. My dad's birthday is Halloween, and we would have giant block parties [on that day]. There was always an adult who said, 'Look out for the Piasa Bird!' My third-grade gym instructor bought [my ancestor's] mansion and turned it into a ['haunted'] tourist attraction. There are a lot of people who believe in ghosts and the Piasa Bird fits into that."

14. Marquette, *Op. cit.*, p. 249.

15. McPike, *Op. cit.*

16. Phillips, Charles, *The Lost History of Aztec and Maya: The history, legend, myth and culture of the native peoples of Mexico and Central America.* London: Select Editions, 2004, p. 180.

17. *Idem*, p. 181.

18. Martin, Simon, "Great Beasts of Legend: Monsters of the Maya Cosmos" (Lecture at Penn Museum), University of Pennsylvania, 1 February 2017.

19. *Ibid.*

20. Henrik, Hans ("Lichtenberg"), "The Dresden Codex—and how to read it before it is too late." *Holybooks.com*, 17 December 2012. Online: https://holybooks.com/dresden-codex-maya-calendar/.

21. See Coe, Michael D., *Breaking the Maya Code.* New York: Thames and Hudson, 1992.

22. *Idem*, p. 107.

23. Miller, Mary and Karl Taube, *An Illustrated Dictionary of the Gods and Symbols of Ancient Mexico and the Maya.* London: Thames & Hudson, 1993, pp. 99–100.

24. Coe, *Op. cit.*, p. 276.

25. Hagège, Claude and Jody Gladding (Trans.), *On the Death and Life of Languages.* Yale University Press, 2009, p. 14.

26. The Cape Verde Islands are one notable exception given that they were uninhabited when Portuguese explorers first arrived, *c.* 1460.

27. See Holm, John A., *Pidgins and Creoles, Volume 1: Theory and Structure.* Cambridge University Press, 1988, pp. 9–10.

28. See http://romani.uni-graz.at/romlex/lex.xml.

29. The exonym *Gypsy* (and its various cognates) belies the common misconception that the Roma originated in Egypt; the confusion likely emerged due to medieval and early modern Europeans' greater familiarity with Egypt than with India.

30. See Matras, Yaron, *I Met Lucky People: The Story of the Romani Gypsies.* London: Allen Lane/Penguin, 2014.

31. Though the Roma/Roms represent a significant portion (~10%) of Romania's population, Matras (*Idem*, p. 15) explains that the similarity in nomenclature is ultimately a coincidence.

32. Wedeck, H.E., *Dictionary of Gypsy Life and Lore.* New York: Philosophical Library, 1973, p. 73.

33. *Ibid.*

34. Lecouteux, Claude and Jon E. Graham (Trans.), *Dictionary of Gypsy Mythology: Charms, Rites, and Magical Traditions of the Roma.* Rochester, Vermont: Inner Traditions, 2018, p. 47.

Chapter 5

1. Job 30:26–29 (all verses in this chapter are taken from the King James Version).

2. Revelation 12:3–4.

3. Souvay, Charles Léon, "Animals in the Bible." *The Catholic Encyclopedia, Volume 1.* New York: The Encyclopedia Press, 1913, p. 522.

4. *Tannin* is cognate with Arabic *tani(y)n* (تنين; see Chapter 2, *Middle East/Central Asia*).

5. Strong's Exhaustive Concordance: "From an unused root probably meaning to elongate; a monster (as preternaturally formed), i.e., A sea-serpent (or other huge marine animal)…"

6. Klein, Ernest, *A Comprehensive Etymological Dictionary of the Hebrew Language for Readers of English.* Jerusalem: Carta, 1987, p. 20.

7. Also see the discussion of Modern Hebrew's "dragon" in Chapter 2.

8. Interview with Anonymous, 21 January 2022.

9. E.g., Psalm 74:14: "It was you who crushed the heads of Leviathan and gave it as food to the creatures of the desert," which directly follows a verse, mentioned above, which includes the more generic *tannin.*

10. Mintz, Samuel L., "Leviathan as Metaphor." *Hobbes Studies*, Vol. II, 1989, p. 5.

11. Leviathan is so called in Psalms, Isaiah, and Job (see Ogden, Daniel, *Drakōn: Dragon Myth and Serpent Cult in the Greek and Roman Worlds.* Oxford University Press, 2013, p. 14).

12. See Psalm 148:7 (King James Version): "Praise the LORD from the earth, ye dragons, and all deeps…"

13. Ogden, Daniel, *Dragons, Serpents, and Slayers in the Classical and Early Christian Worlds: A Sourcebook.* Cary: Oxford University Press USA—OSO, 2013, p. 244.

14. *Ibid.*

15. White, T.H. (Trans., Ed.), *The Book of Beasts: Being a Translation from a Latin Bestiary of the Twelfth Century.* New York: Dover, 1984 [1954], p. 167.

16. Discussed further in Chapter 9.

17. White, *Op. cit.*, pp. 165–6.

18. Ogden, *Op. cit.*, p. 3.

19. Garry, Jane and Hasan El-Shamy (Eds.), *Archetypes and Motifs in Folklore and Literature: A Handbook.* Armonk, NY: M.E. Sharpe, 2005, p. 76.

20. Kuehn, Sara, *The Dragon in Medieval East Christian and Islamic Art.* Leiden and Boston: Brill, 2011, p. 103.

21. Evans, Jonathan D., *Dragons: A Beautifully Illustrated Quest for the World's Greatest Dragon Myths.* Lewes, UK: Ivy Press, 2008, p. 108.

22. Ogden, *Op. cit.*, p. 3.

23. *Ibid.*

24. It is generally agreed that at least fifty Christian saints' legends contain dragons, almost always in the context of a physical and/or spiritual fight (see Rauer, Christine, *Beowulf and the Dragon: Parallels and Analogues.* Cambridge, UK: D.S. Brewer, 2000, p. 52.)

25. Generally, dragons no longer appear in the hagiographies of saints who themselves lived after the sixth century AD (see Ogden, *Op. cit.*, p. 239).

26. White, *Op. cit.*, p. 245.

27. Thompson, Stith, *The Folktale.* Berkeley: University of California Press, 1977 [1946], p. 24.

28. *Ibid.*

29. *Ibid.*

30. See Thompson, *Op. cit.*, p. 27 for the relative distribution of the two motifs among various European and other people-groups.

31. This was the very edition I viewed at the University of Cambridge, as mentioned in the Introduction.

32. The saint's name derives from the Greek *georgós* (γεωργός), "farmer, husbandman," or, more literally, "earthworker" (*gē(o)* "earth" + *ergon* "work").

33. For a discussion of the links between the St. George cultus and the Georgian nation (Republic of Georgia), see Tuite, Kevin, "The Old Georgian version of the miracle of St George, the princess and the dragon: Text, commentary and translation." *Sharing Myths, Texts and Sanctuaries in the South Caucasus*, July 2020, xx.

34. Butler, Alban, *The Lives of the Fathers, Martyrs, and Other Principal Saints; Compiled from Original Monuments and Other Authentic Records, Illustrated with the Remarks of Judicious Modern Critics and Historians*, Vol. 4. London: J. Murphy, 1812–15, pp. 248–9.

35. Reames, Sherry L. *The Legenda Aurea: A Reexamination of Its Paradoxical History.* Madison, WI: The University of Wisconsin Press, 1985, p. 44.

36. Voragine, Jacobus de, *The Golden Legend: Selections.* London: Penguin Books, 1998, p. 117.

37. *Ibid.*

38. *Ibid.*

39. See Whatley, E. Gordon, Thompson, Anne B., and Upchurch, Robert K. (Eds.,), "St. George and the Dragon in the South English Legendary" (East Midland Revision, *c.* 1400). University of Rochester (NY): Saints' Lives in Middle English Collections, 2004.

40. Voragine, *Op. cit.*, p. 118.

41. Itself named for a martyred saint, Catherine of Alexandria, a contemporary of St. George (see Voragine, *Op. cit.*, pp. 333–8).

42. The date may vary depending on denominational tradition.

43. Mortimer, Ian, "Why is St George our patron saint?" *Ian Mortimer* [personal website], 23 April 2006. Online: http://www.ianmortimer.com/essays/George.htm.

44. *Ibid.*

45. One commentator suggests that the red of St. George's Cross is evocative of the blood shed during the Crusades (see Marshall, Tim, *A Flag Worth Dying For: The Power and Politics of National Symbols.* New York: Scribner, 2016, p. 44).

46. See Chapter 12.

47. Voragine, *Op. cit.*, p. 162.

48. Butler, *Op. cit.*, vol. 7, p. 327.

49. Voragine, *Op. cit., ibid.*

50. *Idem*, p. 163.

51. *Idem*, p. 184.

52. *Idem*, p. 183.

53. *Ibid.*

54. The Book of Enoch (60:7–9) describes Leviathan as female, by default implying the sex of Onachus.

55. Voragine, *Op. cit.*, p. 183.

56. Voragine, *Op. cit.*, pp. 183–4.

57. *Idem*, p. 184

58. Ogden, *Op. cit.*, p. 202.

59. *Ibid.* p. 203.

60. *Ibid.*

61. *Ibid.* p. 204.

62. *Idem*, p. 203.

63. *Ibid.*

64. Voragine, *Op. cit.*, pp. 25–30.

65. *Idem*, pp. 343–357.

66. See David M. Lang's introduction to Woodward, G.R. and Harold Mattingly (Trans.), [*John Damascene:*] *Barlaam and Ioasaph.* Cambridge, MA: Harvard University Press/Loeb Classical Library, 1967 [1914], pp. ix–xxxv.

67. Quoted at length in Schulz, Siegfried A., "Two Christian Saints? The Barlaam and Josaphat Legend." *India International Centre Quarterly*, vol. 8, no. 2, India International Centre, 1981, pp. 131–43.

68. *Idem*, pp. 187–89.

69. *Idem*, p. 189.

70. *Ibid.*

71. *Idem*, p. 191.

72. Also discussed in Chapter 3, *South Asia, East/Southeast Asia.*

73. Ogden, *Op. cit.*, p. 218.

74. Rendina, Claudio (Trans. Paul D. McCusker), *The Popes: Histories and Secrets.* Santa Ana, CA: Seven Locks Press, 2002, p. 41.

75. This took place throughout these years and essentially portended the sectarian and furthermore socio-cultural schisms between the Western and Eastern divisions of the waning Roman Empire.

76. Rendina, *Op cit.*, p. 42.

77. Ogden, *Op. cit.*, pp. 221–8.

78. *Idem*, p. 221.

79. *Ibid.*

80. *Idem*, p. 235.

81. *Idem*, p. 236.

Chapter 6

1. Tolkien, J.R.R., "Mythopoeia," quoted in Carpenter, Humphrey, *Tolkien: A biography.* Boston: Houghton Mifflin, 1977, p. 190.

2. From Anglo-Saxon *bona* (or *bana*), a common Germanic convention: "In *Beowulf* it is applied both to heroes and to monsters; the dragon is the subject" (Watkins, Calvert, *How to Kill a Dragon: Aspects of Indo-European Poetics.* Oxford University Press, 1995, p. 418).

3. Tolkien, J.R.R., "*Beowulf*: The Monsters and the Critics." In Mittman, Asa Simon and Marcus Hensel (Eds.), *Classic Readings on Monster Theory: Demonstrare, Volume One.* Leeds, UK: Arc Humanities Press, 2018, p. 7.

4. *Ibid.* p. 9.

5. Evans, Jonathan D., "Medieval Dragon-lore in Middle-earth." *Journal of the Fantastic in the Arts*, Vol. 9, No. 3 (35), The Tolkien Issue (1998), p. 181.

6. Senter, Phil, Uta Mattox, and Eid E. Haddad, "Snake to Monster: Conrad Gessner's *Schlangenbuch* and the Evolution of the Dragon in the Literature of Natural History." *Journal of Folklore Research*, Vol. 53, No. 1 (January/April 2016). Bloomington: Indiana University Press, p. 71.

7. *Idem*, p. 72.

8. Especially in the United States, the Rod of Aesculapius, with its one wingless snake, is often confused with the caduceus of the god Hermes, which features two winged snakes wrapped around a staff.

9. Other interpretations hold that it was the Egyptian pharaoh-sorcerer Nectanebo who seduced Olympias, though in the draconic guise of Ammon. See *Les Faize d'Alexandre*, Ms. Burney 196, f.14, *c.* 1468–1475, or *Alixandre Le Grant*, Paris: Michel le noir, 1506, C.39.d.64, f.?, both held at the British Library.

10. A term used vaguely in Greek literature to refer to the Upper Nile region of what is now southern Egypt, as well as to other points further south in the Horn of Africa.

11. Evans, Jonathan D., *Dragons: A Beautifully Illustrated Quest for the World's Greatest Dragon Myths.* Lewes, UK: Ivy Press, 2008, p. 112.

12. Yet another mythological princess, of Troy. According to legend, she was rescued from sacrifice to a sea-dragon by Heracles (Hercules).

13. Ogden, Daniel, *Dragons, Serpents, and Slayers in the Classical and Early Christian Worlds: A Sourcebook.* Cary: Oxford University Press USA—OSO, 2013, p. 162.

14. More precisely an adnoun, a part of speech that may function as both an adjective and/or a noun, depending on context. Adnouns are somewhat uncommon in modern English but prevalent in the grammars of modern Latin-derived languages.

15. Various modern translators render the word as such, including Howell D. Chickering (1977), Maria Dahvana Headley (2020), and Seamus Heaney (2000).

16. In the early twentieth century, translator Logan Marshall rendered Grendel's mother as "a monstrous witch who dwelt at the bottom of a cold mere [lake]" (see *Myths and legends of all nations; famous stories from the Greek, German, English, Spanish, Scandinavian, Danish, French, Russian, Bohemian, Italian and other sources.* Philadelphia: John C. Winston Co., 1914, p. 169).

17. Ruth Franklin, reviewing Maria Dahvana Headley's 2020 translation for *The New Yorker* ("A 'Beowulf' for Our Moment," 31 August 2020),

writes, "The character is called 'aglaec-wif,' which others have translated as 'wretch,' 'ogress,' 'hell-bride,' and even 'ugly troll lady.' But Headley asserts that it is a female equivalent of the noun 'aglaeca,' which means awe-inspiring. Many versions also call Grendel's mother a 'sea-wolf,' but the Old English equivalent for this is 'brimwylf'— and the manuscript itself reads 'brimwyl,' which, Headley points out, could easily be a scribal error for 'brimwif,' 'sea-woman.'"

18. Roper, Simon, "Wild Animals in the Anglo Saxon Mind." YouTube, 25 September 2020. Online: https://www.youtube.com/watch?v=y5cgb1nDCMg.

19. Brown, Cecil H. "Folk Zoological Life-Forms: Their Universality and Growths." In *American Anthropologist*, Vol. 81 No. 4, 1979, pp. 791–812.

20. The only extant copy is mounted in a codex (along with several other manuscripts from the era) and housed at the British Library under the catalog code Cotton MS Vitellius A XV. The text was digitized and has been available in its entirety online since 2013 at http://www.bl.uk/manuscripts/Viewer.aspx?ref=cotton_ms_vitellius_a_xv_f094r.

21. See Chickering, Howell D., Jr. (Trans.), *Beowulf: A Dual-Language Edition*. New York: Anchor Books, 2006 [1989; 1977].

22. To great, eerie effect, the film has Grendel (voiced by Crispin Glover) speak only in Old English.

23. Tolkien, J.R.R. (Trans.), *The Legend of Sigurd & Gudrún*. Boston/New York: Mariner Books, 2009, p. 3.

24. See Chapter 10.

25. Headley, Maria Dahvana (Trans.), *Beowulf: A New Translation*. New York: MCD x FSG Originals; Farrar, Straus and Giroux, 2020, p. 40.

26. Chickering, *Op. cit.*, p. 256.

27. Heaney, Seamus (Trans.), *Beowulf: An Illustrated Edition*. New York and London: W.W. Norton & Company, 2008 [2000], p. xiv.

28. *Idem*, p. xv.

29. *Ibid.*

30. Campbell, Joseph, *Joseph Campbell and The Power of Myth*, Episode 1: "The Hero's Adventure." PBS, 1988. Online: https://billmoyers.com/content/ep-1-joseph-campbell-and-the-power-of-myth-the-hero%e2%80%99s-adventure-audio/.

31. See Monmouth, Geoffrey of and Lewis Thorpe (Trans.), *The History of the Kings of Britain*. London: Penguin Books, 1966, p. 171: "The Boar of Cornwall shall bring relief from these invaders, for it will trample their necks beneath its feet."

32. Also extant are the Brythonic (and highly endangered) languages of Cornish and, in France's Brittany region, Breton. Contrast with the Goidelic-Celtic languages: Irish, Scottish (Gaelic), and Manx.

33. See Ashe, Geoffrey, *Merlin: The Prophet and His History*. Thrupp, UK: Sutton, 2006.

34. Saint Patrick, so his legend goes, was the child of a Celtic British (Welsh) woman and a Roman soldier.

35. Though the town of Monmouth lies on the Welsh-English border, some scholars have contended that Geoffrey may have been a French-speaking Norman. At any rate, he was most likely Welsh or possibly Breton. See Monmouth, *Op. cit.*, pp. 10–14.

36. *Idem*, p. 14.

37. Ashe, *Op. Cit.*, p. 2.

38. Namely, in the tales "Lludd and Llevelys" and "Peredur Son of Evrawg."

39. In an earlier Welsh source by an author named Nennius, the wizard's name was *Myrddin*. Geoffrey of Monmouth likely altered the spelling since the name's Latin version, *Merdinus*, would have brushed distractingly close to the vulgar French word for feces.

40. Monmouth, *Op. cit.* p. 168.

41. By Geoffrey's time, not only were the Welsh politically marginalized by the English, but furthermore by the Normans who had invaded and conquered Britain starting in 1066.

42. Monmouth, *Op. cit.*, p. 171.

43. Unlike all the other Romance languages, Romanian syntax places the article after the noun: *Drac-* ("devil") + *-ul-* ("the") + *-a* ("son of").

44. Dacian was probably an Indo-European language but otherwise its categorization is hotly disputed.

45. An honorific more consonant with "warlord," though Vlad III was also a prince.

46. Rezachevici, Constantin, "From the Order of the Dragon to Dracula." *Journal of Dracula Studies*: Vol. 1, Article 1, 1999, n.p.

47. *Idem*, n.p.

Chapter 7

1. Fort, Charles, *The Book of the Damned*. New York: Boni and Liveright, 1920, p. 239.

2. Quoted in Carpenter, Humphrey, *Tolkien: A Biography*. Boston Houghton Mifflin, 1977, p. 139.

3. *Idem*, p. 59.

4. See Evans, Jonathan D., "Medieval Dragonlore in Middle-earth." *Journal of the Fantastic in the Arts*, Vol. 9, No. 3 (35), The Tolkien Issue, 1998, pp. 175–191.

5. Tolkien, J.R.R., *The Hobbit*. Boston: Houghton Mifflin, 1966 [1937], pp. 234, 238, 252, 274, respectively.

6. Heaney, Seamus (Trans.), *Beowulf: An Illustrated Edition*. New York and London: W.W. Norton & Company, 2008 [2000], v. 2520–3070.

7. Tolkien, *Op. cit.*, p. 28.

8. *Cf.*, "smuggle."

9. Carpenter, *Op. cit.*, p. 178.

10. Symons, Victoria, "Monsters and Heroes in Beowulf." *Discovering Literature: Medieval*. The British Library, 31 January 2018. Online: http://www.bl.uk.

11. *The Hobbit: The Battle of the Five Armies*, Dir. Peter Jackson, New Line Cinema, 2014.

12. *Idem*, p. 317.

13. Evans, *Op. cit.*, p. 178.

14. *Idem*, p. 183.

15. Carpenter, *Op. cit.*, p. 191.

16. Tolkien, J.R.R., interview with Denys Gueroult for BBC Radio, 1964 (released 1971). Online: https://youtu.be/bzDtmMXJ1B4.

17. Evans, *Op. cit.*, p. 189.

18. Tolkien, *Op. cit.*, 1966, p. 207.

19. *Idem*, p. 211.

20. This phenomenon is discussed further in Chapter 11.

21. Hanlon, Tina L., "The Taming of the Dragon in Twentieth Century Books." *Journal of the Fantastic in the Arts*, Vol. 14, No. 1 (53), Spring 2003, p. 7.

22. *Idem*, p. 14.

23. Also see Chapter 10.

24. Hanlon, *Op. cit.*, p. 18.

25. See Barrier, Michael, *The Animated Man: A Life of Walt Disney*. University of California Press, 2007.

26. *Guinness World Records*. Vol. 60 (2015 ed.), 2014, pp. 160–61.

27. Navarro, José Gabriel, "Total assets of the Walt Disney Company in the fiscal years 2006 to 2021." *Statista*, 19 January 2022. Online: https://www.statista.com/statistics/193136/total-assets-of-the-walt-disney-company-since-2006/.

28. Titled *The Sorcerer's Stone* in the United States.

29. According to various posts on George R.R. Martin's personal blog, https://georgerrmartin.com/notablog/, it seems possible that the author may complete the manuscript to novel number seven, *The Winds of Winter*, sometime in 2023 or '24. But as of the time of writing no formal announcement has been made.

30. Bright, Martin, "Harry Potter's creator richer than the Queen." *The Guardian*, 27 April 2003. Online: https://www.theguardian.com/uk/2003/apr/27/harrypotter.books.

31. Cecire, Maria Sachiko, *Re-enchanted: The Rise of Children's Fantasy Literature in the Twentieth Century*. Minneapolis: University of Minnesota Press, 2019, p. 241.

32. Rowling, J.K. and Olivia Lomenech Gill (Illustrator), *Newt Scamander: Fantastic Beasts and Where to Find Them*. New York: Arthur A. Levine Books/Scholastic, 2017, p. 25.

33. Such a creative choice bears further scrutiny given Rowling's recent remarks on gender issues starting in June of 2020. The author, primarily via Twitter, has argued that though she supports the rights of transgender individuals, referring to trans women as, simply, "women" threatens to erase the historical and ongoing oppression of cis-gender women by men. (Rowling herself had experienced domestic abuse at the hands of her ex-husband. Soon after leaving him she became, quite famously, a struggling single mother on government assistance. It was during this hard-scrabble period that she created Harry Potter and his storyworld in the early 1990s.) When confronted with opposing views on transgender issues following her tweets,

Rowling has tended towards even more reactionary positions, including her self-identification as a "TERF" (trans-exclusionary radical feminist). All the stars of the *Harry Potter* films, as well as its studio, Warner Bros., conversely, have made public statements condemning Rowling's comments on the matter and have affirmed their support of the rights of transgender individuals to freely and openly identify as men, women, or non-binary. The polemic was further intensified when stand-up comedian Dave Chappelle voiced support of Rowling and her "TERF war" in a Netflix special released in October of 2021. Many former *Harry Potter* fans have since disavowed Rowling entirely and have threatened to boycott any of her future creative output.

34. Rowling, *Op. cit.*, p. 25.

35. *Idem*, pp. 24–37.

36. Cecire, *Op. cit.*, p. 182.

37. *Ibid*.

38. Rowling, *Op. cit.*, p. 28.

39. *Idem*, p. 27.

40. As stated in the book's front matter: "Publisher's note: This book purports to be the facsimile of an original, published on a print run of 100 copies in 1895, of which a copy was recently found in a bookshop near the Seven Dials in London. Unfortunately, the publisher has been unable to ascertain whether a real Dr. Ernest Drake ever lived in St. Leonard's Forest or wrote a book called *Dragonology* and so, with regret, is unable to make any claim as to the truth of this and must present this volume merely as an interesting curiosity." (Drake, Ernest (Pseud.) and Wayne Anderson, Douglas Carrel, and Helen Ward (Illustr.), *Dragonology: The Complete Book of Dragons*. Cambridge, MA: Candlewick Press, 2003, n.p.)

41. *Idem*, n.p. (Chapter I).

42. *Ibid*.

43. *Idem*, n.p. (Chapter II).

44. *Idem*, n.p. (Chapter I).

45. *Idem*, n.p. (Chapter III).

46. *Ibid*.

47. Cowan, Douglas E., *Magic, Monsters, and Make-Believe Heroes: How Myth and Religion Shape Fantasy Culture*. University of California Press, 2019, p. 22.

Chapter 8

1. Wilhelm, Richard (Trans.), *I Ching* [*The Book of Changes*]. New York: Pantheon Books, 1950, p.3: *Chi'en* ["The Creative," the first hexagram].

2. Harvey, Chris, "Ai Weiwei: 'It's obvious Covid is not a natural disease, it's something that leaked out.'" *The Telegraph*, 29 January 2022. Online: https://www.telegraph.co.uk/art/artists/ai-weiwei-obvious-covid-not-natural-disease-something-leaked/.

3. One recent semi–viral tweet comes to mind, wherein a young student brought home a worksheet purporting to show how to write one's name "in Chinese." Much to the child's parent's chagrin

(they knew Mandarin), the characters given were not the correct logograms but instead characters that were superficially similar to the letters of the Latin alphabet.

4. O'Connell, Mark and Raje Airey, *Symbols, Signs & Visual Codes: A Practical Guide to Understanding and Decoding the Universal Icons, Signs and Symbols That Are Used in Literature, Art, Religion, Astrology, Communication, Advertising, Mythology and Science.* London: Hermes House, 2009, pp. 114–15.

5. Quoted in Ingersoll, Ernest, *Dragons and Dragon Lore. Cryptozoology and Mythology.* Public domain reprint, 2017 [1928], p. 51.

6. *Ibid.*

7. *Idem,* p. 53.

8. Visser, Marinus Willem de, *The Dragon in China and Japan.* Amsterdam: J. Müller, 1913, p. 44.

9. *Idem,* p. 40.

10. See Carr, Michael, "Classical Dragon Names." *Linguistics of the Tibeto-Burman Area,* Vol. 13, No. 2, Fall 1990.

11. Dobson, Kenneth and Arthur Saniotis, "Dragons: Myth and the Cosmic Powers." *Prajñā Vihāra: Journal of Philosophy and Religion,* Vol. 15, No. 1, January-June 2014, p. 86.

12. *Ibid.* pp. 86–7.

13. See Chapter 2, *Middle East/Central Asia.*

14. Hessler, Peter, "How China Controlled the Coronavirus." *The New Yorker,* August 10–17, 2020, p. 35.

15. Visser, Marinus Willem de, *The Dragon in China and Japan.* Amsterdam: J. Müller, 1913, p. 38.

16. Krishna, Bai, "Fact Check: Animated video of 'Coronavirus leaving earth' as a Chinese dragon goes viral." *India Today,* 22 March 2020. Online: https://www.indiatoday.in/coronavirus-outbreak/story/fact-check-animated-video-of-coronavirus-leaving-earth-as-a-chinese-dragon-goes-viral-1658392-2020-03-22.

17. Barati, Mikael, "یه کار سریع برای جوون مردایی که عبدشونو تو این وضعیت گزروندن" [A quick piece for those who spend their Eid in this situation]." https://www.instagram.com/mikaelbarati/, 8 March 2020.

18. Duma, Narjust, "The Dragon." *The Oncologist* 25.10 (2020), p. 903.

19. See Goodkind, Daniel, "The Astonishing Population Averted by China's Birth Restrictions: Estimates, Nightmares, and Reprogrammed Ambitions." *Demography* 1 August 2017; 54 (4), pp. 1375–1400.

20. A notable exception was made for rural families in the mid–1980s: they were permitted to have two children if the first was a daughter; *Ibid.*

21. See Fong, Mei, *One Child: The Story of China's Most Radical Experiment.* Boston: Houghton Mifflin Harcourt, 2016.

22. See Goodkind, Daniel, "Chinese Lunar Birth Timing in Singapore: New Concerns for Child Quality amidst Multicultural Modernity."

Journal of Marriage and Family, Aug. 1996, Vol. 58, No. 3, pp. 784–795.

23. Goodkind, Daniel, "Creating New Traditions in Modern Chinese Populations: Aiming for Birth in the Year of the Dragon." *Population and Development Review,* Dec. 1991, Vol. 17, No. 4., pp. 672–3.

24. *Ibid.*

25. Goodkind, Daniel, "If Science Had Come First: A Billion Person Fable for the Ages (A Reply to Comments)." *Demography* 1 April 2018; 55 (2), pp. 743–768, Fig. 2.

26. Goodkind, *Op. cit.,* 1991, pp. 664–5.

27. Fong, Mai, *Op. cit.,* p. 193.

28. Interview with Courtney "Coco" Cone, 25 July 2021.

29. Lee, Min Jin, "Asian-Americans Have Always Lived with Fear." *The New York Times,* 18 March 2022.

30. Yep, Laurence, *Dragonwings.* New York: HarperCollins, 2000 [1975], p. 169.

31. On March 16, 2021, a young white man shot to death eight people, six of whom were women of Asian origin, at three separate massage parlors or "spas" in Atlanta and its suburbs. Though the shooter's motives were unclear—uncontrolled sexual addiction and evangelical-Christian-inspired shame have been suggested as two major factors—given the context the optics of the tragedy were hard to avoid. The words of the spokesman of law enforcement in Cherokee County, where one of the shootings had occurred, implied yet another insidious aspect: that these murders were somehow less grave because mostly foreign-born, non-white individuals had died. "[Y]esterday was a really bad day for him," said Captain Jay Baker, seemingly recentering the narrative on the wellbeing of the murder suspect, Robert Aaron Long, "and this is what he did." Many critics were outraged by what they perceived as an apologia on behalf of the alleged white murderer of non-white people, especially given the fraught history of Asian-American immigration, from its beginnings in the nineteenth century to the present day.

32. Alexander, Kwame (Ed.) et al., "Today I Am a Witness to Change" [A Crowdsourced Poem Against Anti-Asian Hate], *Morning Edition.* National Public Radio (NPR), 12 April 2021. Online: https://www.npr.org/2021/04/12/985374483/today-i-am-a-witness-to-change-a-crowdsourced-poem-against-anti-asian-hate.

33. See Wilkerson, Isabel, *Caste: The Origins of Our Discontents.* New York: Random House, 2020.

34. Niemann, Christoph, *The Pet Dragon: A Story about Adventure, Friendship, and Chinese Characters.* New York: Greenwillow Books/HarperCollins, 2008, n.p.

35. *Mulan* grossed $120,620,254 in the United States but was only the fifteenth-highest grossing movie in 1998 (see https://www.boxofficemojo.com/year/1998/).

36. Schwartzel, Erich, *Red Carpet: Hollywood, China, and the Global Battle for Cultural*

Supremacy. New York: Penguin Press, 2022, pp. 3–22.

37. San Souci, Robert D. and Jean & Mou-Sien Tseng (Illustr.), *Fa Mulan*. New York: Hyperion Books for Children, 1998, n.p. (Author's Note).

38. Hong Kingston, Maxine, *The Woman Warrior: Memoirs of a Girlhood Among Ghosts*. New York: Vintage Books, 1977, p. 24.

39. "Chinese unimpressed with Disney's Mulan." *BBC News*, 19 March 1999. Online: http://news.bbc.co.uk/2/hi/entertainment/299618.stm.

40. Schwartzel, Erich, *Op. cit.*, pp. 62–3.

41. Carr, *Op. cit.*, p. 88.

42. "Traditional Chinese Artistic Motifs: The Skies and Heaven Beyond." *Shen Yun Performing Arts*, n.d. Online: https://www.shenyun.org/explore/view/article/e/m4NudX9jfTI/phoenix-dragons-cloud-lightning-chinese-artistic-motifs.html.

43. The CCP-ruled People's Republic of China is officially atheist. However, party leadership tolerated Falun Gong in its early years because it was based on systems of thought—such as Confucianism, Taoism, and Buddhism—so deeply embedded in Chinese culture as to be virtually inextricable from it.

44. Ownby, David, *Falun Gong and the Future of China*. Oxford University Press, 2008, p. 126.

45. "The Performance." *Shen Yun Performing Arts*, n.d. Online: https://www.shenyun.org/classical-chinese-dance-music-costumes-singers-and-more.

46. "Misconception 2: Shen Yun Dances about Falun Gong are 'Political,'" *Shen Yun Performing Arts*, 15 September 2011. Online: https://www.shenyun.org/explore/view/article/e/Pwua6-S5xXk/misconception-2-shen-yun-falun-gong-political.html.

47. See Zeng, Jing and Mike S. Schäfer, "Conceptualizing 'Dark Platforms': Covid-19-Related Conspiracy Theories on 8kun and Gab." *Digital Journalism*. Routledge. 9 (16 June 2021), pp. 1321–1343. DOI: 10.1080/21670811.2021.1938165.

Chapter 9

1. Grahame, Kenneth, *The Reluctant Dragon*. New York: Holiday House, 1966 [1938; 1898], n.p.

2. According to the "Pokédex" of pokemon.com, of the 898 total cryptids there are fifty-six categorized under the "dragon" label.

3. The Japanese franchise debuted as a game for Nintendo Game Boy in 1996 and is now a multimedia franchise.

4. Boodhoo, Niala et al., "'Look at You Now,' A Memoir; Millennium Park Protest; Pokémon Go Goes To College (And Everywhere)." *Illinois Public Media*, 12 July 2016. Online: https://will.illinois.edu/21stshow/program/look-at-you-now-a-memoir-pokemon-go-goes-to-college-and-everywhere.

5. Silva, Caroline, "Man who spent $50K in COVID-19 funds on Pokémon card sentenced." *The Atlanta Journal-Constitution*, 9 March 2022, p. A10.

6. Online: https://www.pokemon.com/us/pokedex/charizard.

7. *Meet the Parents* (Dir. Jay Roach). Universal Pictures/Dreamworks Pictures, 2000.

8. Garnick, Darren, "Puff the Urban Legend." *The Jerusalem Report*, 15 January 2001, p. 39.

9. Lipton, Lenny, "Thank you, Puff the Magic Dragon." *Lenny Lipton* [personal blog], 24 February 2009. Online: https://lennylipton.wordpress.com/2009/02/24/thank-you-puff-the-magic-dragon/.

10. Chelin, Pamela, "The Man Who Wrote 'Puff, the Magic Dragon' Swears It's Not About Drugs." *LA Weekly*, 3 February 2015, https://www.laweekly.com/the-man-who-wrote-puff-the-magic-dragon-swears-its-not-about-drugs/.

11. Kilgallen, Dorothy, "Voice of Broadway." *Edmonton Journal*, 29 August 1963, p. 23.

12. *Idem, Montreal Gazette*, 4 December 1964, p. 38.

13. *Idem, Springfield (Missouri) News-Leader*, 29 September 1965, p. 6.

14. *Idem, Wilkes-Barry (Pennsylvania) Times Leader*, 3 February 1964, p. 6.

15. Kilgallen's official cause of death was given as an overdose of alcohol and barbiturates. To this day many suspect that she was murdered for getting too close to uncovering the conspiracy behind the assassination of President John F. Kennedy in 1963. See Israel, Lee, *Kilgallen*. New York: Delacorte Press, 1979.

16. Nash, Ogden, "Custard the Dragon." In *The Best of Ogden Nash*. Chicago: Ivan R. Dee, 2007, pp. 21–3.

17. See Chapter 1.

18. Greenberg, Robert, "Music History Monday: Puff the Magic Dragon." *Robert Greenberg* [personal blog], 16 March 2020, n.p. Online: https://medium.com/@rgreenbergmusic/music-history-monday-puff-the-magic-dragon-a4b8d2a4276b.

19. Kendrick, Denny, "Letters to the Editor." *Newsweek*, 30 May 1966, p. 4.

20. "The Magic Dragon." *Newsweek*, Vol. 68, Iss. 18 (31 October 1966), p. 48.

21. Associated Press, "New Chapter in Verse Tiff Results in Huff Over 'Puff,'" *The Hartford* [Connecticut] *Courant*, 24 October 1984, p. A2.

22. Lipton, *Op. cit.*, n.p.

23. *Ibid.*

24. Singapore's Ministry of Culture banned the song because of its purported drug associations in March of 1970 (see "'Drug Songs' Banned." *Pacific Daily News (Guam)*, 6 March 1970, p. 10).

25. *C.f.*, the sorceress Maleficent in *Sleeping Beauty* (1959).

26. White, T.H., *The Sword in the Stone*. London: Collins, 1938, p. 83.

27. Thompson, Stith, *The Folktale*. Berkeley: University of California Press, 1977 [1946], pp. 96–7.

28. *Idem*, p. 97.

29. Gabler, Neal, *Walt Disney: The Triumph of the American Imagination*. New York: Alfred A. Knopf, 2006, pp. 334–5.

30. *Idem*, p. 393.

31. Barrier, Michael, *Hollywood Cartoons: American Animation in Its Golden Age*. Oxford University Press, 1999, pp. 306–7.

32. Parkin, Simon, *An Illustrated History of 151 Video Games: A Detailed Guide to the Most Important Games*. Wigson, Leicestershire, UK: Lorenz Books, 2013, p. 41.

33. The ingenuity of the game was the result of the prodigious and complementary talents of former Disney animator Don Bluth (*Sleeping Beauty, The Sword in the Stone, Robin Hood*, among others) and Rick Dyer of Advanced Microcomputer Systems. Their collaboration was first conceived when Dyer saw Bluth's latest directorial opus, *The Secret of NIMH*, in 1982. Dyer realized at that moment in the theater that if he could somehow combine high-framerate, cinematic cel animation with a relatively dynamic player interface (made possible only with the new technology of LaserDisc), he would have a hit. And, since Bluth was serendipitously available after the success of *NIMH*, all it took was a meeting for Dyer to convince the ex–Disney visionary to partner up. Bluth then brought onboard his team of 300 animators and, in seven frantic months, they had their game.

34. Parkin, *Op.cit., Ibid.*

35. Skelly, Tim, "The Rise and Fall of Cinematronics." In Wolf, Mark J.P. (Ed.), *Before the Crash: Early Video Game History*. Detroit: Wayne State University Press, 2012, p. 163.

36. Notoriously difficult and doubly expensive (50¢ USD as opposed to the usual 25¢), *Dragon's Lair* was only a hit for as long as the allure of its amazing graphics held sway. Yet it unmistakably succeeded as an arcade game during this early window, buttressing a video-game industry already in turmoil as the transition from the arcade to the home had begun. Because of its unique operating system, *Dragon's Lair* was at first only available in arcade format while many other popular games of the era began to be offered on home consoles, such as the Atari 2600.

37. Scoggin, Lisa and Dana Plank (Eds.), *The Intersection of Animation, Video Games, and Music: Making Movement Sing*. New York: Routledge, 2023, p. 105.

38. According to most accounts, Donkey Kong got his name from Miyamoto's (mis)interpretation of "donkey" as a synonym of "stubborn" in a Japanese-English dictionary ... plus the "Kong" of King Kong, naturally.

39. Like his namesake, Segale was reportedly also short in stature and wore suspenders. However, it appears unlikely that he had a mustache. The original Jumpman sprite's facial hair was merely a workaround due to the limitations of graphic design when limited by only 8 bits per pixel.

40. Interestingly, the original idea was for the game's hero to be the American comic-strip and cartoon stalwart Popeye. Copyright restrictions, however, quickly altered Nintendo's plans.

41. Parkin, *Op. cit.,* p. 32.

42. *Ibid.*

43. Paumgarten, Nick, "Master of Play: The Many Worlds of a Video-Game Artist." *The New Yorker*, 12 December 2010. Online: https://www.newyorker.com/magazine/2010/12/20/master-of-play.

44. See "The Great Bowser Debate: Is he a dragon or a turtle?" *Easy Allies Forums*, 7 February 2019. Online: https://forums.easyallies.com/topic/5262/the-great-bowser-debate-is-he-a-dragon-or-a-turtle.

Chapter 10

1. Danielewski, Mark Z., "That Place." In *House of Leaves*, 2nd Edition. New York: Pantheon Books, 2000, p. 558.

2. Blumberg, Nick, "George RR Martin Talks Northwestern, Writing and 'Game of Thrones.'" *WTTW-Chicago*, 16 June 2021. Oneline https://news.wttw.com/2021/06/16/george-rr-martin-talks-northwestern-writing-and-game-thrones.

3. Online: https://www.shirepost.com/collections/a-game-of-thrones-coins/products/targaryen-set.

4. Cogman, Bryan, *Inside HBO's Game of Thrones*. San Francisco: Chronicle Books, 2012, p. 176.

5. Price, Rob, "How big will the 'Game of Thrones' dragons get? Let's do the math." *The Daily Dot*, 27 April 2014. Online: https://www.dailydot.com/parsec/how-big-are-game-of-thrones-dragons/.

6. Martin, George R.R., *Fire and Blood: Being a History of the Targaryen Kings of Westeros*. New York: Bantam Books, 2018, p. 5.

7. *Idem*, p. 68.

8. "Dragonfire!" in Martin's constructed language of Valyrian.

9. Curley, Michael J. (Trans.), *Physiologus: A Medieval Book of Nature Lore*. University of Chicago Press, 2009 [1979], pp. 28–9.

10. Then again, "warm-" and "cold-blooded" in their modern pseudo-scientific usages are also somewhat archaic and inaccurate notions; endothermic mammals and ectothermic reptiles, for example, regulate their temperature not by an inherent or static temperature of their blood as much as by their different means of capturing, retaining, or releasing heat.

11. See Curley, *Op. cit.*, pp. 29–32.

12. Pliny the Elder (Trans. Philemon Holland), *The Historie of the World. Commonly called, the Naturall Historie of G. Plinius Secundus. The first Tome*. London: Imprensis G.B., 1601, p. 199 (book viii, ch. 12). [The spelling of this passage has been modernized.]

13. *Idem*, book xxxiii, ch. 8.

14. Druce, George C., "The Elephant in Medieval

Legend and Art." *Journal of the Royal Archaeological Institute.* Vol. 76. London, 1919, p. 34.

15. One need only refer to the expansionist Muslim Arabs of the seventh to ninth centuries AD, or the Catholic Spaniards of the sixteenth, for particularly stark examples of this phenomenon.

16. Though its provenance is unclear, this sentiment has been documented online since at least 2003. For a discussion, see https://quoteinvestigator.com/2016/10/24/privilege/.

17. Online: https://www.facebook.com/photo/?fbid=699645487702994&set=a.243547736646107. Accessed 8 March 2022.

18. Allen, Danielle, "Our democracy is menaced by two dragons. Here's how to slay them." *The Washington Post*, 20 July 2023. Online: https://www.washingtonpost.com/opinions/2023/07/20/gerrymandering-electoral-college-solution-democracy/.

19. See Martis, Kenneth C., "The original gerrymander." *Political Geography*, Vol. 27, Issue 8, 2008, pp. 833–839. DOI: 10.1016/j.polgeo.2008.09.003.

20. *Idem*, p. 835.

21. *Ibid.*

22. The Governor's name was actually pronounced with a hard *g*, as in "Gary."

23. Lester, John C. and Daniel Love Wilson, *Ku Klux Klan: Its Origin, Growth and Disbandment.* Nashville, TN: Wheeler, Osborn & Duckworth Manufacturing Co., 1884, p. 52.

Chapter 11

1. Asia, "Heat of the Moment" (John Wetton/ Geoff Downes), *Asia.* Geffen, 1982.

2. Manganiello, Joe (as told to Megan Carpentier), "Dungeons & Dragons isn't a weird game for nerds. It's a creative outlet for people like me." *THINK (NBC News)*, 21 April 2018. Online: https://www.nbcnews.com/think/opinion/dungeons-dragons-isn-t-weird-game-nerds-it-s-creative-ncna867906.

3. Kushner attributes this response to Gygax's eldest daughter, Elise (2017, p. 60). However, Witwer contends that it was Gygax's youngest daughter, Cindy, six years old at the time, who exclaimed, "Oh, Daddy, I like Dungeons and Dragons best!" (2016, p. 101). Ewalt supports the latter as well (2013, p. 70).

4. Gygax, E. Gary and Dave Arneson, "Monsters & Treasure (Volume 2 of Three Booklets)." *Dungeons & Dragons: Rules for Fantastic Medieval Wargames Campaigns Playable with Paper and Pencil and Miniature Figures.* Lake Geneva, WI: Tactical Studies Rules, 1974, pp. 11–14.

5. *Idem*, p. 11.

6. *Ibid.*

7. *Idem*, p. 12.

8. *Idem*, p. 13.

9. For a full listing of attributes, see Gygax, E. Gary, *Advanced Dungeons & Dragons Monster Manual*, 4th Edition. Lake Geneva, WI: TSR Games, 1979, pp. 31–34.

10. Evans, Jonathan D., "Medieval Dragon-Lore in Middle-earth." *Journal of the Fantastic in the Arts*, Vol. 9, No. 3 (35), The Tolkien Issue (1998), p. 184.

11. Gygax, *Op. cit.*, 1979, pp. 29–30.

12. *Idem*, pp. 34–5, 61, 79.

13. Tiffany, Kaitlyn, "A Chart to Explain Your Entire Worldview: A simple grid from Dungeons & Dragons has become a way to categorize people, food, fonts, Shia LaBeouf acting roles, and everything else." *The Atlantic*, 5 March 2020, n.p. Online: https://www.theatlantic.com/technology/archive/2020/03/alignment-chart-memes-moral-worldview-fantasy/607561/.

14. *Ibid.*

15. Gygax, *Op. cit.*, p. 32.

16. See Chapter 2, *Middle East/Central Asia*.

17. *Ibid.*

18. *Idem*, p. 33.

19. Also the source of the English word behemoth; see Chapters 1 and 4.

20. This animal-collective term—along with *clan*, *tribe*, *council*, and others—is suggested by user Frost MacMahon, a so-called "Dragon enthusiast and self-proclaimed 'dragon expert'" on the popular question-and-answer website Quora: https://www.quora.com/What-is-a-group-of-dragons-called.

21. Perkins, Christopher, et al., *D&D Monster Manual: A menagerie of deadly monsters for the world's greatest roleplaying game.* Renton, WA: Wizards of the Coast, 2014, p. 6.

22. *Idem*, p. 86.

23. *Idem*, p. 103.

24. *Idem*, p. 6.

25. *Idem*, p. 83.

26. *Idem*, p. 84.

27. *Idem*, p. 303.

28. *Ibid.*

29. White, *Op. cit.*, p. 230.

30. Gygax, *Op. cit.*, p. 29.

31. White, *Op. cit.*, pp. 61–68.

32. Witwer, Michael, *Empire of Imagination: Gary Gygax and the Birth of Dungeons & Dragons.* New York: Bloomsbury, 2016, p. 151.

33. The first edition run of 1,000 copies of *D&D* sold out in less than ten months (see Ewalt, David M., *Of Dice and Men: The Story of Dungeons & Dragons and the People Who Play It.* New York: Scribner, 2013, pp. 91–2). At the time of writing (July 2020), a complete, first edition copy of the game is currently on sale via AbeBooks.com for $1,073.48 (plus shipping from the UK).

34. For an excellent overview of this series of incidents and their implications, see Joseph P. Laycock's *Dangerous Games: What the Moral Panic over Role-Playing Games Says about Play, Religion, and Imagined Worlds.* University of California Press, 2015.

35. Gygax, Gary, "The Influence of J.R.R. Tolkien on the D&D and AD&D Games." *Dragon*, vol. 9, no. 95 (March 1985), pp. 12–13.

36. Quoted in Kushner, David, "Dungeon

Master: The Life and Legacy of Gary Gygax." *Wired.* 10 March 2008. See also: Witwer, Michael, *Empire of Imagination: Gary Gygax and the Birth of Dungeons & Dragons.* New York and London: Bloomsbury, 2016, p. 86.

37. Carpenter, Humphrey, *Tolkien: A biography.* Boston: Houghton Mifflin, 1977, p. 221.

38. See Ewalt, *Op. cit.*, pp. 140–41 for a concise relation of the episode. Dragons, of course, remained an integral component of *Dungeons & Dragons.*

39. Witwer, *Op. cit.*, p. 131.

40. Laycock, Joseph P., *Op. cit.*, p. 70.

41. Kushner, David and Koren Shadmi, *Rise of the Dungeon Master: Gary Gygax and the Creation of D&D.* New York: Nation Books, 2017, p. 134.

42. The addition of "Advanced" to the game's title was partially related to ongoing intellectual-property disputes but also implied a considerable number of changes to the game's underlying operating system; the level of explanatory detail and many other aspects were revised considerably between the 1974 and 1977 editions (see Ewalt, *Op cit.*, pp. 134, 137–39).

43. See Laycock, *Op. cit.*

44. Heaney, Seamus (Trans.), *Beowulf: An Illustrated Edition.* New York and London: W.W. Norton & Company, 2008 [2000], p. xv.

Chapter 12

1. Waters, Roger, "Sunset Strip." *Radio K.A.O.S.* EMI Records, 1987.

2. Ipsos, "More Americans Have Tattoos Today Than Seven Years Ago." Online: https://www.ipsos.com/en-us/news-polls/more-americans-have-tattoos-today.

3. Anecdotally, I would estimate that half of my friends (most of whom fall into the millennial cohort—born between 1980 and 1995) have at least one tattoo, myself included.

4. Interview via email with Daniel "Danny" Frank, 2–3 January 2022.

5. Interview via email with Errol Packard, 21–24 March 2022.

6. Palmer, Harry Clay (Ed.) et al., *Athletic Sports in America, England, and Australia.* New York: Union Pub. House, 1889, p. 160.

7. *Ibid.*

8. Online: https://drexeldragons.com/sports/2006/9/15/Mascot.aspx.

9. Interview with Trevor Neumann, 26 March 2021.

10. The top-seeded Illinois happened to trounce the Dragons, 78–49 … though Illinois later lost to Loyola-Chicago in the second round.

11. Runevitch, Jennie, "March Madness | 'Queen of Fuzz' creates mascots in Indy studio." Toledo, OH: WTOL-11, 2 March 2021. Online: https://www.wtol.com/article/money/business/small-business/ncaa-basketball-mascots-avantgarb-indianapolis/531-16154533-b039-47bb-b1fc-67ce49e71351#:~:text=When%20March%20Madness%20comes%20to,or%20mascots%20at%20the%20tournament.

12. "Dragon Mascot School List." Online: https://www.ranker.com/list/dragon-mascot-school-list/reference.

13. Oddy, Lou, "The Name 'Dragons.'" *The Drexel Triangle,* 16 April 1928, p. 4.

14. Anonymous, "Drexel Dragon Rejuvenated." *The Drexel Triangle,* 7 November 1930, p. 1.

15. For a broad survey of dragons in vexillology, see Denny, Kieran, "Dragons Add Mystique and Strength to European and Asian Flags." In *Vexillum: Research and Information from the North American Vexillological Association*, No. 17 (March 2022), pp. 16–20.

16. 肖吟新 (Xiao Yinxin), *The story of the Qing dynasty national flag (*清代国旗的故事). 世纪, 2002, p. 63.

17. "係為雇船捕盗而用, 並未奏明定為萬年國旗", "[the flag] is used for ferry and policing, but is not explicitly designated as the permanent national flag," from 《北洋水師章程》 (Regulations of the Beiyang Fleet).

18. As opposed to more "common" four-clawed Chinese dragons, only the five-clawed imperial dragon, associated with the legendary Yellow Emperor who supposedly founded the Empire, was worthy of adorning The Great Qing's pennant.

19. "今中國兵商各船日益加增, 時與各國交接, 自應重定旗式, 以崇體制。應將兵船國旗改為長方式, 照舊黃色, 中畫青色飛龍。", "Nowadays the number of both Chinese military and commercial ships is growing. When our ships meet those of other nations they should display a flag based on a conformed system. [The government] should change the military flag to a pennant with an azure dragon in the middle," 《北洋水師章程》 (Regulations of the Beiyang Fleet).

20. At this point, the "five-colored flag" representing the major ethnic groups of China (Han, Manchus, Mongols, Hui, and Tibetans) was adopted.

21. George VI is also known to history as the younger brother of King Edward VIII (who famously had abdicated the throne to marry his American paramour Wallis Simpson), and as the father of Queen Elizabeth II.

22. Sensen, Mark et al., "The George Cross." *Flags of the World,* 7 November 1995. Online: https://www.crwflags.com/fotw/flags/mt)gc.html#gc.

23. Perrin, W.G., *British Flags: Their Early History, and Their Development at Sea; with an Account of the Origin of the Flag as a National Device.* London: Cambridge University Press, 1922, p. 30.

24. Loeser, Peter, "Introduction: Kingdom of Wessex." *Flags of the World,* 18 May 2021. Online: https://www.crwflags.com/fotw/flags/gb-wessx.html#intro.

25. In 927 CE, all of England was unified under King Æthelstan, the grandson of Alfred the Great.

26. Dennys, Rodney, *The Heraldic Imagination.* London: Barrie & Jenkins; Toronto: Anson-Cartwright Editions, 1976, p. 26.

27. Association of British Counties, "Somerset." *ABC Flag Blog*, 4 July 2013. Online: http://abcounties.com/flags/2012/01/01/somerset/.

28. Ayer, John (Trans.), "Supposed historical emblems of the Kazan Khanate." *Flags of the World*, n.d. Online: https://www.crwflags.com/fotw/flags/ru-16_h.html#kaz.

29. *Ibid.*

30. See Chapter 2, *Middle East/Central Asia.*

31. In heraldic jargon: "Gules issuant from three mounts vert a city tower argent port and windows sable on which is sitting a dragon of the second" (See https://www.crwflags.com/fotw/flags/si-061.html#coa).

32. City of Ljubljana, "City emblems and city holiday." *City of Ljubljana*, n.d. Online: https://www.ljubljana.si/en/about-ljubljana/city-emblems-and-city-holiday/.

33. *Ibid.*

34. https://worldpopulationreview.com/country-territories/macau-population

35. Master, Farah, "In Macau, Portuguese elites feel squeezed out by Chinese history." *Reuters*, 5 October 2018. Online: https://www.reuters.com/article/us-macau-china-law/in-macau-portuguese-elites-feel-squeezed-out-by-chinese-influence-idUSKCN1MF0OQ.

36. Portuguese Colonial Ministry, Ministerial Decree no. 8:098, *Diário do Governo: I Série* 104, 8 May 1935, p. 599 (translation by the author).

37. Koh, Tom, "Colonial Hong Kong: The end of British rule." *Flags of the World*, 1 July 1997. Online: https://www.fotw.info/flags/hk-colon.html.

38. This is a common vexillological term and does not have a negative connotation. Rather, it refers to a badge or seal appearing on a military ensign, also seen above in colonial Macau vis-à-vis Portugal. This is still the case of several Commonwealth countries, including Australia and New Zealand.

39. Regarding the status of vexillology in pop-culture consciousness, the supporting character Sheldon Cooper of the long-running CBS sitcom *The Big Bang Theory* (2007–2019) may be illustrative. The socially inept theoretical physicist, played by Jim Parsons, is periodically shown throughout the series as the host of an absurdly overwrought YouTube series called "Sheldon Cooper Presents Fun with Flags."

40. Cuhaj, George S. (Ed.) et al., *2015 Standard Catalog of World Coins, 1901–2000* (42nd Ed.). Iola, WI: Krause Publications, 2014, pp. 387–461; 1327–34.

41. *Idem*, pp. 462–540.

42. *Idem*, pp. 235–43.

43. *Idem*, pp. 996–1022.

44. *Idem*, p. 1480.

45. *Idem*, p. 787; see Chapter 2, *Africa.*

46. *Idem*, p. 1523; see Chapter 4, *Central/South America.*

Whither the Dragon?

1. Delaney, Rob, Tweet sent 31 August 2020. Online: https://twitter.com/robdelaney/status/1300349010960617472. Accessed 2 August 2023.

2. Online: https://www.urbandictionary.com/define.php?term=Big%20Dick%20Energy. Accessed 25 June 2023.

3. See Simon, Felix and Chico G. Comargo, "Autopsy of a metaphor: The origins, use and blind spots of the 'infodemic.'" *New Media & Society*, Vol. 25, Issue 8, 2021, pp. 2219–2240. DOI: 10.1177/14614448211031908.

4. "infodemic, n." *Wiktionary*, January 2023, https://en.wiktionary.org/wiki/infodemic. Accessed 5 April 2023.

5. "infodemic, n." *OED Online*, Oxford University Press, March 2023, www.oed.com/view/Entry/88407009. Accessed 6 April 2023.

6. A notable exception would be words formed by onomatopoeia, or mimicry of sounds found in nature.

7. Most English speakers should be familiar enough with these two pronunciations from mass media and/or common usage, even if the symbols (phonemes) of the International Phonetic Alphabet (IPA) may be obscure.

8. Chabria, Anita, "How QAnon hijacked Hollywood narratives; Story lines meld into conspiracies. 'It's terrifying. It's weird.'" *Los Angeles Times*, 7 December 2021, p. A-1.

9. Need citation

10. Blust, Robert, "The Origin of Dragons." In *Anthropos*, Vol. 95, No. 2, 2000, p. 520.

11. Wilson, Edward O., *The Social Conquest of Earth*. New York: Liveright, 2012, p. X.

12. Or "dream." Regardless, the sense implies the suspension of reason.

13. Interview with Kylie McCormick, 17 February 2021.

14. McCormick, Kylie, "About." *The Circle of the Dragon*. Accessed 16 February 2021. Online: http://www.blackdrago.com/about.htm.

15. Daniel 14 describes an exchange between the eponymous noble Jewish priest and members of the Babylonian royal court. (Like many Jews of this era, Daniel had been exiled to Babylon.) In addition to a god named Bel (or Baal), who corresponds to the same Marduk detailed in Chapter 2 (*Middle East/Central Asia*), the Babylonians also worshipped a supposedly "living dragon." Daniel knew that this was another case of idolatry, so he "gathered some pitch, fat, and hair. He boiled them together and formed the mixture into cakes, which he placed into the mouth of the dragon. When the dragon swallowed them, he burst open. Daniel said, 'Behold what you have been worshiping'" (14:27). None too pleased, the Babylonians then threw Daniel into a lions' den. But he was ultimately saved by God.

16. McCormick, Kylie, *Op. cit.*, n.p.

17. See Perry, S.D., *Alien: The Weyland-Yutani Report*. London: Titan Books, 2016.

18. Jones, David E., *An Instinct for Dragons.* New York: Routledge, 2002, p. 4.

19. Perry, *Op. cit.*, p. 21.

20. Interpretations of the specific mechanics of this process vary within the *Aliens* canon.

21. Scott, Ridley (Dir.), *Alien*, 20th Century Fox, 1979

22. User: zeitgeist08 (@zeitgeistamericas08), "Elon Musk, CEO and CTO, Space Exploration Technologies Corp (SpaceX), Peter Diamandis, CEO, X Prize Foundation and John Doerr, Venture Capital, Kleiner Perkins Caufield & Byers." You-Tube, 18 September 2008. Online: https://youtu.be/s3RlCVtQ6mA.

23. Dunigan, Maeve, "Dragon Hoarding Enormous Pile of Treasure Seeks Unpaid Intern." *McSweeney's Internet Tendency*, 22 February 2021. Online: https://www.mcsweeneys.net/articles/dragon-hoarding-enormous-pile-of-treasure-seeks-unpaid-intern.

24. See Chapter 1.

25. See Chapter 8.

Bibliography

Ashe, Geoffrey, *Merlin: The Prophet and His History*. Thrupp, UK: Sutton, 2006.

Barrier, Michael, *Hollywood Cartoons: American Animation in Its Golden Age*. Oxford University Press, 1999.

Blust, Robert, "The Origin of Dragons." *Anthropos*, Vol. 95, No. 2, 2000.

Borges, Jorge Luis (Trans. Andrew Hurley), *The Book of Imaginary Beings*. New York: Penguin, 2005 [1967].

Bruce, Scott G. (Ed.), *The Penguin Book of Dragons*. New York: Penguin, 2021.

Butler, Alban, *The Lives of the Fathers, Martyrs, and Other Principal Saints; Compiled from Original Monuments and Other Authentic Records, Illustrated with the Remarks of Judicious Modern Critics and Historians*, Vol. 4. London: J. Murphy, 1812–15.

Campbell, Joseph, *The Hero with a Thousand Faces*, 2nd Ed. Princeton, NJ: Princeton University Press, 1968 [1949].

Carpenter, Humphrey, *Tolkien: A biography*. Boston: Houghton Mifflin, 1977.

Carr, Michael, "Classical Dragon Names." *Linguistics of the Tibeto-Burman Area*, Vol. 13, No. 2, Fall 1990.

Cecire, Maria Sachiko, *Re-enchanted: The Rise of Children's Fantasy Literature in the Twentieth Century*. Minneapolis: University of Minnesota Press, 2019.

Chickering, Howell D., Jr. (Trans.), *Beowulf: A Dual-Language Edition*. New York: Anchor Books, 2006 [1989; 1977].

Cowan, Douglas E., *Magic, Monsters, and Make-Believe Heroes: How Myth and Religion Shape Fantasy Culture*. University of California Press, 2019.

Cuhaj, George S. (Ed.) et al., *2015 Standard Catalog of World Coins, 1901–2000* (42nd Ed.). Iola, WI: Krause Publications, 2014.

Curley, Michael J. (Trans.), *Physiologus: A Medieval Book of Nature Lore*. University of Chicago Press, 2009 [1979].

Dobson, Kenneth, and Arthur Saniotis, "Dragons: Myth and the Cosmic Powers." *Prajñā Vihāra: Journal of Philosophy and Religion*, Vol. 15, No. 1, January-June 2014.

Drake, Ernest (Pseud.), and Wayne Anderson, Douglas Carrel, and Helen Ward (Illustr.), *Dragonology: The Complete Book of Dragons*. Cambridge, MA: Candlewick Press, 2003.

Evans, Jonathan D., *Dragons: A Beautifully Illustrated Quest for the World's Greatest Dragon Myths*. Lewes, UK: Ivy Press, 2008.

Evans, Jonathan D., "Medieval Dragon-lore in Middle-earth." *Journal of the Fantastic in the Arts*, Vol. 9, No. 3 (35), The Tolkien Issue, 1998.

Ewalt, David M., *Of Dice and Men*. New York: Scribners, 2013.

Gabler, Neal, *Walt Disney: The Triumph of the American Imagination*. New York: Alfred A. Knopf, 2006.

Garry, Jane, and Hasan El-Shamy (Eds.), *Archetypes and Motifs in Folklore and Literature: A Handbook*. Armonk, NY: M.E. Sharpe, 2005.

Goodkind, Daniel, "Chinese Lunar Birth Timing in Singapore: New Concerns for Child Quality Amidst Multicultural Modernity." *Journal of Marriage and Family*, Vol. 58, No. 3, Aug. 1996.

Goodkind, Daniel, "Creating New Traditions in Modern Chinese Populations: Aiming for Birth in the Year of the Dragon." *Population and Development Review*, Vol. 17, No. 4, Dec. 1991.

Grahame, Kenneth, *The Reluctant Dragon*. New York: Holiday House, 1966 [1938; 1898].

Gygax, E. Gary, *Advanced Dungeons & Dragons Monster Manual*, 4th Edition. Lake Geneva, WI: TSR Games, 1979.

Gygax, E. Gary, and Dave Arneson, "Monsters & Treasure (Volume 2 of Three Booklets)." *Dungeons & Dragons: Rules for Fantastic Medieval Wargames Campaigns Playable with Paper and Pencil and Miniature Figures*. Lake Geneva, WI: Tactical Studies Rules, 1974.

Hanlon, Tina L., "The Taming of the Dragon in Twentieth Century Books." *Journal of the Fantastic in the Arts*, Vol. 14, No. 1 (53), Spring 2003.

Headley, Maria Dahvana (Trans.), *Beowulf: A New Translation*. New York: MCD x FSG Originals; Farrar, Straus and Giroux, 2020.

Heaney, Seamus (Trans.), *Beowulf: An Illustrated Edition*. New York and London: W.W. Norton & Company, 2008 [2000].

Hislop, Susanna, *Stories in the Stars: An Atlas of Constellations*. New York: Penguin Books, 2015.

Huxley, Francis, *The Dragon: Nature of Spirit, Spirit of Nature.* New York: Collier Books, 1979.

Ingersoll, Ernest, *Dragons and Dragon Lore. Cryptozoology and Mythology.* Public domain reprint, 2017 [1928].

Isbell, Lynne A. *The Fruit, the Tree, and the Serpent: Why We See So Well.* Harvard University Press, 2009

Jones, David E., *An Instinct for Dragons.* New York: Routledge, 2002.

Jung, C.G., and Violet Staub de Laszlo (Ed.), *The Basic Writings of C.G. Jung.* New York: Random House/The Modern Library, 1993 [1959].

Kuehn, Sara, *The Dragon in Medieval East Christian and Islamic Art.* Leiden and Boston: Brill, 2011.

Laycock, Joseph P., *Dangerous Games: What the Moral Panic Over Role-Playing Games Says About Play, Religion, and Imagined Worlds.* University of California Press, 2015.

Leeming, David Adams, and Margaret Adams Leeming. *Oxford Reference.* Oxford University Press, 2009 [1994]

Martin, George R.R., *Fire and Blood: Being a History of the Targaryen Kings of Westeros.* New York: Bantam Books, 2018.

Mayor, Adrienne, *The First Fossil Hunters: Dinosaurs, Mammoths, and Myth in Greek and Roman Times.* Princeton University Press, 2011.

Miller, Mary, and Karl Taube, *An Illustrated Dictionary of the Gods and Symbols of Ancient Mexico and the Maya.* London: Thames & Hudson, 1993.

Mintz, Samuel L., "Leviathan as Metaphor." *Hobbes Studies,* Vol. II, 1989.

Monmouth, Geoffrey of, and Lewis Thorpe (Trans.), *The History of the Kings of Britain.* London: Penguin Books, 1966.

O'Connell, Mark, and Raje Airey, *Symbols, Signs & Visual Codes: A Practical Guide to Understanding and Decoding the Universal Icons, Signs and Symbols That Are Used in Literature, Art, Religion, Astrology, Communication, Advertising, Mythology and Science.* London: Hermes House, 2009.

Ogden, Daniel, *Dragons, Serpents, and Slayers in the Classical and Early Christian Worlds: A Sourcebook.* Cary: Oxford University Press USA-OSO, 2013.

Ogden, Daniel, *Drakōn: Dragon Myth and Serpent Cult in the Greek and Roman Worlds.* Oxford University Press, 2013.

Palmer, Harry Clay (Ed.) et al., *Athletic Sports in America, England, and Australia.* New York: Union Pub. House, 1889.

Parkin, Simon, *An Illustrated History of 151 Video Games: A Detailed Guide to the Most Important Games.* Wigson, Leicestershire, UK: Lorenz Books, 2013.

Perkins, Christopher, et al., *D&D Monster Manual: A Menagerie of Deadly Monsters for the World's Greatest Roleplaying Game.* Renton, WA: Wizards of the Coast, 2014.

Perrin, W.G., *British Flags: Their Early History, and Their Development at Sea; with an Account of the Origin of the Flag as a National Device.* London: Cambridge University Press, 1922.

Phillips, Charles, *The Lost History of Aztec and Maya: The History, Legend, Myth and Culture of the Native Peoples of Mexico and Central America.* London: Select Editions, 2004.

Porada, Edith, *Monsters and Demons in the Ancient and Medieval Worlds: Papers Presented in Honor of Edith Porada.* Mainz on Rhine: P. von Zabern, 1987.

Rauer, Christine, *Beowulf and the Dragon: Parallels and Analogues.* Cambridge, UK: D.S. Brewer, 2000.

Reames, Sherry L. *The Legenda Aurea: A Reexamination of Its Paradoxical History.* Madison, WI: The University of Wisconsin Press, 1985.

Rendina, Claudio (Trans. Paul D. McCusker), *The Popes: Histories and Secrets.* Santa Ana, CA: Seven Locks Press, 2002.

Rowling, J.K., and Olivia Lomenech Gill (Illustrator), *Newt Scamander: Fantastic Beasts and Where to Find Them.* New York: Arthur A. Levine Books/Scholastic, 2017.

Schwartzel, Erich, *Red Carpet: Hollywood, China, and the Global Battle for Cultural Supremacy.* New York: Penguin Press, 2022.

Senter, Phil, Uta Mattox, and Eid E. Haddad, "Snake to Monster: Conrad Gessner's *Schlangenbuch* and the Evolution of the Dragon in the Literature of Natural History." *Journal of Folklore Research,* Vol. 53, No. 1 (January/April 2016). Bloomington: Indiana University Press, 2016.

Smith, G(rafton) Elliot, *The Evolution of the Dragon.* Manchester, UK: The University Press, 1919.

Souvay, Charles Léon, *The Catholic Encyclopedia, Volume 1.* New York: The Encyclopedia Press, 1913.

Thompson, Stith, *The Folktale.* Berkeley: University of California Press, 1977 [1946].

Tolkien, J.R.R., "*Beowulf*: The Monsters and the Critics." In Mittman, Asa Simon and Marcus Hensel (Eds.), *Classic Readings on Monster Theory: Demonstrare, Volume One.* Leeds, UK: Arc Humanities Press, 2018.

Tolkien, J.R.R., *The Hobbit.* Boston: Houghton Mifflin, 1966 [1937].

Visser, Marinus Willem de, *The Dragon in China and Japan.* Amsterdam: J. Müller, 1913.

Voragine Jacobus de, *The Golden Legend: Selections.* London: Penguin Books, 1998.

Watkins, Calvert, *How to Kill a Dragon: Aspects of Indo-European Poetics.* Oxford University Press, 1995.

White, T.H., *The Sword in the Stone.* London: Collins, 1938.

White, T.H. (Trans., Ed.), *The Book of Beasts: Being a Translation from a Latin Bestiary of the Twelfth Century.* New York: Dover, 1984 [1954].

Wilhelm, Richard (Trans.), *I Ching* [*The Book of Changes*]. New York: Pantheon Books, 1950.

Williams, George, *A Handbook of Hindu Mythology*. Oxford University Press, 2008.

Wilson, Edward O., *The Social Conquest of Earth*. New York: Liveright, 2012.

Witwer, Michael, *Empire of Imagination: Gary Gygax and the Birth of Dungeons & Dragons*. New York: Bloomsbury, 2016.

Index

Numbers in **bold italics** indicate pages with illustrations

www.ingramcontent.com/pod-product-compliance
Lightning Source LLC
Chambersburg PA
CBHW080551270326
41929CB00019B/3266